CURRENT
INTELLIGENCE

CURRENT
INTELLIGENCE

HOW THE CIA'S TOP-SECRET
PRESIDENTIAL BRIEFING
SHAPED HISTORY

DAVID CHARLWOOD

First published 2022

The History Press
97 St George's Place, Cheltenham,
Gloucestershire, GL50 3QB
www.thehistorypress.co.uk

© David Charlwood, 2022

British Library Cataloguing in Publication Data.
A catalogue record for this book is available from the British Library.

ISBN 978 0 7509 9880 2

Typesetting and origination by The History Press
Printed and bound in Great Britain by TJ Books Limited, Padstow, Cornwall.

Trees for LYfe

For Dad (1942–2020)

and

Harvey Thomas (1939–2022)

Contents

List of Illustrations

Introduction

President Harry S. Truman stared at the sheet of white paper, his brown eyes magnified by the thick lenses of his glasses. It was marked 'TOP SECRET', and beneath the dramatic capital letters were two pages of typed text arranged under six headings. The paper was the first 'Daily Summary' created by US intelligence services, a report that would go on to become the President's Daily Brief, informing every occupant of the Oval Office of the goings-on in the world. Truman received the first on Friday, 15 February 1946, the day *The New York Times* ran a front-page article on the unveiling of the world's first electronic computer, which the paper conceded 'may speed [up] engineering'.

The President had specifically requested the document's creation. He had arrived in office with what he admitted were 'gaps in my information'. The short summary from the intelligence services helped to fill them. Truman was delighted with it, declaring, 'at last, a coordinated method had been worked out, and a practical way had been found for keeping the President informed as to what was known and what was going on'.

There were a number of warning signs in Truman's first Daily Brief, including a note under the heading 'French Indochina' that reported difficulties between the French, who had controlled the area as a colony prior to the end of the Second World War, and Chinese forces, who had liberated it from Japanese occupation. In the coming decades, part of the region would take on far greater significance for the USA's Commanders-in-Chief, under its local name of Vietnam. At the moment of the Brief's birth, however, Truman was simply pleased the document existed. From February 1946 onwards, the neat pages of classified text became a crucial part of the President's day.

★ ★ ★

This book tells the story of the key events of the last three-quarters of a century for which the secret daily reports of the Central Intelligence Agency (CIA) have been declassified, or where information has leaked out about the daily intelligence presidents received. It covers the beginnings of the Cold War, the 1950s 'missile gap', the Cuban Missile Crisis, CIA covert operations, the Vietnam War, 9/11 and the fall of Afghanistan to the Taliban in 2021. The information contained in the Daily Briefs provides a unique insight into decisions and events. Sometimes it is revelatory, sometimes prophetic or even embarrassing. In a few cases there are deliberately blanked-out spaces where the CIA's redactors have hidden insights from the eyes of history, but the vast majority of the thousands of pages, which for decades were kept as far from public view as possible, are now openly available on the CIA's online archive. They shed new light on what presidents knew.

In 1946, when the Second World War had only just ended, Truman received repeated warnings that the ally that had jointly defeated the Nazis was now the single greatest threat to global peace. The day-to-day intelligence that crossed the President's desk painted a chilling picture and reveals the first manoeuvrings in the decades-long rupture between East and West that would become known as the Cold War.

For Truman's successor, Dwight D. Eisenhower, one of the primary worries of the new divided world was the threat from above: the fear that the destructive power of nuclear weapons, which the USA had unleashed on Japan, might fall on US cities, delivered by unstoppable ballistic missiles. When the Soviets launched the first satellite into the earth's orbit, it was a moment met with wonder on newspaper front pages, but with consternation in the CIA's secret Brief to the President. For the years that followed, the Briefs were concerned – wrongly, as it later transpired – that the USA lagged behind the Soviet Union (USSR) in missile development.

Following his ascension to office, the USA's youngest ever President warned the nation, 'The path we have chosen is full of hazards.' And every day, John F. Kennedy read about them in his Daily Brief. Almost hidden half-way down one page on 4 August 1962 was a note that eleven Soviet merchant ships were on their way to Cuba. The analysts added, 'we suspect they are carrying arms'. The report was the first move in the dramatic chess game of the Cuban Missile Crisis, which brought the world to the brink of nuclear war. As the crisis unfolded, the Briefs provided critical intelligence to the President.

The Daily Brief of 22 November 1963 never reached its intended recipient. Kennedy lay dead; his bullet-holed body was carried back from Dallas on Air Force One. His Vice President, Lyndon B. Johnson, received the next day's intelligence report and the ones that followed. It was Johnson who pushed the USA into active combat operations in Vietnam, but the threads of the web that enmeshed Johnson to fight a conflict that changed the culture of his country can be traced back as far as the very first Daily Brief and the reports to Truman on Indochina. Vietnam was a war long in the making and a concern for multiple presidents before it became the bloody conflict it is known as today.

The Daily Briefs also reveal the secret actions of the CIA. Eisenhower's first briefing concerned a Prime Minister that the CIA were about to overthrow, and the following year, a 'late item' added to another Brief told of how a newly installed military government in Guatemala had outlawed the Communist Party in the Central American nation. The Brief deliberately did not mention the role US covert operations had played in the turn of events. The CIA also involved itself in Africa, fuelling a brutal conflict in the Congo that lasted half a decade and claimed thousands of lives. When it comes to covert operations, we must often read between the lines of the Briefs, but by collating the intelligence given to presidents before, during and after key moments, it is possible to piece together the picture of the CIA's actions overseas.

The President's Daily Briefs from the 1980s onwards remain under lock and key, but excerpts from a tiny number have been made public. They reveal some disturbing truths about pivotal events of recent history, including that George W. Bush was warned that a shadowy jihadist in Afghanistan named bin Laden had threatened to hijack passenger aircraft to attack the USA in advance of 9/11. We know, because that was exactly what was mentioned in at least one Daily Brief. It was that attack that triggered the invasion of Afghanistan, a two-decades-long conflict that ended in a chaotic evacuation in 2021, leaving the country once more in the hands of the Taliban. The intelligence President Joe Biden received before and during the retreat from the USA's longest-running war is the subject of the final part of this book.

★ ★ ★

The Daily Brief has proved a resilient document, critical to presidential decision making. The first one was created while nations still reeled from the deadliest war in history, and the last has not yet been written; the CIA still compiles a Brief for the President, every working day. This book is the story of the top-secret pages that sit on the President's desk each morning and how they, and the leaders who read them, have shaped history.

Part I

The Curtain Falls:
The Start of the Cold War

1

Long Telegrams

On 22 February 1946, the Deputy Ambassador at the US Embassy in Moscow was in bed. George F. Kennan was suffering from a nasty cold, a fever and a seemingly connected toothache; and in the absence of the Ambassador, Kennan was managing the USA's relations with the Soviet Union from underneath a thick layer of blankets. Outside the elegant, columned front of the US Embassy, Muscovites scuttled through the cold, the only stationary figures in the grand park across the road the heroes monumentalised in stone. A few hundred metres away from Kennan's window, beyond the dormant flower beds and the statues, were the outer walls of the Kremlin, the seat of power of the Soviet government.

Kennan's secretary, Dorothy, brought incoming telegrams to him in his room. On receiving a message that the US Treasury was perplexed at the Soviet government's apparent refusal to keep in step with the requirements of the International Monetary Fund, he finally concluded that his Washington superiors were blind to reality. He called Dorothy in and dictated an 8,000-word telegram for the attention of the State Department. 'Here was a case where nothing but the whole truth would do,' he later noted in his memoirs. 'They had asked for it. Now, by God, they would have it.' He split it into five parts so it would not be so 'outrageously long', justifying his flagrant abuse of the supposedly succinct telegraphic system by claiming a single message would be an oversimplification. None of Kennan's previous missives had 'seemed to evoke even the faintest tinkle from the bell at which they were aimed', but this time Kennan's musings from his sick bed on the post-war world reached the Oval Office.

The man officially in charge of the Daily Brief's contents was the Director of Central Intelligence, Rear Admiral Sidney Souers. The dogged, neatly moustached 54-year-old had spent the war in the Navy and only agreed to take the job of heading up the newly created Central Intelligence Group if he could give it up six months later, once the new organisation had discarded its training wheels. When he was asked what he would like to do following his appointment, he said, 'I want to go home.' He was handed the role at a formal ceremony, where the grinning President presented Souers with a black hat and cloak, along with a wooden dagger, and announced to the room that the naval reservist businessman-turned-admiral from Ohio was now 'Director of Central Snooping'. Souers, however, was aware of the weight of responsibility that came with the job. At the first meeting of the new intelligence leaders, he told his colleagues around the table that the President had asked him 'to make a digest of significant developments ... there was no intention that he should interpret ... or advise the President on any matters of foreign policy'. As he phrased it to an aide, the evaluation of what came in was 'not an exact science', and 'every safeguard should be imposed to prevent one department from having the opportunity to interpret information in such a way as to make it seem to support previously accepted policies or preconceived opinions'. Perhaps it was partly that rationale – or perhaps the fact that Kennan's telegram was 8,000 words long – that meant it was not included in detail in the Daily Brief. Souers' team did, though, make mention of it. Three days after Kennan had dispatched his assessment, the President of the United States read the words, 'US charge [d'affaires] Kennan has submitted to the State Department a detailed analysis of Soviet foreign policy in the post-war world and has presented recommendations from the standpoint of American foreign policy.' The President did not know it, but the 'long telegram' would become one of the markers of the beginning of the Cold War.

In February 1946, Truman had been President for barely ten months, and he had become President by accident. Harry S. Truman – the 'S' was simply a letter and did not stand for anything – was only the seventh man in history to find himself in power because of the death of the sitting President. He was the son of a Missouri farmer who had gone from a clapboard farmstead to the White House, promoted from Vice President when Franklin Delano

President Truman presenting Sidney Souers with the Distinguished Service Medal in 1952. Shortly afterwards he was (finally) allowed to go home.

Roosevelt finally succumbed to his litany of maladies in April 1945. Where Roosevelt had been urbane and thoughtful and was descended from a political aristocracy, Truman was a man of simple tastes from the Midwest. A number of the Washington elite were of the opinion that it was not just his tastes that were simple. At Roosevelt's funeral, one senior US official told the UK Foreign Secretary, Anthony Eden, who had come to pay his respects, that the incoming President 'knows absolutely nothing of world affairs'. Disturbingly, it was a largely true observation. Truman was a liberal Democrat who championed what would today be considered typical Democrat domestic positions: expanding social care, increasing wages for the low-paid and improving public housing. The former County Judge was not a diplomat, as Roosevelt had been, but Truman would give a straight answer to a question and possessed what one UK Prime Minister described as 'power of decision'. When it came to foreign policy, however, the new President was learning as he went along, and he was doing so while the war was still not yet won.

Truman took it upon himself to go to night school. He carried on the practice Roosevelt had initiated with the State Department of receiving a two-page daily summary of diplomatic goings-on, recording later in his memoirs that he went over them in detail every evening and 'never went to bed until I had thoroughly digested the information they contained'. The creation of a similar summary, but for intelligence instead of diplomacy, had seemed a good idea.

★ ★ ★

The text from Kennan's telegram was not printed in the Daily Brief, but Truman apparently asked to read it. The diplomat had not minced his words. He asserted 'in the long run there can be no peaceful coexistence [with the USSR]', quoting the Soviet leader Joseph Stalin's own claim that there would emerge a 'socialist centre' and a 'capitalist centre' that would battle for supremacy. He warned that the Soviets would look to weaken the influence of Western nations around the world and that the USA was confronting 'a political force committed fanatically to the belief that … our traditional way of life be destroyed, [and] the international authority of our state be broken'. Kennan added that the Soviets were 'impervious' to the logic of reason but 'highly sensitive' to the logic of force, although he hoped the threat could be countered without 'a general military conflict'.

Kennan's message made waves in Washington departments and was widely circulated. The next time he wrote a memo, its contents were included in the Daily Brief. Under the heading 'Conciliation of Soviet Government considered futile', it was noted, 'Kennan considers that the "breath of life" for the prevailing political system of the USSR is the existence, real or imagined, of a hostile international environment.' Having a collective enemy was 'the lifeblood' of the Soviet political system and post-war, Japan and Germany had simply been replaced by the UK and the USA. For Kennan, 'Attempts to reassure the Soviet leaders of our peaceful intention are futile, since the Soviets trust no one, not even their own officials.' The analysts added, 'Kennan feels that US diplomacy should be adjusted to this situation.' The Deputy Ambassador to the Soviet Union was not the only person who held that view. It was also shared by a recently demoted politician, who had crossed the Atlantic with the intention of telling any Americans who would listen exactly the same thing.

Winston Churchill had arrived in New York aboard the liner *Queen Elizabeth* several weeks before, officially for a holiday. He first went to Miami, where he relaxed by trying to paint and acquired a taste for the card game gin rummy, which he had never played before. The 71-year-old Prime Minister had been unceremoniously rejected by voters in the UK's first post-war election, and for the first time since 1939, he found himself out of government. Churchill remained leader of the Conservative Party, but the British public wanted peacetime politics and the pugnacious wartime premier seemed no longer suited to the times. Before they met up, Churchill wrote to his friend Harry Truman: 'I have a Message to deliver to your country and the world and I think it very likely that we shall be in full agreement about it.'

Nine days after Kennan's telegram had reached Washington, Winston Churchill was in the capital. There he spent a few days preparing his 'message', which he would deliver in a pre-agreed speech at Westminster College in Fulton, Missouri. On 4 March 1946, Churchill was driven to the White House, where the same car picked up Truman. From there, the two men travelled to the railway station for the twenty-four-hour journey west. On the train, Truman and Churchill played poker and Churchill shared the draft of his speech with the President. Truman told Churchill it was 'admirable', but added 'it would make a stir'. Truman was right.

At Fulton, Churchill uttered the now immortal line: 'From Stettin in the Baltic to Trieste in the Adriatic, an iron curtain has descended.' Behind that 'curtain' was what he called a Soviet sphere with 'police governments' and 'no true democracy'. The Soviet Union did not, Churchill insisted, want war. But he asserted, 'I am convinced there is nothing they admire so much as strength, and there is nothing for which they have less respect for than weakness.' Britain had fought side by side with the Soviet Union – 'wartime comrades', as Churchill phrased it – but ideologically, the political systems of East and West could not comfortably coexist. Within days of each other, the US Deputy Ambassador in Moscow and the UK's revered wartime leader had articulated the same sentiment: that the new world was a divided one and that a conflict between the Soviet Union and the West – although perhaps not a direct military one – now loomed.

Churchill's words caused a storm in the press. The *Chicago Sun* slammed them as 'poison', declaring Churchill had suggested 'world domination, through arms, by the United States and the British Empire'. The concerned *Wall Street Journal* pointed out in its editorial that Truman's presence alongside Churchill at Fulton implied support for his view: it now seemed, the paper said, 'The United States wants no alliance, or anything that resembles an alliance, with any other nation.' Truman ended up scheduling a special press conference in which he openly lied, vowing that he had had no prior knowledge of Churchill's words.

A week later, the fallout from Fulton was a topic in Truman's Daily Brief. The Embassy in Moscow reported a set of attacks on Churchill's speech in the Soviet press which, it said, 'was only initiated after the Soviet leaders noted hostile reactions to the speech in US and Britain and therefore concluded that Soviet influence could be exerted on international opinion'. The private view of Moscow Station was that the real response was 'relief, and the belief that the Western democracies will not likely succeed in organising an effective military block against the USSR'. Churchill had been right, but many Western politicians – used only to the Soviets as their ally – found his assertions too problematic, while much of the press had spent years publishing thinly veiled government propaganda about the brave Soviet war machine that had defeated Nazi Germany. The spectre of conflict with the Soviet Union was a shift too vast to contemplate, but the new threat was being clearly spelled out in Truman's Daily Briefs. A few months after the Fulton speech, news of the existence of the Daily Briefs was leaked to the US press. A *New York Times* journalist ran a splash entitled 'The President's Secret Daily Newspaper'. The article noted that the Brief, 'in the opinion of his [Truman's] intimate staff, makes him the best-informed Chief Executive in history on foreign affairs'.

2

Helping Friends

The fault lines of the new world were being formed at the same time as Americans were rejoicing in the end of hostilities. By the middle of February 1946, the Daily Brief reported that more than 6 million Army personnel had been discharged and that General Douglas MacArthur forecast that the force occupying defeated Japan would total 173,000 by the summer but would drop to 51,000 by the following year. The difference in perspective in the USA was well summed up by a UK newspaper correspondent who narrated a brief *Letter from America* for BBC radio a few weeks later. 'America,' Alistair Cooke told his listeners, 'while it is a throbbing arsenal and a swarming training camp, has been so far, in relation to the battle fronts, a stadium and the American civilian population the anxious but comparatively comfortable crowd.' The crowd were now cheering their heroes' arrival home and were not willing to welcome an interruption to the party. Across the Sea of Japan, however, the news was less promising, as the end of open hostilities had brought dangerous uncertainty.

★ ★ ★

The Korean Peninsula juts out from north-eastern China, with the Yellow Sea on one side and the Sea of Japan on the other. The port city of Busan is less than 200 miles, as the crow flies, from Hiroshima; the city's residents would, on a clear day, potentially have been able to glimpse the mushroom cloud that rose 60,000ft above Honshu island on 6 August 1945 as Hiroshima was vaporised by the first atom bomb dropped in anger. Korean and Japanese affairs had been interwoven for centuries, but in 1910, Korea was annexed by the Japanese Empire. The Japanese administration banned the teaching of Korean, burned Korean historical documents and even uprooted native trees to plant Japanese cherry and junipers, a seasonal reminder to Koreans that their land and culture were subordinate to another. For Koreans, the arrival of the Allied armies in September 1945 was a liberation after a generation of subjugation. As with Germany, Korea was freed from both sides: the Soviets came from the north and the Americans from the south.

The latitude line of the 38th Parallel had been decided as the line above which Soviet forces would accept the surrender of the occupying Japanese and below which US forces would accept the Japanese surrender. The logical line for dividing responsibility became the dividing line which placed northern Korea in Soviet hands and the south in American. Instead of seeking to unify the country, it soon became clear that the Soviets were intent on dividing it. The armies of two former allies now faced each other, with the 38th Parallel increasingly becoming a no man's land between enemies. On 6 March 1946, Truman's Daily Brief noted that the number of Soviet troops in northern Korea was increasing and 'there is much talk among them of a possible war with the US'. One Soviet officer had claimed they could conquer southern Korea in five days. The analysts stated that this was 'braggadocio', but admitted Soviet troops were 'in a state of readiness for combat'. The Soviets were spreading rumours that the Americans would 'abandon' Korea within three years, which was not helping to persuade Koreans in the south that they should support US efforts to create a provisional government. Near the end of April, Lieutenant General John Reed Hodge, who was military governor in the south, dispatched a blistering message to Washington, which was printed in the President's Daily Brief. He recommended the withdrawal of both US and Soviet forces from Korea, asserting that dual occupation 'will result either in war between the US and the USSR or the complete discrediting of Americans in Asia'. In the months that followed, Hodge grew even more concerned, reporting there was 'growing evidence' that the Soviets were 'planning to use a Soviet-trained Korean army for an invasion of South Korea, after the rice season this fall'. The military governor of South Korea seemed, to his superiors in

Washington, to be crying wolf, but his intelligence was not wrong. He was merely premature in his predictions.

★ ★ ★

The world stage now had two major players. It was a fact that Winston Churchill had admitted during one of the wartime meetings between himself, the Soviet leader Joseph Stalin and then US President Franklin D. Roosevelt. On one side, he had said, was 'the big Russian bear with its paws outstretched – on the other the great American elephant'. At the top of his Daily Brief of 8 April 1946, Truman was greeted with the line, 'British now believe USSR aims at world domination.' The UK Foreign Office now believed the Soviet Union did not want simply internal security but instead 'world domination to be achieved indirectly through propagation of Communist doctrine and directly through extension of pressure across Soviet frontiers'. The argument Kennan had put forward in his telegram was now shared on both sides of the Atlantic. Intelligence from the British Zone in Germany – revealed in the Brief a few months later when a UK civil servant met up with a US military attaché in London – suggested the Soviet Union had prepared a twenty-year plan for 'complete communization of Western Europe'. The post-war world did not look like it would remain peaceful for long.

The most obvious frontier was in divided Germany. The conquered country was split into 'zones of occupation' between the different wartime allies. The map was apportioned roughly into four, with the Soviets controlling the top-right-hand side east of Hamburg and south to Dresden; the British had the top left north of Cologne; the western remainder was one-third French; and a large southern section from Frankfurt to Munich the responsibility of the Americans. Berlin was in the heart of the Soviet Zone, but the city itself was divided into sectors between the former wartime allies. East Berlin was Soviet controlled, and the Soviets seemed intent on parading their military hardware along the border.

In early June 1946, Truman's Daily Brief reported that the French were increasingly concerned about troop concentrations in the Soviet-controlled zone near the Western demarcation line. The French view was that 'the Soviets may desire a) to impress the German people with their strength, and b) to engage in a "little war of nerves"'. It was a message backed up by news from

Moscow the following day. The Soviets, it was reported, were engaged 'in an old fashioned Eastern-European show of force'. Moscow, the US Ambassador said, was very 'sensitive' to what it saw as underestimation of its strength. While Soviet officials in Berlin were 'making unusual efforts to be socially friendly and agreeable' over the summer of 1946, there were more and more armed men on the Soviet side of the line. On 2 August, the Brief stated there were 100,000 Soviet troops around the area of Berlin. Trains carrying Soviet soldiers, vehicles and ammunition arrived for the rest of the month, with the ammunition declared as shipments of corn in an attempt to fool watching American eyes. Not long afterwards, there were reports of Soviet tanks crossing into Germany through Poland with slogans painted on the side, including, 'We destroyed Germany; now we shall destroy England and America.'

The broader picture was that the Soviet Union, while it was officially demobilising after the end of the war, was still preparing to fight. Tank factories in the Ural Mountains were operating at full capacity, and Soviet total armed strength was estimated at 3.1 million men, including an air force of 550,000 personnel. The impression, crystallised by the reports in Truman's Daily Briefs, was one of ongoing Soviet militarism.

At the start of the autumn, the President was in a melancholic mood. In a musing diary entry, Truman recalled 'a man of my acquaintance' (that is to say, himself) who twenty-nine years before had stood behind an artillery battery near the French town of Neuvelle. After that war his country had quickly moved to disarm; now after another war, 'the same elation filled the home people ... they were happy to have the fighting stop and to quit worrying about their sons and daughters in the armed forces'. But then Truman noted: 'The reaction set in. Selfishness, greed, jealousy ... [with] No wartime incentive.' The world was different now, facing 'absolute and complete destruction', and it led Truman to consider his own capabilities. He wrote, 'my acquaintance tried to meet every situation and has met them up to now. Can he continue to outface the demagogues, the chisellers [swindlers], the jealousies? Time only will tell.' Truman would shortly face the sternest test yet of his post-war resolve as the Cold War witnessed its first significant escalation in Berlin, but the threat of Communism really did seem global.

★ ★ ★

Five thousand miles east of Washington, the birthplace of democracy itself was apparently at risk of becoming another Soviet satellite. Greece had been in a state of semi-civil war since the end of German occupation in 1944. Many of the partisans who had bravely fought back against Nazi tyranny either espoused Communist ideology or were sympathetic to it, and their visions for a free Greece did not include the country's exiled monarch or former government. When UK forces arrived to assist Greece's liberation, they were under orders to aid the reinstallation of the pre-war administration. When violence broke out in Athens, Churchill (then Prime Minister) sent British soldiers into the city, where they opened fire on Communist demonstrators. UK military action helped install a temporary government in 1945, but the Communists boycotted elections early the following year and violence escalated. By mid-1946, Communist guerrillas were hiding out in the same mountains where they had evaded the Germans, but now they were fighting a nationalist government run by their own countrymen.

Greece barely appeared in Truman's Daily Briefs until the summer of 1946, when the US Ambassador in Athens shared an appeal from Communist political groups that the actions of the Greek government, including the rounding-up of political prisoners, 'have brought Greece to the verge of civil war'. The Ambassador added his own note, admitting that 'while the present Royalist Government secured control on the strength of popular reaction against Communist excesses, the Government's present measures for "law and order" are in the hands of "unscrupulous reactionaries"'. Four weeks later, there was news that the Greek government planned to outlaw the Communist Party completely, while 'serious fighting' was under way in the north, as Greek soldiers, supported by Royal Air Force Spitfire squadrons, attacked Communist guerrillas. The US Ambassador was unequivocal: the policy of the Greek government was, he said, 'extremist' and a certain way of 'making enemies'. Greece was swiftly descending into a full-scale civil war, but the UK forces, which had not left since marching into Athens in 1944, were being gradually withdrawn; the plan was that they would be down to one brigade by March 1947 and gone by that summer.

The first item on Truman's Daily Brief on 26 September 1946 was a copy of a note from the Secretary of State. Truman's lead foreign policy man believed the situation in the world 'has so hardened' that, in the light of the Soviet attitude, the USA should 'reorientate its economic policy in Europe and the Near East'. The Secretary insisted, 'we must now act on the policy of helping our friends in every way', adding it was of the 'highest importance' to help Greece. The great irony of the Greek situation was that the Soviet Union was not directly aiding Greek Communists at the time, but the assumption in Washington was the opposite. Throughout the autumn and early winter there was more negative news, and the reports from the ground were equally discouraging.

In January 1947, a 49-year-old Kentucky-born journalist was dispatched to Greece as a member of a fact-finding mission on behalf of the US State Department and the fledgling United Nations (UN). Mark F. Ethridge, along with representatives from a number of countries including the Soviet Union, was officially examining 'border incidents' between Yugoslavia and Greece. Instead he found himself reporting on a country on the verge of political and financial collapse. With the help of the US Ambassador, Ethridge dispatched a cable to Washington from the Embassy in Athens. He later recalled, 'we just felt the situation was desperate ... felt that Greece would go down the drain if the United States didn't do something'. On 18 February, Truman read the words, 'Ethridge reports the situation in Greece is deteriorating ... the Soviet delegate and satellite representatives, [are] convinced Greece will shortly fall within the Soviet orbit'. The journalist reported that the government was losing popular confidence, Communist forces were gaining ground and soldiers were deserting the Greek Army to join the Communists. He stated, 'the Soviet belief in the imminent fall of Greece is justified'. Action was now the order of the day, and Truman moved to push the suggestion from his Secretary of State a few months before that the USA 'act on the policy of helping our friends'.

On 12 March 1947, the thirty-third President of the United States addressed Congress. In a smart dark suit and tie, a measured Truman carefully read from the notes in front of him. He told his legislators:

> The United States has received from the Greek Government an urgent appeal for financial and economic assistance. Preliminary reports from the American Economic Mission now in Greece and reports from the American Ambassador in Greece corroborate the statement of the Greek Government that assistance is imperative if Greece is to survive as a free nation.

Calmly, with no movement other than an occasional upward glance to his audience and the turning of the pages of his speech with his right hand, Truman outlined to his listeners the reality of the world they now lived in. 'At the present moment in world history nearly every nation must choose between alternative ways of life. The choice is too often not a free one.' He went on to assert, 'I believe that it must be the policy of the United States to support free peoples who are resisting attempted subjugation by armed minorities or by outside pressures.' His request was simple: $400 million from Congress as 'assistance' for Greece and other nations under threat. Truman concluded, 'The free peoples of the world look to us for support in maintaining their freedoms. If we falter in our leadership, we may endanger the peace of the world – and we shall surely endanger the welfare of our own nation.'

The next day Truman's Daily Brief reported that a military campaign by the Greek Army against guerrillas was to start in early April, with the Greeks reportedly 'delighted' with US promises of support. Five days later the 'broad results' of Truman's speech were noted. There were already statements of political unity from everyone except the Communists. The Greek currency had strengthened, and activity had resumed in the domestic property market. For many, it was the 'clear assurance of political security' that was 'more important to Greece's recovery than [the] economic aid'.

The news was welcomed with joy by many: 'My God, it was greeted with the wildest demonstration on the part of Greeks', Ethridge recalled twenty-seven years later. 'My Russian opposite number [in Athens] said to me "What does this mean, Mr Ethridge?" I said, "It means you can't do it [turn Greece Communist]." He said, "I understand that kind of language."' Ethridge was convinced his desperate message from the Athens Embassy that had made its way into Truman's Daily Brief was the catalyst for the sudden move to promise huge support to Greece. 'In our own minds, we gave Greece about five weeks, no more. And Truman reacted in ten days.'

In his memoirs, Truman later stated that the doctrine was 'the turning point in America's foreign policy'. The Cold War was now an open ideological confrontation, in which the USA would aggressively support its perceived allies and intervene in the peacetime affairs of nations in a new way. For just over a year, Truman had received a daily document that detailed the escalation of the Communist threat and its global nature. It is perhaps wishful thinking to draw a direct line between Truman's Daily Briefs and his policies, as there were always wider discussions between staff, and he would have received far more information than just the short summaries of the Briefs. But Truman liked the pithy snapshots of world goings-on. When narrating his daily routine in his diary a few years later, the President recorded that once he had finished with his mail, calendar and business relating to legislation, he dismissed personal staff and then 'the Intelligence service reports what goes on around the world'. It was, he noted, 'all "Top Secret" and most interesting. It helps the President to make decisions on foreign and domestic policy.'

3

Winged Angels

On 14 June 1948, President Truman's Daily Brief contained a note from the US Ambassador in the isolated enclave of the German capital. Freight movements across the Soviet Zone into the Western-controlled sectors of Berlin were being delayed by pedantic Soviet officials. The advisor observed that it 'may well be that the USSR is now preparing to cut Berlin off completely from supplies originating in the west'. The analysts of the Central Intelligence Agency, who occasionally annotated Truman's Brief, felt the need to add their own comment: 'Ambassador Murphy's alternative suggestion that the USSR may be trying to create an "emergency" situation [in order to force talks] is more likely to represent Soviet intentions.' But the CIA was wrong.

★ ★ ★

In the fifteen months since Truman had announced his 'doctrine', the dividing line between East and West had hardened further. In the spirit of 'helping friends', Truman had also persuaded Congress to endorse a European Recovery Program that gave $15 billion to rebuild the war-ravaged nations of Europe. Officially, the programme, which became known as the Marshall Plan after the former US commander who had devised it, was not political. Its architect insisted, 'Our policy is not directed against any country, but against hunger, poverty, desperation and chaos.' The Soviet Ambassador in

Washington was less convinced, however. He reported to Moscow that 'the outlines of a Western European block directed against us are patently visible'. The reality was that neither the Americans nor the British or the French wished to see US taxpayers' money going to areas under Soviet control. An Under Secretary of State for Economic Affairs was dispatched to Paris where he secretly met with the UK Foreign Secretary Ernest Bevin; the two discussed ways of making sure the Soviet Union did not take part in the plan, and the hope that US economic aid might lure away from Soviet orbit some of the Eastern European states. The Soviets, correctly perceiving the political intent behind the promises of free cash, refused to take part in the European Recovery Program, which suited Washington perfectly. It was hardly a coincidence that the formula devised for handing out the money resulted in huge sums heading to the Allied-controlled areas of western Germany. The CIA also managed to secure 5 per cent of the funds, which it used to roll out clandestine operations across Europe. The Soviet response was to launch their own recovery fund for sympathetic satellite states, with the result that by the summer of 1948 the Cold War had a clear economic dimension. And the anomaly of Berlin – under Western influence but surrounded by Soviet-controlled German territory – was an obvious weak point.

Berlin often cropped up in Truman's Daily Briefs. Sidney Souers, however, was no longer supervising them. After six months in post as Director of Intelligence he had finally been allowed to go home, although it was a short-lived retirement. Souers was pulled back to Washington by Truman to assist with a new organisation: the National Security Council (NSC). The NSC was the top of a new security pyramid that had been created by a national security act earlier that year. The NSC would coordinate national security policy, with the Army, Navy and Air Force's squabbling resolved by the establishment of the positions of Joint Chiefs of Staff, who would be military advisors to the President. The dynamic moving part of the new structure was a replacement for the Central Intelligence Group that Souers had originally been brought in to lead. The new intelligence organisation would have no jurisdiction on US soil and no law-enforcement powers, but it was authorised in deliberately vague language to perform 'functions and duties relating to intelligence affecting the national security'. The Central Intelligence Agency had been born. And Truman's Daily Briefs were now the CIA's responsibility. One of the questions that had to be resolved was to define what 'current intelligence' actually meant.

It was decided it was 'spot information or intelligence of all types and forms of immediate interest and value to operating or policy staffs'. It was that 'current intelligence' that the CIA was responsible for placing in front of the President every day. The content of the Briefs did not change significantly, but the new agency discarded Souers' original insistence that there should be no interpretation of information. The analysts began adding notes to the Brief.

Six days after the CIA officially came into being, it published a 'Review of the World Situation as it Relates to the Security of the United States'. The whole first page was taken up with the Soviet threat, with the authors conceding that 'the USSR, at will, could speedily overrun most of continental Europe, the Near East, northern China and Korea'. But they concluded that the USSR did not seek a war and 'the immediate threat was the economic collapse of Western Europe'. And at the heart of Western Europe was Berlin.

★ ★ ★

On 26 June 1948, US military aircraft began flying supplies into the now cut-off city, and Truman ordered the use of every single available plane in the European Command. A former advertising man turned soldier, Colonel Frank L. Howley, held the difficult post of military governor of Berlin. The genial-faced, wavy-haired 46-year-old could give off an impression of wholly good-naturedness, which he used to cover his steely determination. For Berlin's residents, the first days of the blockade were simply days of marginally greater hunger than they had already endured in the ravaged, defeated city, with its war-wrecked economy. But Howley knew how close the spectre of starvation was. When he was asked how many planes he could receive, he said he would accept them as fast as they could come in; and he asked for flour to be the first cargo. The first arrivals were C-47 Dakotas – the same transport aircraft that had dropped sticks of Allied paratroopers over Europe – and many of them were flown by pilots who had previously navigated their way to Berlin to deliver bombs, not food. 'They wobbled into Tempelhof [airport],' Howley later recalled:

> … coming down clumsily through the bomb-shattered buildings around the field, but they were the most beautiful things I had ever seen. As the planes touched down, and bags of flour began to spill out of their bellies,

I realized that this was the beginning of something wonderful – a way to crack the blockade. I went back to my office almost breathless with elation, like a man who has made a great discovery and cannot hide his joy.

Across the Atlantic, the US press was waking up to the realities of what the Soviet blockade of Berlin might mean. The morning after the first aircraft touched down at Tempelhof, *The New York Times* informed its readers, 'Today, the two great power groups of the West and East are moving toward a showdown across the shattered capital of the enemy they joined to defeat.' The Soviets, however, had a right to be peeved. Amidst the hand-wringing and howling at the cutting off of Berlin, most Western observers did not publicise the awkward fact that the action had been immediately precipitated by a provocative economic act. The day Berlin was fully cut off was also the day that the USA and UK had introduced their own new currency, the Deutschmark, across all their zones of occupation in Germany, and in the areas they controlled in Berlin. The threat of the plan had been enough for the Soviets officially to pull out of the post-war Allied Control Council, which coordinated policy between the zones. When the Deutschmark was introduced without the Soviets being notified, it was viewed as an insulting escalation of the economic Cold War.

Any notions of justified indignance on the Soviet side were ignored at the CIA, whose analysts believed Soviet intentions were fairly clear. 'The Soviet action,' they noted in one Brief, 'has two possible objectives: either to force the Western powers to negotiate on Soviet terms regarding Germany or, failing that, to force a Western power withdrawal from Berlin.' Truman was determined not to buckle. The same day that aircraft began shuttling food and fuel into Berlin, Truman's Brief revealed that the city had stored sufficient food to meet the minimum ration requirements for six weeks, while fuel supply for light, power and water would last three. After the update on the situation in Berlin, there was a stark warning. '[The] CIA considers that: a) the Berlin population is basically anti-Soviet; and b) the people of Berlin will, from the point of view of self-interest, support the stand of the Western powers unless it becomes obvious that the US can no longer feed the Germans.' Staving off starvation for the 2 million inhabitants of the war-ravaged ruins of Berlin was outwardly an act of heroic humanitarianism. In truth, however, it was the opening salvo in a battle for hearts and minds that would be seen, with hindsight, as the first real confrontation of the Cold War. Truman would later narrate the events in Berlin in war-like language: 'The blockade in Berlin was international Communism's counterattack.'

On 19 July 1948, Truman recorded in his diary that it had been 'quite a day', starting with a meeting on Berlin and the Soviet situation. He wrote, 'I have to listen to a rehash of what I know already and reiterate my "Stay in Berlin" decision. I don't pass the buck.' Truman then attended the funeral of General John J. Pershing at Arlington National Cemetery in the sweltering summer heat, returning to 'the great white jail [the White House]' feeling 'hot and humid and lonely'. He ended the day's entry, 'Why in the hell does anybody want to be a head of state? Damned if I know.'

The next day, four weeks after Berlin had been cut off, US officials in the German capital had completed their detailed number crunching. They estimated that minimum daily requirements for the summer months were 1,178 tons of food, 73 tons of medical supplies, 20 tons of gasoline and diesel fuel, and 2,380 tons of coal. In the coming winter, they warned, the western areas of the city would need 4,431 tons of coal daily. Any reduction in that total 'would mean considerable hardship to the population'. The final line of the section in Truman's Brief admitted that it might be possible to cut the coal requirement in half to reduce the daily airlift to 3,000 tones, but as of 19 July they had only been managing 2,400 tons.

The knife-edge nature of the situation was summarised in the Brief the following day: the 'physical and economic plight' of the population of West Berlin was 'worsening daily'. The Ambassador added, 'The air lift is providing the population with enough food to sustain life but not to sustain morale over an extended period.' The end of August and early September was identified as the critical period because by then, even with the current effort, food and fuel would have run out. By mid-July, the daily airlift operation involved fifty-two C-54 Skymaster transport planes and eighty of the venerable twin-engined Douglas C-47 Dakotas. Every aircraft was making two round trips a day. But it would be touch and go whether Berliners starved or froze to death.

It was the combined efforts of wartime allies that turned the corner. The British added their weight to the operation, and the logistics became well oiled. Tempelhof Airport was witnessing a plane land or take off every thirty seconds, while any pilot who missed their first approach was banned from making another attempt, as it would hold up other aircraft, and simply ordered to fly back to their starting base to refuel and go again. Pilots were making multiple trips a day, with some even finding time to fling candy tied to parachutes out of their cockpit windows on the final approach, as a treat for children. By the middle of August, it was clear that the seemingly implausible idea of feeding an entire city by air was becoming a deliverable reality. Combined US and UK efforts were now averaging 3,300 tons of supplies per day, with a daily record of 4,575 tons. Miraculously, stockpiles in Berlin were now growing: there was a thirty-day food reserve and a twenty-five-day coal reserve.

Berlin was still a regular feature in the Daily Briefs, but the focus from August onwards was the progress of negotiations with the Soviets over the German situation and ending the blockade, rather than the threat of the starvation of the population. Despite apparent overtures from the Soviet side, it seemed discussions were at an impasse. At the start of 1949, the US Embassy in Moscow messaged:

> There is absolutely no indication of any Soviet willingness to reach an agreement on the Berlin dispute at any price which the US could conceivably pay … the Kremlin will continue to welcome any delays which do not interfere with the maintenance of the blockade and permit the strengthening of the German Communist puppets.

The Soviets were actively increasing control over institutions – including German police – outside of West Berlin, leading to reports to Truman that the Soviets were trying to 'split' the city. However, there was a sudden shift in tone a few months later. On 21 April 1949, the Brief passed on from UK sources that there seemed to be 'feelers' and rumours the Soviets might consider lifting the blockade. The CIA analysts wrote: 'The USSR is likely in the near future to make proposals for an East–West settlement involving lifting the Berlin blockade.' This time, the CIA was right.

In only eight days of negotiations, the Soviets agreed to free the city's supply links, in exchange for a high-level meeting between foreign ministers to discuss the future of occupied Germany. Instead of forcing the Western allies into a corner, or making them abandon Berlin, Moscow now appeared to all the world to be the aggressor, who would threaten the starvation of civilians as leverage. On 12 May 1949, eleven months after it began, the Berlin blockade officially ended. '[The] Berlin [airlift],' Truman would later assert, 'had become a symbol of America's – and the West's – dedication to the cause of freedom.'

4

Genbaku

A nightmare had disturbed Terufumi Sasaki's sleep the night before. The newly qualified 25-year-old Japanese doctor had dreamt he was at the bedside of a patient, but that the police burst in, dragged him outside and beat him up for not having a medical permit. His nightmare was not unfounded: the young doctor was unofficially treating patients in the country town where he lived with his mother, and the dream stayed with him as he sat, bleary eyed, on the commuter train into the city Red Cross hospital where he worked.

He arrived early on the morning of 6 August 1945 and his first procedure of the day was to draw blood from a patient who was being tested for syphilis. Terufumi was taking the vial to the lab on the third floor of the hospital when he saw what seemed to be a huge camera flash. Instinctively, he ducked down, before a shockwave tore through the building, ripping his glasses from his face and shattering the vial of blood against the wall. He rushed to fetch bandages to treat his now wounded patients and colleagues, assuming that a bomb must have directly hit the roof. Soon it became clear that the flash he had seen was something more, as people from all around the local area converged on the Red Cross hospital in Hiroshima. The sky, which had started the day blue, had turned dark purple, and when one of the doctors went to the basement to fetch a plate to take an X-ray, he found the entire hospital stock was already exposed and useless. The city had been hit by what the Japanese would come to call a *genbaku* – an atomic bomb. The young doctor worked to treat the wounded and dying for the next three days with only one hour's sleep. The atom bomb dropped on Hiroshima killed around 70,000 people immediately and caused tens of thousands more deaths in the weeks and months that followed, killing in total perhaps as much as 40 per cent of the city's population.

Truman had made the decision to deploy nuclear weapons twelve days previously. That night the President had recorded in his diary, 'We have discovered the most terrible bomb in the history of the world ... it is certainly good that Hitler's crowd, or Stalin's, did not discover this.' But within a few short years, the prospect that 'Stalin's crowd' might soon be a nuclear power was keeping US politicians up at night. And the progress of Soviet efforts to obtain 'the Bomb' was an important topic of the President's Daily Briefs from as soon as Truman began receiving them.

★ ★ ★

On 30 May 1946, Truman's Daily Brief warned, via a military attaché in Paris, that '[the] Soviets reportedly expect to have [the] atomic bomb next year'. Such rumours were commonplace and appeared frequently. In public, the Soviets insisted that they wanted an international agreement that would mean the USA committed not to use atomic weapons, to stop production and to destroy stockpiles. Truman was supportive of removing the threat of nuclear weapons, but the Soviet position, he would later write, would mean the USA would be 'deprived of everything except their [the Soviets'] promise to agree to controls'. He phrased it more candidly in a letter to a US representative at the UN: 'We should not under any circumstances throw away our gun until we are sure that the rest of the world can't arm against us.' Truman's position was logical and understandable, but it exemplifies the primary stumbling block that has bedevilled every effort at nuclear disarmament. More news appeared in Truman's Brief in September 1946. A US naval attaché in Odessa had spoken to an unnamed source who claimed to have been co-pilot of a plane which dropped the first of three atom bombs in tests successfully conducted in the Chita region near Mongolia in June or July of 1946. There had been previous rumours of atom bomb tests around that time, but in Kazakhstan the 'descriptions of the bomb and its effect are not in keeping with the US experience', the analysts noted. It was concluded the story was probably unfounded. For the next two years, the reports were the same: rumours here and there, always unsubstantiated.

The scepticism on the part of the Americans came from an underestimation of Soviet capacity, not necessarily capability. They had the scientists, but knowing how to construct a nuclear weapon was not the same as doing it. The Soviets had not only put to work German physicists captured near the end of the war, but they had also – unknown to the Americans – succeeded in penetrating the top-secret Manhattan Project, the codename for the US atom bomb-building programme. Through an unassuming German refugee scientist named Klaus Fuchs, the Soviets obtained details of what was needed to detonate a plutonium weapon, knowledge which certainly helped to speed along their work, as it narrowed down their design options. In May 1949, Truman's Daily Brief warned that known Communist Frédéric Joliot-Curie, a French physicist who was part of the French atomic programme, was likely to be dropped by the French government because of his awkward politics. It was reported from a supposedly 'trustworthy source' that Joliot-Curie had already claimed that, if he were fired, he would lend his services to the Soviets. The CIA was sceptical, suggesting that his defection would 'bolster Soviet propaganda more than Soviet science', adding that it was 'doubtful' the Frenchman would ever actually go to the USSR. But by May 1949, the Soviets did not need defecting foreign scientists anyway.

Three months later, on 29 August, Soviet scientists detonated the first Soviet nuclear bomb at Semipalatinsk in modern-day Kazakhstan. The valley on the Kazakh Steppe had been chosen two years before. It was a bleak, barren place, with little flora or fauna, a suitable location for unleashing a weapon that could instantly kill every living thing within 2 miles. The bomb was set up on the top of a tower and then triggered. One of the witnesses remembered that the explosion 'reached us like the roar of an avalanche … The atomic mushroom was blown away to the south, losing its outlines, and turning into the formless torn heap of clouds one might see after a gigantic fire.' The scientists embraced one another; privately, several had feared facing a firing squad if they failed.

Five days after the bomb test, a modified US B-29 bomber took off from Misawa Air Force Base in Japan climbed to its maximum altitude and cruised for several hours before later landing at Eielson in Alaska. The plane was one of a handful operated by the secretive Air Force Office of Atomic Energy and, officially, it was measuring the weather. When the scientists looked through the data the plane had brought back, they immediately triggered an alert. A piece of filter paper exposed in the thin air had recorded something invisible: radioactive debris. The scientists and pilots scrambled to dispatch more flights to double check, and five days after the first B-29 had scudded its way over the most eastern tip of Soviet territory, the CIA Director entered the room and handed the President a one-page memo. It read, 'Samples of air masses recently collected over the North Pacific have shown abnormal radio-active contamination.' There were four possible causes: volcanic activity, waste from a US nuclear facility in Washington State being swept up into the atmosphere, leakage from an atomic plant in the Soviet Union, or 'an Atomic explosion on the continent of Asia'. The scientists and spies were being careful with their written words. In person, the CIA Director was less guarded. The first hypothesis, he told Truman, was that the Soviets had successfully detonated a nuclear bomb.

The new head of the CIA, Roscoe Henry Hillenkoetter, was a Navy admiral and an able and affable leader. The 52-year-old had been wounded in the Japanese attack on Pearl Harbor when executive officer on the battleship *Virginia*, but had recovered and commanded a destroyer in the Pacific during the war, while also working with naval intelligence. He was the first Director of the CIA. He frequently briefed the President on events, but on that morning he was handing to the Commander-in-Chief an admission of failure. It was the Air Force that had discovered the fact that the Soviet Union had exploded the first atom bomb: Hillenkoetter and the CIA knew nothing about it. Worse, in July 1948, Hillenkoetter had sent a personal memo to Truman which read, 'the earliest date by which it is remotely possible the USSR may have completed its first atomic bomb is mid-1950, but most people believe this to be mid-1953'. In July the following year, just over a month before the bomb code-named 'Joe-1' atomised miles of the Kazakh Steppe, the CIA had reiterated the same assessment. The deeply disturbing reality was that neither the President nor anyone else had had any idea quite how close the Soviets were to having their own nuclear weapons.

Truman was shaken by the news and at first refused to believe it. There had been no warning in his Daily Briefs. News of the Soviet test was apparently not included in the days that followed either, although there are pages missing from a number of the Briefs surrounding the September date, and the entire first sheet of the 10 September 1949 Brief is a white, blank, redacted space. (The practice of redacting sections of the Daily Briefs is largely confined to the 1960s and '70s, but there are earlier occasions when some details have been removed from documents.) It was the greatest change in the balance of power in the post-war world, and the CIA – and the entire US intelligence community – had thought it was an event still in the far-off future. After a heated internal debate, Truman decided that it was better for the American people to hear the news direct from their President, rather than from the mouth of Moscow media; at least then they would feel that the Soviets could not just go detonating a nuclear bomb without American leaders knowing about it. The announcement would also serve to shock the Soviets, who had no idea of the sophistication of US detection capabilities. On 23 September, almost a month after the nuclear test, Truman released a calmly worded media statement. 'We have evidence that within recent weeks an atomic explosion occurred in the U.S.S.R.,' it read:

> Ever since atomic energy was first released by man, the eventual development of this new force by other nations was to be expected. The probability has always been taken into account by us … it was emphasized that no single nation could in fact have a monopoly of atomic weapons. This recent development emphasizes once again, if indeed such emphasis were needed, the necessity for that truly effective enforceable international control of atomic energy which this Government and the large majority of the members of the United Nations support.

The President successfully poured oil over troubled waters, but there was no denying that the balance of power had changed. On 30 September, a week after Truman had announced the Soviet test to the world, the Daily Brief reported the thoughts of the US Embassy in Moscow on what was described as 'unanticipated Soviet progress in the atomic field'. They did not think it meant imminent war, but stated the obvious: 'the Kremlin will consider its hand strengthened'. Successfully testing a bomb was not the same as having an arsenal ready to be dropped from aircraft at a moment's notice. But it was now only a matter of time before the USA ceased to have a monopoly on 'the most terrible bomb in the history or the world'. For Truman, the shock of not knowing urged him toward a new, more aggressive stance. He had been persuaded not by what he read in his Daily Briefs, but by what was absent.

5

A Re-Examination

The memo from the President, when it landed on the desks of the Secretaries of State and Defense, contained a one-sentence demand of the sort that ruins the working week of government officials and everyone under them. Truman requested they 'undertake a re-examination of our objectives in peace and war and of the effect of those objectives on our strategic plans'. In other words, the President was asking them to rip up the USA's foreign policy and military strategy and start again. His reason was 'the probable fission bomb and possible thermonuclear bomb capability of the Soviet Union'.

The Soviets' successful nuclear test had well and truly spooked the President. Since the first Soviet test in August 1949, there had been little news. The Soviets' next atom bomb test would not in fact be for another two years, but no news was definitely not good news; in early October 1949, Truman's Brief contained reports that one of the new estimates was that the Soviets would now have 'a substantial supply' of atomic bombs by 1952. As the world entered a new decade, the President's concern only increased. On 31 January 1950, Truman sent his 'directive' to his Secretaries of State and Defense. Just over two months later he got a reply.

The first draft of the report was delivered to Truman on 7 April. The front page of *The New York Times* that Friday was entirely filled with domestic issues: the death of a famous gambler in Missouri, the progress of a housing bill through Congress and Truman's announcement of a new 'jobless pay rise' to support the unemployed. Truman's Daily Briefs that week had been busy with the situation in Germany – there was concern over the increasing 'militarization' of police units in eastern Germany – as well as a crisis in Belgium where the king, who had surrendered his country to the invading Germans in 1940, was trying to return from exile. In contrast, the document that would become known as National Security Council Report NSC-68 was singly focused on what was seen as the threat of the Soviet Union. The contents of the report's sixty-six pages would remain classified for a quarter of a century.

After a preamble outlining the terms of reference, the report gave a page of background on 'the present world crisis'. It made for sobering reading. 'Within the last thirty-five years the world has experienced two global wars of tremendous violence ... It has also seen the collapse of five empires ... [in] the span of one generation, the international balance of power has been fundamentally altered.' The now-looming prospect of nuclear conflict had focused minds too: 'in this context ... this Republic [of the USA] and its citizens in the ascendency of their strength stand in their deepest peril'. The page concluded that the US government 'must now take new and fateful decisions' in the shadow of the threatened destruction, 'not only of this Republic but of civilization itself'. Truman sent the first draft on to his National Security Council and asked them to provide him 'with further information on the conclusions contained therein'. The final document would become the blueprint for the USA's approach to the Cold War for the next half-century.

Central to the document were the concerns over the Soviet nuclear weapons programme:

> The Soviet nuclear threat is more immediate than had previously been estimated ... within the next four or five years the Soviet Union will possess the military capability of delivering a surprise atomic attack of such weight that the United States must have substantially increased general air, ground, and sea strength, atomic capabilities, and air and civilian defences to deter war.

While adding a huge caveat that the authors could not know accurately what the Soviet weapons capability might be, they pulled together CIA estimates, which they ran past the State Department and intelligence officers in the Army, Navy and Air Force, as well as some US nuclear scientists. They claimed that by mid-1950 the Soviets would have between ten and twenty bombs and by mid-1953 over a hundred. There was also another concern: that the Soviets would develop a more powerful 'thermonuclear' (hydrogen) bomb, which would have destructive power orders of magnitude greater than the weapons dropped by the USA on Japan.

In the face of the military threat to Western Europe, the new nuclear armaments of the Soviet Union and the efforts to push the international spread of Communism, the document outlined four possible courses of action. Negotiation was considered but discounted: 'Clearly under present circumstances we will not be able to negotiate a settlement which calls for a change in the Soviet [Communist] system. What, then, is the role of negotiation?' The alternative options were: a continuation of current policies; isolation; 'preventative' war; or a rapid build-up of political, economic and military strength in the free world. Isolation had 'some attractiveness', but it was noted, 'There is no way to make ourselves inoffensive to the Kremlin except by complete submission to its will. Therefore isolation would in the end condemn us to fight alone and on the defensive.' The considerations against war were 'so compelling that the free world must demonstrate that this argument is wrong', while it was conceded that the only war that could be launched was a pre-emptive nuclear strike, after which it was still thought that the Soviets would be able to conquer the whole of Eurasia with conventional forces. The final course, the authors insisted, was 'the only course which is consistent with progress toward achieving our fundamental purpose'. 'Time is short,' it was noted, 'and the risks of war attendant upon a decision to build up strength will steadily increase the longer we defer it.'

The only option presented to Truman was a massive military build-up which would be significant economically and also perhaps politically costly. At the same time, the political and economic spheres also needed to be strengthened to project the interests of 'the free world' and fund an armaments programme to enable the USA to stay ahead of the Soviet Union. NSC-68 concluded, 'The whole success of the proposed program hangs ultimately on the recognition by this Government, and the American people … that the Cold War is in fact a real war in which the survival of the free world is at stake.'

NSC-68 was not a report compiled in isolation or the product of a single individual assessment, like Kennan's Long Telegram had been three years previously. It came from the heart of the State Department and reflected military analysis and foreign policy considerations; it was a Washington insider view of the uncomfortable new world reality. The events of the past few years, along with intelligence that Truman received every day, seemed strongly to bear out the conclusions: unless resisted, the Soviets would push to take Berlin and expand into Western Europe; they would support Communism wherever it could gain a foothold, from Greece to the Far East; and, while calling for nuclear disarmament, they would press ahead with their own programme to build the bomb. However, agreeing with the conclusions in principle was much more difficult than enacting the recommendations in practice. As the writers of the report had observed, unless the US government and the American people could be convinced that the Cold War was a 'real war', it would be difficult to demand huge increases in military expenditure, including turbo-charging US nuclear scientists' own efforts to create the hydrogen bomb so they could stay ahead in the nuclear race. Well-argued points about the state of the world would have to become a budget Truman could get through Congress. Contrary to popular myth, NSC-68 was not immediately signed off by Truman. To enact the proposed vast programme of armament, the President would need some political cover. Truman only had to wait eleven weeks.

★ ★ ★

On Saturday, 24 June 1950, the President was home for the first time since Christmas. On the way back to Missouri his plane had stopped for a ribbon-cutting ceremony at a new airport in Baltimore, before flying on to Kansas City. From there it was a half-hour drive to the town of Independence. The Truman family's elegant, two-storey home was now marooned behind a chain-link fence for the sake of security, but it was sweet isolation at the end of a hot and humid southern summer's day. After dinner, Truman chatted with his wife Bess and then retired to the library. Just before half past nine, the telephone rang. It was Truman's Secretary of State, Dean Acheson. He was brief and to the point. 'Mr President,' he said. 'I have very serious news. The North Koreans have invaded South Korea.'

Since the warnings that South Korea would be invaded by the north in Truman's Briefs in 1946, the situation on the peninsula had hardened.

The temporary demarcation line along the 38th Parallel had become a permanent border, dividing a nation in two; an ideological splintering of a country that had nothing to do with race or creed, but everything to do with the Cold War. There were governments on either side of the line, one supported by Western nations and the other supported by Moscow. The huge foreign armies had gone – the Soviets in late 1948 and the Americans the following year – but advisors remained behind, and each side trained and equipped its own Korean troops. Throughout the spring of 1950, the CIA passed on reports that the North Koreans were potentially planning a full-scale attack, but each week only brought news of new incursions across the 38th Parallel. Until 24 June.

Truman had wanted to return to Washington straight away when he heard the news of the invasion, but Acheson had told him to hold off until the following day, so he could fly back in daylight; on 23 June, a Northwest Orient Airlines flight from New York to Seattle had crashed, killing all fifty-eight people on board, and there was an understandable wariness over the President taking a rushed night flight in the same week. On the three-hour journey on the Sunday, Truman pondered the turn of events. 'This was not,' he would later recall, 'the first occasion when the strong had attacked the weak ... Communism was acting in Korea just as Hitler, Mussolini and the Japanese had acted ten, fifteen, twenty years earlier.' The Daily Brief Truman received when he arrived in Washington contained a message from the US Embassy in Moscow, which warned that the North Korean offensive 'constitutes a clear-cut Soviet challenge to the United States' and called for the USA to make clear to the world it was prepared to assist Korean independence 'by all means at US disposal, including military assistance'. The CIA analysts agreed that action was needed; otherwise, the Soviets would exploit the 'Western failure' in Korea.

Six days after news of the invasion broke, Truman was already up and shaved at 5 a.m. when he got a call. It was an aide, passing on the message that General Douglas MacArthur was asking for two divisions of ground troops to be rushed to Korea. Truman had no issues with the additional commitment, but it was a sombre moment. Five years after the end of the Second World War, a US President was again sending American soldiers into battle. Truman narrated the day's events in his diary that night, adding, 'Must be careful not to cause a general Asiatic war.'

As Secretary of State Acheson later admitted, NSC-68 had nothing to do with Korea, but the invasion of the south by the Communist north 'proved our thesis'. It was the cover Truman needed. At a National Security Council meeting on 30 September, five months after the initial draft of NSC-68 had been secretly circulating around the corridors in Washington, Truman approved it as 'a statement of policy to be followed over the next four or five years', and requested implementation by all government agencies and departments. For the 1951–52 budget, the first after NSC-68 and the outbreak of the Korean War, military spending was more than quadrupled to $60 billion. It was the start of a new arms race.

6

Information of Vital Importance

By the time the Korean War broke out, Truman had been in office for five years. The 66-year-old was working eighteen hours a day and struggling under the strain. In principle, Truman was not fighting in Korea alone. The decision to counter the North Korean aggression had been unanimously supported by the UN Security Council, the first time the body had voted for military intervention in a conflict; there was no Soviet veto, as the USSR had been boycotting the Security Council and no Soviet representative was therefore present. When openly asked at his first press conference after the commitment to action, Truman insisted to journalists 'we are not at war', instead asserting it was a 'police action under the United Nations'. However, in practice, although US soldiers would go on to be supported by twenty other nations, it was Americans who did the vast majority of the fighting. At the start of the 'police action', nearly all the home press had shared similar sentiments to *The Washington Post*, whose editorial eulogised the President for giving 'the free world the leadership it desperately needed'.

The narrative of the Korean War is one of periods of stalemate alternating with dramatic reversals of fortune. Initially, North Korean forces swept all before them: the southern capital Seoul fell within a week, and the reports that graced Truman's desk were dire. One read, 'many [South] Korean soldiers showed a reluctance to hold under artillery fire and in several instances withdrew without contacting enemy infantry'. While reinforcements were rushed in by sea, a small number of US soldiers, along with what was left of the South Korean Army, fought to slow the onrushing tide. By mid-August, US casualties had already totalled more than 6,000. The generals drew a line 130 miles from the southern port city of Busan, where reinforcements were landing night and day, and decreed the retreat would end. Facing the prospect of potential annihilation, Truman ordered ten nuclear-capable B-29 bombers from the Strategic Air Command to Andersen Air Force Base on Guam in the Pacific, within striking distance of Korea. Each carried an assembled nuclear bomb, missing only the plutonium core. It was the first time an atom bomb had been deployed outside the USA since the end of the Second World War.

The threat of a wider war, which Truman had confided in his diary, was an ever-present concern. In one Brief during the fraught, high-temperature summer of 1950, as North Korean forces flooded across the 38th Parallel, Truman received news from Havana, Cuba. Smoke and 'the odour of burning paper' had been reported a few nights before at the Soviet Embassy. Earlier that day, the CIA's watching eyes had spotted the delivery of a batch of six 35mm film cameras: the suggestion of the CIA analysts was that sensitive documents had been photographed and transferred to microfilm before being burned. 'In the absence of evidence of systematic destruction of files by Soviet diplomatic missions in other countries,' they noted, 'the burning of files in Havana is probably a local or routine administration ... rather than an indication of Soviet expectation of global war in the near future.' With no other indications of imminent war, it was rather obvious the Soviet diplomats in Cuba were simply doing some housekeeping, but the CIA still felt the need to pass the report on and at the same time calm fraying nerves.

The Soviets had provided arms and training to the North Koreans, but the intervention that was feared in Washington was that of China, which had turned Communist following the 1949 revolution that brought Mao Zedong to power. As one early autumn Brief warned, 'The Chinese Communists have long had the capacity for military intervention in Korea on a scale sufficient to materially affect the course of events.' Twelve days later, contacts through the Netherlands government reported that four divisions of unidentified troops 'presumed to be Chinese' had crossed the Manchurian border into North Korea. The analysts were dismissive in their attached comment: 'The CIA continues to believe that the Chinese Communists, while continuing to assist the North Koreans, probably will not intervene openly in the present fighting in Korea.'

A dramatic change of fortune altered the equation. On 15 September 1950, US Marines mounted a daring amphibious landing at Inchon, flanking the North Korean troops encircling Busan; a fortnight later US soldiers were back in Seoul, and at the start of October, UN-backed forces crossed the 38th Parallel heading north. On 30 October, Truman's Brief contained reports of captured Chinese soldiers fighting in Korea, who had been wearing new cold-weather uniforms and spoke in the North Manchurian dialect. The CIA discounted them, but the following day there were reports from the US Eighth Army of facing regiments of Chinese Communist troops. The CIA analysts were still reticent to make a call on Chinese involvement, noting in Truman's Brief, '[The] CIA does not believe that the appearance of these Chinese Communist Soldiers indicates that the Chinese Communists intend to intervene directly or openly in the Korean war.' Two days later, they changed their mind.

On 2 November 1950, the Daily Brief led with an item on Chinese 'intervention' in Korea. Parts of the entry have been redacted, but the visible sections reveal intelligence of a meeting on 24 October, attended by Mao Zedong himself, in which open Chinese action in Korea was approved. The same Brief item also noted that 'twenty jet fighters of unknown nationality' had appeared over the city of Mukden. They were cutting-edge Soviet-designed fighter aircraft: MiG-15s. Unbeknown to anyone in Washington, a number of them were also being flown by Soviet pilots, who had repainted their planes and donned North Korean uniforms, a fact the Kremlin would vehemently deny for half a century.

The day before the 2 November report, the CIA Director had met with Truman to admit that it had now been 'clearly established' that there were Chinese soldiers opposing the UN 'police action' in Korea. The estimate of their numbers was as high as 20,000, and it was going up. Hillenkoetter had now been replaced as Director by a former Army man, General Walter Bedell Smith. Smith had been US Ambassador to the Soviet Union in 1946–48; it was he who had been away on official business when the feverish George Kennan dispatched his Long Telegram from the Moscow Embassy. Known as 'Beetle', the second Director of the CIA would go on to redefine the organisation's focus and make the CIA responsible for clandestine operations around the world. A few weeks after he met with Truman, Chinese forces crossed into North Korea and the momentum of the war swung back the other way, turning the US advance into a retreat. A melancholy note in the President's

Brief described US Commander MacArthur's crossing of the 38th Parallel (which Truman had approved) as 'walking into a baited trap'. In the eyes of many of the American public, the Korean War had quickly gone from a morally sound action to a disaster that was costing US lives. The daily news that Truman read was still mostly bad news.

★ ★ ★

Sobering reading though they mostly may have been, the Daily Briefs appeared to be serving their purpose. Truman was certainly not complaining: one of few pieces of feedback to the writers was that 'the President normally reads every item in the Daily [Brief] with interest'. But not everyone was happy. When the NSC conducted a review in 1949, its members criticised the Brief as a 'fragmentary publication' that was 'based largely on abstracts of State Department materials, not in historical perspective, lacking in full knowledge of the background'. Worse, it was suggested, 'There is an inherent danger it will be misleading to its customers.' There was some truth to the criticisms. While the document itself could be snappy and current on a good day, it relied on the reader to know the context behind each snippet of information and rarely, other than for communications from overseas employees of the State Department, were there significant extracts of actual intelligence. The 'Daily Summary', as Truman's Briefs were known, was simply that. The President received briefings around it and sometimes in parallel to it, but there had also been gaping holes in it: the severity of the situation in Greece, the imminent blockade of Berlin, the Soviets' atom bomb test and the real and pressing threat of Chinese intervention in Korea; all had been either underreported, analysed incorrectly or missed completely. A change seemed in order. After discussions between the CIA, the State Department and the NSC, a new draft was prepared for publication. There were still only a handful of items, but each was longer, with more context, and included comments and, for the first time, direct quotes from intelligence itself.

On 28 February 1951, five years after the two sheets of paper with six items had first landed on Truman's desk, the Daily Summary ceased to exist. Now, there was the Current Intelligence Bulletin. CIA Director Smith enclosed a note for Truman: 'It is hoped that the broad representative current intelligence presented in the new Bulletin, with immediate comments of analysts, will be of more comprehensive value to you.' Truman read his first copy of the newly adapted Daily Briefs while he was on holiday in Key West, Florida. Key West was Truman's favourite vacation spot, which he visited perhaps more than ten times while in office. He holed up in a former commandant's residence on the US Navy base, ensuring easy security, and spent his days swimming in the sea, reading or listening to records of classical music, and playing poker on the porch with family or any staff members he could coerce into joining him. Just over a week into his spring break in 1951, he wrote to Walter Bedell Smith to thank him personally for the new Briefs, which arrived with the other papers in the pouch flown out each day from the White House. 'I have been reading the Intelligence Bulletin and I am highly impressed with it. I believe you have hit the jackpot with this one.' That day, Truman's Brief had contained the CIA assessment of the apparent disappearance of Chinese leader Chairman Mao (and the suggestion he had heart trouble), a report of ongoing conflict in Indochina, rumours of a coup plot in Panama and news of the assassination of the Prime Minister of Iran. It seemed an impressive return to form.

It was while at Key West – on an earlier visit – that Truman had made the considered decision not to run for office again. The newly passed Twenty-Second Amendment to the US Constitution would prohibit all future presidents from holding office for more than two terms, but specifically exempted the sitting President, meaning Truman could have been on the ticket in 1952. He had been thrust into the position of leader of the free world on the death of his running mate Roosevelt, but since securing his own stunning election victory in 1948, the bitter reality of the Cold War and the reversal of fortunes in Korea were bringing him down. Added to that, Truman faced a flurry of domestic political scandals, including corruption investigations of senior administration officials. Public polls put his ratings at an all-time low; he may have been the 'most informed Chief-Executive in history', but he was no longer popular.

The daily intelligence assessments Truman received in his final eighteen months in office were still often occupied with Korea; the war on the peninsula would drag on beyond his presidency and conclude as it began, with a stalemate along the 38th Parallel. There was other news too, including an escalating crisis in the Middle East over Iranian relations with the West, and

French difficulties in their pre-war colony of Indochina, which will be the subject of later chapters. And throughout, there was the Cold War context of the Soviet threat in Europe and the spectre of a nuclear war, as the Soviet bomb-making programme carried on its seemingly inevitable progression.

The Daily Brief was rarely an easy read, but the President who had created the document hugely valued it. In a farewell speech to CIA officers two months before he left office, Truman told them that, when he had arrived in post, if the President wanted information 'he had to send to two or three departments to get it, and then he would have to have somebody do a little digging'. He thanked them for putting 'information of vital importance to the President in his hands', adding, 'I am briefed every day on all the world.' There is no doubt that Truman's Daily Briefs shaped his outlook on world events, which surely had an impact on US foreign policy. As he prepared to leave, he wanted his successor, whoever that was, to be equally well equipped to face the coming challenges.

Truman invited former wartime general and Republican candidate Dwight D. Eisenhower to visit the White House during the November 1952 election campaign, along with Adlai Stevenson, the Democrat pitching to replace Truman in post. Eisenhower turned down the invitation, as his advisors thought it would hurt his campaign, and a mortified Truman penned a personal note to apologise if he had caused any embarrassment, adding: 'What I've always had in mind was and is a continuing foreign policy … Partisan politics should stop at the boundaries of the United States. I am extremely sorry that you have allowed a bunch of screwballs to come between us.' Eisenhower did, however, receive four special CIA intelligence briefings over the course of the election campaign. Each was labelled 'Eyes Only' and wrapped in a spiral-bound cover. He was handed the second while he was on his campaign train going from Silver Spring to Baltimore, Maryland, in late September. It contained updates on the war in Korea, the developing situation in Indochina, the global Communist threat and unrest in the Middle East. When he read it, Eisenhower remarked to an aide, 'This certainly presents a picture of a gradually deteriorating situation all over the world. Sometimes I wonder if it has gone beyond the point from which it can be retrieved.'

President Truman's parting words to the American public were delivered in a televised address to the nation shortly before the 1953 inauguration. He acknowledged, 'I suppose that history will remember my term … as the years when the Cold War began to overshadow our lives.' Five days later, Eisenhower stood on the steps of the Capitol facing the Chief Justice and raised his right hand to take the oath of office. To one side was a grey-haired, grim-faced Truman. From that moment on, the President's Daily Briefs would be written for a new audience.

Part II

The Threat from Above: The Missile Gap

7

Briefing the Commander-in-Chief

For most of the world's population, the small silver sphere entered their lives in the form of a metronomic rising beep, audible for three weeks if they battled the static and tuned their radio set carefully in the 20-megacycle frequency. Many responded with wonder and with good reason: what they were hearing was the start of a new age. On 5 October 1957, the banner headline of *The New York Times* read, 'Soviet Fires Earth Satellite Into Space, It Is Circling The Globe At 18,000 M.P.H., Sphere Tracked In Four Crossings Over US.'

The intelligence bulletin prepared for the eyes of President Dwight D. Eisenhower the following day contained the more sobering side of the story: 'The launching of a satellite of this weight would require a launching vehicle approaching ICBM [intercontinental-ballistic-missile] proportions.' There were a number of advantages to having a man-made piece of metal hurtling around the globe, including gaining information about the ionosphere, but the blunt truth at the heart of the matter was that if the Soviet Union had a rocket that could blast a satellite into space, it also had a missile that could deliver a nuclear bomb halfway around the world. On Sunday, the staff of the CIA who carefully prepared each day's Daily Brief took a day off work, but when the new week began there was more troubling news. The cheerful beep that would fade a fortnight later as Sputnik's batteries died had been heard differently in China. As recorded in the Monday briefing, one 'authoritative' newspaper from the Communist nation boldly declared that 'Soviet missile successes have shattered "[American] hopes for world hegemony".'

★ ★ ★

By the time of the Sputnik launch, Eisenhower had been President for more than four years. Before that, he had spent the previous three decades in the military; never had a new President so easily adopted the Commander-in-Chief aspect of the role. Eisenhower looked like a soldier, with a straight jaw and clear eyes, and he carried himself like a man who had lived his life in uniform. He also had a legendary temper, which he tried, and occasionally failed, to contain. But he was a born leader. At one point, both parties had attempted to persuade the wartime general to run for the presidency on their ticket. Eisenhower had been quiet about his political affiliations, personally regarding himself as an issues voter who did not want to be labelled as liberal or conservative, but ahead of the New Hampshire primary in March 1952, senior Republican Party figures leaked to the press their knowledge that Eisenhower had voted Republican since he had left active military service four years before. 'I was now publicly known as a Republican,' Eisenhower later wrote in his memoirs, 'but would say no more.' He ran for the Grand Old Party and at the age of 63 secured a landslide 442 out of 531 votes in the Electoral College, campaigning under the meaningless but profoundly popular slogan 'I like Ike'.

The first few years of his first term had finally witnessed the end of fighting in the Korean War (with a negotiated armistice), multiple CIA clandestine operations (covered in detail in Part IV), as well as an increased threat from nuclear weapons. On 12 August 1953, the Soviets completed their first test of a hydrogen bomb, laying waste to an even larger area of the Kazakh Steppe. This time the bomb test had been pre-announced by Moscow, but it was hardly a surprise: US scientists had detonated their own first 'H-bomb' on a Pacific atoll ten months previously, as the sun set on Truman's time in the White House, and the working assumption of NSC-68 was always that the Soviets would be hot on the heels of the USA when it came to expanding their nuclear arsenal. The comment from the CIA analysts in the Brief the day after the announcement from Moscow – four days before the bomb detonation – assessed it as a reassertion of the strength of the Soviet regime. It was rather a statement of the obvious, although Eisenhower never read it. The uncomfortable truth was that since Truman had left the White House, the President was no longer actually reading the President's Daily Brief.

Eisenhower took a rather different view of intelligence to his predecessor. Truman had religiously taken his Daily Briefs back to the Residence to read carefully each evening, with discussions on the contents taking place the following day. In contrast, Eisenhower disliked reading reports of any kind and from his arrival in office simply refused to invest any time in the Daily Brief. One of the few he did pass his eyes over led him to complain that the document 'failed to differentiate between what the Soviets could do and what they were likely to do'. Instead, he asked for in-person briefings from a White House aide, Colonel Andrew Goodpaster. Eisenhower liked to do things the Army way, with a spoken report, a wide involvement of key staff and lots of charts and graphics. Each week, Goodpaster would pore over the Daily Briefs from the CIA – alongside reports from the State Department, the Department of Defense and the Joint Chiefs of Staff – and would work them up into a presentation which he would give to the President typically twice a week, on Wednesdays and Fridays. The President did not even consider that his primary intelligence briefing, which in his view was the presentation each Thursday at 9 a.m. ahead of the National Security Council meeting; on occasion there were so many maps and charts for the pre-NSC presentation that aides would have to load them into their own limousine to get them to the White House.

For the CIA analysts used to years of curating a highly personalised presidential intelligence report with an extremely tight-knit circulation, it was a painful readjustment. Intelligence from the CIA was part of the weekly NSC Briefing and it is hard to prove Eisenhower missed critical information by failing to read his Briefs, but the mystique of 'The President's Secret Daily Newspaper' had rather been lost. As one pained internal CIA memo noted the same month as the Sputnik launch: 'It [the Brief] is not established as a "must" read [at the White House]. At best, portions of it may be conveyed [to the President] ... by briefing officers.'

The production team had some right to be peeved. The preparation of the Brief was a significant amount of work. It was a product of the CIA's Office of Current Intelligence (OCI), which in the early 1950s was staffed by more than 150 people and operated out of buildings that were part of the grounds of the US Navy Bureau of Medicine and Surgery on 2430 E. Street in downtown DC. The OCI staff were in 'Q-Building', where each afternoon a chairman would sit with three regional intelligence division chiefs to consider what were called 'submissions' for the following day's Brief. Different branches of intelligence would put forward items and an assigned editor was responsible for making sure they were clear and in the preferred style before going to the board meeting each afternoon. Overnight, watch officers and an intelligence duty officer kept a close eye on all incoming material bearing on the items that would be in the next day's Brief. If something new came up, the original analyst who wrote the item would be hauled out of bed to update it.

The Brief itself was getting more complicated to produce. The mimeographed pages that had made up Truman's first Brief were long gone. Since early 1954, the Brief had come with occasional pictures, produced with a decidedly antique-looking Robertson graphic camera, which could reduce or enlarge an image to a desired size; the first image appeared on 22 February and was a military map of French positions against Communist guerrilla forces in Indochina. But all the daily hours of effort were not reaching the 'First Customer', as the President had been called during the Truman years. The exasperated authors of what was supposed to be the most exclusive daily intelligence document in the world found they had to checkmark the key items in the 'number one' Brief that went to the White House, in the hope they would be noted by the aide reading it on the Commander-in-Chief's behalf, and hopefully therefore make it to the President's twice-weekly presentation.

In Truman's last year, only fourteen copies of the President's Daily Brief had gone outside the Agency. One went to the Oval Office, another to the Secretaries at the State and Defense Departments, another to the President's Chief of Staff and the remainder to the Joint Chiefs and the key leaders at the NSC. The circulation was so small that the list of recipients was printed on the document: it was only ever intended that a handful of people would know what the President knew each day when it came to intelligence. The Eisenhower administration changed everything. Instead of the analysts putting together a key document for the President and his closest foreign and defence policy advisors, the Daily Brief was now one of a batch of sources of information that was fed to the President. Given that the President wasn't reading it, it seemed sensible to make sure more other people were. By mid-1954, thirty-three copies were going outside the Agency and by 1957, when the news about Sputnik was splashed across newspaper front pages around the world, the Brief's analysis of the event was going to forty-eight recipients, including one copy to the naval Commander-in-Chief of the US Pacific Fleet in Hawaii, nearly 5,000 miles from Washington. Not surprisingly, the quality and exclusivity of the information in the Brief was watered down as a result. It still covered critical information, but it was not the source of secrets it had once been.

A few months after they had produced the item on the first ever satellite, the Brief production team launched yet another redesign. Now in its twelfth year, the Brief was growing with age. The new design was sometimes ten to twenty pages long, although it still opened with a short summary of six items. There were now also often longer backup articles, which were in part an acknowledgement that many of the document's increasingly diverse readership needed more than just a summary of events if they were to understand what was going on around the world. The revised version also had lots of maps, not least because the Agency had learned that the former military commander in the Oval Office liked them. Each Brief now came with a map of the two hemispheres of the globe, with red arrows pointing at the areas covered by the document. The name of the new Brief was changed from the Current Intelligence Bulletin to the Central Intelligence Bulletin. It wasn't just so the CIA could stick their name on the front (in bold); it was also in the wish that Eisenhower might personally read it more often. The Director of the OCI, which produced the Brief, rather hopefully declared that the new version would be a publication that 'a responsible policymaker will be able to ignore only at his own peril'. Sadly for the analysts and authors, there is little evidence the changes attracted the personal attention of the President. But the added detail did give the revised Daily Brief an even better reputation outside of the Agency as a catch-all source for information about what was going on in the world.

The CIA itself was headed by a new man. Walter Bedell Smith had moved on to work for the State Department in 1952, just as Truman left office, and he had been replaced by Allen Dulles, who was the first civilian Director of the CIA. The 'civilian' title was somewhat of a misnomer. The spectacled, always smartly dressed Dulles had run an agent ring out of Switzerland in the Second World War; he was an experienced hardcore spy who embraced covert operations with vigour. Under his ten years in charge, the CIA carried out numerous actions to destabilise or bring down foreign governments from Iran in the Middle East to Cuba in the Caribbean, most of which were vehemently denied until decades later.

Dulles had a good relationship with Eisenhower, and it was he who led the pre-NSC meeting briefings every Thursday morning, which the President used as his substitute for reading his Daily Briefs. Often, the Executive Secretary of the NSC would ask for Dulles' input on topics already planned for discussion; on other weeks, the CIA would come up with its own suggestions for what should be covered in the intelligence briefing. The OCI, which wrote the Daily Brief, also produced the written content for NSC briefings, so while its star publication was still being ignored by the President, it still had significant input on the current intelligence that was regularly presented to Eisenhower ahead of NSC meetings.

Every Thursday at about 8.15 a.m., Dulles would pick up that week's graphics from Q-Building and be driven in a limousine to the White House, arriving about 8.50. An assistant would then set up the charts on an easel by the fireplace in the Cabinet Room of the West Wing, ready for Eisenhower to arrive at nine. Dulles presented his intelligence briefing directly to the President as if he were the only one in the room, but he would take questions and not move on to the next item until Eisenhower said, 'Ok, Allen. Let's go ahead.' The NSC's role in deciding on the topics predetermined what was covered most weeks, but the perception at the CIA was that the President was being kept well informed. He just could not be bothered to read his Briefs. As Eisenhower once reportedly told one CIA officer, 'I would much rather have it [an intelligence briefing] at the NSC level so all my staff and all of us can hear the same thing each time rather than to have a personal briefing.'

8

Reconnaissance

Missiles were not a new threat. Eisenhower's predecessor, Truman, had read multiple warnings in his President's Daily Briefs about them and the technology had already existed for more than a decade. The precursors to the huge rocket the Soviets had used to fling Sputnik into space were the brainchild of German wartime weapons developers, and one man in particular: Wernher von Braun. Von Braun was a suave scientist descended from Prussian aristocracy whose passion for space flight had led him to study physics. Immediately following completion of his doctorate, the 20-year-old von Braun was commandeered to develop rockets for the German Army. By 1935 he and his team were creating liquid-fuelled designs and, three years later, the entire research and development operation was relocated 200 miles north to Peenemünde, on the bleak Baltic coast.

By the time Hitler plunged Europe into war, Braun was already trying to turn rockets into weapons. In 1942, the first A-4 liquid-propelled rocket blasted off from Peenemünde and went 60 miles up into the atmosphere. A few months later, Braun was invited to explain the rocket project in detail to the Führer. At a movie hall at Hitler's headquarters, Braun introduced the project and then dimmed the lights. A projector whirred into life and played a colour film 'of a great rocket rising from its pad and disappearing into the stratosphere'. Hitler was enraptured, and when Braun had left, he told an aide, 'This is the decisive weapon of the war ... God help us if the enemy finds out about it.' Mass production was ordered immediately, with the rockets to have a new name under the *Vergeltungswaffen* (reprisal weapons) programme; the A-4 became the V-2.

More than a thousand were launched at London in the final years of the war, killing several thousand people, an experience more terrifying than anything before because the V-2 travelled so fast it arrived without warning. There were also other casualties of the V-2 programme. In order to try and meet Hitler's demands for 5,000 missiles that would rain death on London from the sky, prisoners from concentration camps, especially those with any manufacturing experience, were pressed into working day and night. As many as 20,000 may have perished building the V-2s, with eyewitnesses recalling how guards hanged prisoners who refused to work from cranes above the rocket assembly lines.

At the end of the war, Braun gave himself up to US forces, and he and a number of his colleagues, along with other German war scientists, were spirited away to the USA to work for their former enemy. Many inconvenient pasts, including Braun's membership of the *Schutzstaffel* (SS) and the Nazi Party, and his knowledge of the working conditions at the rocket plants, were conveniently forgotten. While the Americans had taken Braun, the Soviets had taken over Peenumünde, its remaining scientists and the V-2 production programme. The rocket race was on.

★ ★ ★

Presidents knew little about the Soviet rocket programme, but there were hints here and there in the Daily Briefs in the years before Eisenhower took office. One August 1946 Brief for Truman concerned news that German weapons experts were working on propulsion and radio guidance systems for Soviet rockets that were developed to fly 'over 700 miles'. They were calling them the V-3 and V-4. Four days later, the Brief revealed that a ship in the north Baltic Sea had been discovered sending coded Soviet messages to a station ashore, apparently concerning the flight of rockets launched over the sea from Peenemünde. By the time Eisenhower arrived in the White House, what the US intelligence services did not know about the Soviet missile programme was becoming a pressing concern.

On 25 November 1954, CIA Director Allen Dulles penned a memorandum for the President entitled 'Reconnaissance', which opened with the depressing line, 'You are familiar with the large gaps in our Intelligence coverage of the Soviet Union.' The gaps related to Soviet capabilities for launching a nuclear strike and Dulles' judgement was 'there is not the prospect of gaining this vital intelligence without the conduct of systematic and repeated air reconnaissance over the Soviet Union itself'. The US Air Force was already equipped with British-designed Canberras, a reconnaissance version of a jet bomber which could be modified to reach a ceiling of around 65,000ft, at which height it was noted 'the expectation that it would be detected is very low indeed, and the possibility that it would be intercepted and shot down is practically nil'. But the CIA wanted a specialist, more advanced aircraft that could get up to 70,000ft or higher. There was a 'possibility' that any aircraft flying over the Soviet Union might have to make a forced landing, but Dulles insisted 'the chances of that are low'. The desperate need for intelligence outweighed the risk.

The CIA Director did not have to wait long for a reply. The same day, Eisenhower gave a green light to the funding. In Dulles' memo, the requested figure is redacted, but the approval document for the project

The U-2 spy plane, built to fill the gaps in President Eisenhower's intelligence on the Soviet missile programme.

notes authorisation for the production of thirty aircraft 'at a cost of about $35 million'. The authorisation memo added, 'Mr. Allen Dulles indicated that his organisation could not finance this whole sum without drawing attention to it, and it was agreed that [the Department of Defense] would seek to carry a substantial part of the financing.' In short, the new, secret plane was going to be so expensive, the funding would have to be made deliberately murky. The specialist high-altitude aircraft design eventually selected for the programme was made by Lockheed and designated the CL-282, and it conducted its first flights two years later. In operation, it had a shorter, simpler name: the U-2.

The aircraft was to be equipped with a specially designed camera that, over the course of a whole mission, could photograph an area 200 miles wide and 2,200 miles long. In the CIA's project outline document, it was stated that in clear weather '[the] spotting camera will take pictures in which the individuals in a city street can be counted from 70,000 feet'. But its purpose was not to discover the number of people loitering in Moscow's Red Square. The two main objectives of the U-2 project were to 'improve estimates of [the] Soviet ability to deliver nuclear weapons' and to uncover 'Soviet guided missile development through photographs of testing ranges, etc.'. In his memoirs, Dulles staunchly defended the U-2 spy plane programme as vital to national security:

> We required the information necessary to guide our various military programs and particularly our missile programme. This we could not do if we had no knowledge of the Soviet missile programme. Without a better basis than we then had for gauging the nature and extent of the threat to us from surprise nuclear missile attack, our very survival might be threatened.

As it had with Truman, it was lack of knowledge which pushed Eisenhower into more aggressive action. However, the former general was deeply reticent to approve spy-plane flights over Soviet territory. Three years before Sputnik was launched into space, Eisenhower was already desperate for details of the Soviet missile programme, but the wheels he set in motion that day would lead to the greatest crisis of his presidency.

★ ★ ★

In the years immediately preceding the Soviets' launch of Sputnik, there was still scant information, even less of it verifiable, on Soviet missile programmes. The top item on the Daily Brief on 6 April 1955 reported the creation of a new Soviet ministry of 'General Machine Building', which the CIA suggested was a cover for a specialist missile-development ministry. It was headed by a Soviet minister who had held several armament production posts and had spent the last eighteen months as Deputy Minister in the Ministry of Defence Industry, where it was strongly suspected he had been steering the Soviet guided missile programme. As with all the intelligence about the Soviet missile programme, however, it was almost all guesswork. The Brief noted that 'in the past the USSR has set up specialist organizations to handle the series production of new weapons ... recent developments suggest that large-scale production of missiles may be imminent or may have commenced'. It was noted by the analysts that 'current estimates' credited the Soviets with a surface-to-surface ballistic missile with a range of 500 nautical miles.

Two weeks later, the Daily Brief shared the news of a missing US reconnaissance plane. The aircraft was a Boeing RB-47, a vast six-engine bomber, which had been designed as the replacement for the Boeing B-29 series that had dropped the atom bomb on Hiroshima and Nagasaki, and had formed the mainstay of US long-range bomber wings for the past decade. With its jet engines, the RB-47 could fly faster and higher, and the Strategic Air Command was fitting them with cameras instead of bombs and using them for reconnaissance flights as close as they dared, or sometimes directly over Soviet territory. On 18 April, one aircraft went missing on its flight from Alaska to the Kuril Islands, the easternmost tip of the Soviet land mass. The Brief stated there was 'no direct evidence' the missing aircraft had been intercepted by the Soviets, but it was noted that the most recent intercept attempt had been on a flight only three days earlier. Getting the U-2 in the air could not come soon enough. Thirty-eight years later, after the Iron Curtain had lifted, Soviet officials admitted that the missing RB-47 had in fact been deliberately intercepted and shot down by Soviet fighters. It was one of thirteen reconnaissance aircraft shot down over the course of the Cold War, and in many cases the crews did not survive. Desperately trying to fill what the CIA Director had described to the President as 'gaps in intelligence' was costing lives as well as money.

By the start of 1957, the situation was little improved. The top-secret spy plane project that Dulles had pushed the President to support two years previously was now live, and since June 1956, U-2s had made thirteen flights over Soviet bloc territory, including six over the Soviet Union itself. The preparations for the start of flights were exhaustive. As well as the secret training of pilots, logistics crews and the preparation of the aircraft themselves, the CIA expanded its photographic intelligence division and moved teams into a whole new building in preparation for the vast reels of film that would need instantly analysing after each flight. U-2 planes even made dummy runs across US airspace and photographed US nuclear weapons installations to give the picture interpreters some practise in what they were looking for. In February 1956, Dulles met two members of the Senate Armed Services Committee to inform them of the existence of what was referred to as 'project AQUATONE'. He also told two members of the House Appropriations Committee. For the next four years, those four men were the only elected politicians outside of the President's inner circle who had ever heard of the U-2. Ahead of the first flights over Soviet territory, Goodpaster – the White House aide who read Eisenhower's Daily Briefs for him – met with the CIA Deputy Director of Plans and agreed the cover story to be used if a U-2 was ever shot down. The answer (to everything) would be that the odd-looking aircraft was conducting 'weather research'.

Up until the month before, Eisenhower still harboured grave reservations about mounting direct, regular reconnaissance flights over the Soviet Union, which he feared could start a war. He sent Goodpaster to grill Dulles on the worst-case scenario: if a U-2 malfunctioned and crashed in the Soviet Union. The CIA Director was seemingly unconcerned, telling Goodpaster, 'If we did lose one, the pilot would not survive … [and] it was almost certain that the plane would disintegrate.' Anyway, he added, it would be difficult for the Soviets to prove 'in any convincing way' that they were being spied on. On 4 July 1956, a U-2 took off from Wiesbaden in Germany and flew over Poland, Belorussia and on to Leningrad (St Petersburg). The following day, a U-2 skimmed its way past Moscow, taking a few images of the Soviet capital through hazy cloud, before heading east to capture pictures of Soviet bomber airfields and the Kaliningrad missile plant. But the Soviets had been able to track the U-2 flights for much of their course. On 10 July, the US Embassy in Moscow received a strong note of protest and Eisenhower was spooked. U-2 flights over the Soviet Union were immediately halted. It was a year before Eisenhower again permitted flights across Soviet territory and, this time, he specifically requested the U-2s target Soviet missile development sites.

At the start of August 1957, U-2s flying out of Peshawar, in northern Pakistan, conducted nine flights: two over China and seven over Soviet-controlled Central Asia. There were rumours of a huge Soviet missile launching facility east of the Aral Sea in Kazakhstan, and in the absence of any other intelligence to go on, the pilot of the flight on 5 August followed the railway lines until they converged on a spot in the middle of nowhere. The U-2's camera captured oblique images of a facility with what appeared to be a massive missile launchpad. The image interpreters back at the CIA were still sifting through the stills when, on 26 August, Soviet state media reported the launch of an Intercontinental Ballistic Missile. They claimed that it was 'now possible to send missiles to any part of the world'. Unknown to the CIA and the President, US spy planes had flown right over the very spot it was launched from two weeks before.

The President's Daily Brief on 28 August 1957 contained an evaluation of the Soviet ICBM launch. There was, the analysts noted, 'no evidence' of a successful launch. But they added, 'since it has been estimated that the USSR could, in the relatively near future, have the capability to launch an ICBM test vehicle, the Soviet claim cannot be completely discounted'. The writers of the Daily Briefs, like the vast majority of CIA analysts, had no access to U-2 imagery, and given the astronomical increase in the Brief's circulation, they would hardly have mentioned it if they did. Six weeks later, by which time the Soviets had blasted a satellite into orbit, the Daily Brief was less sceptical.

Despite spending $35 million on a top-secret reconnaissance plane programme, the President had still found out about the Soviet missile success at the same time as the rest of the world. A U-2 overflew the launch site a few days later and captured wonderfully clear images of the main launch complex, but hindsight was no substitute for foreknowledge. A few months later, a new National Intelligence estimate concluded that, since August 1957, the Soviets had fired 'at least four and possibly six missiles, to a distance of 3,500 nautical miles'. They suggested that an operational version would be able to launch a nuclear warhead in excess of 5,000 miles. In short, by 1960, the Soviets would be able to fire a missile from Moscow that could destroy Washington, and they might have as many as a hundred of them.

9

'There was Created a Myth'

The 'missile gap' soon ceased to be the concern solely of US policy makers. Eisenhower's paralysis over Soviet protests and intercept attempts meant the U-2s were relegated to flights along the borders of Soviet territory, leaving the White House once more in the dark. In early 1959, a year after the Sputnik launch, a subcommittee of the Senate's Armed Services Committee called a series of witnesses to examine the perceived problem. Neil McElroy was one of them. The smartly attired 54-year-old had been parachuted in as Defense Secretary just five days after the Soviet satellite had begun orbiting, his main qualification for the post being that he was a good friend of the President; he had spent his previous decades as a brand manager and later president of the Procter & Gamble Company. When the senators interrogated McElroy, he answered questions truthfully. The result was a media storm. As *Time* magazine phrased it, '[He] told the Senators that in the early 1960s the U.S.S.R. will be ahead of the U.S. in operational ICBMs by a substantial margin, perhaps three to one.' A nuclear Armageddon seemed closer than it had ever been.

The US missile programme had come on leaps and bounds since the mid-1950s, and the first American ICBM had been launched only four months after the Soviets'. The USA was also considerably ahead in its development of solid-fuelled missiles. These missiles were more complex to construct than liquid-fuelled designs but were far easier to deploy, as their fuel could be permanently stored inside the missile, rather than needing to be carefully pumped in immediately before launch. However, perception was everything. Over the following year, there were a series of grand announcements from Moscow and the pressure for definitive proof was growing. After the weekly NSC meeting on 12 February 1960, Defense Secretary McElroy, along with the Chairman of the Joint Chiefs of Staff, stayed behind after the meeting to talk to the President about authorising more U-2 overflights. They badgered Eisenhower into approving a programme of spy plane flights for that spring.

In the pleasantly warm early dawn hours of a Sunday in May, a U-2 spy plane gently lifted into the inky-coloured sky above Peshawar, Pakistan, and turned north-east toward Afghanistan. The pilot was Gary Powers, an Air Force captain who had left behind his uniform to fly secret missions for the CIA. Powers was the most experienced U-2 pilot on the programme, with twenty-seven operational missions under his belt, including one penetrative mission over Soviet territory. The previous 9 April flight over the Soviet Union had proceeded successfully, although it was clear that Soviet radar was becoming more sophisticated in its tracking capabilities. The targets for the next photographic mission were the known Soviet missile launching site in Kazakhstan, the nuclear-testing site at Severodvinsk and two other suspected ICBM complexes. Bad weather pushed the flight to 1 May, which was unfortunate timing. The May Day holiday meant there was less civilian air traffic, so tracking the U-2 was easier for Soviet radar operators. As it entered Soviet airspace, all non-military flights were grounded, and a concerted effort was made to shoot the U-2 down. Thirteen fighters were scrambled unsuccessfully, but four-and-a-half hours into the flight, at an altitude of 70,500ft, the U-2 was rocked by an explosion from behind. It was a surface-to-air missile. Flung against the cockpit roof, Powers could not eject and had to open the cockpit manually as the U-2 began spiralling towards the ground. After fighting to free his oxygen hose, which was dragging him down with the plane, he got free and fell several thousand feet before his parachute opened.

Goodpaster was the bearer of the bad news to Eisenhower. 'One of our reconnaissance planes ... is overdue and probably lost,' he told the President over the phone that afternoon. Eisenhower later recalled: 'I knew instantly this was one of our U-2 planes, probably over Russia.' The pre-planned cover story was immediately deployed, and it was announced that an aircraft of the joint NASA–USAF Air Weather Service mission flying out of Turkey had apparently gone down after the pilot reported 'experiencing oxygen difficulties'. A U-2 was hastily painted in a NASA livery and paraded in front of journalists' cameras, but the narrative unravelled completely when, five days later, the Soviet premier Nikita Khrushchev announced that Powers had been captured alive. It was everything Eisenhower had feared. Walking into his secretary's office after he had been informed of Powers' capture, Eisenhower said, 'I would like to resign.' He rowed back from that melancholy pronouncement, and instead pivoted to take full, personal responsibility. He rejected Dulles' own offer of resignation and told his aides, 'We will now just have to weather the storm.'

On 11 May, the President's Daily Brief contained the first mention of what was described as an 'aircraft incident' over the Soviet Union, in which it noted there would be an imminent press conference in Moscow 'to produce the "evidence"'. The following day's Brief remarked on activity at the missile launching site in Kazakhstan, which was one of the targets Powers had been sent to spy on. The evidence of activity was not images but second-hand reports that aircraft that had previously been suspected of flying to Kazakhstan for missile tests had been spotted taking off from Moscow in the preceding days. The Soviets did launch another rocket three days later, which carried the largest payload into space so far, and which the Brief rumoured was an attempt at a 're-entry' to bring a payload back to earth. The 12 May Brief went on to share the intelligence assessment that the Soviets might be capable of putting a man in orbit by the end of the year, but the attention of the document's readers would have been focused elsewhere. The Soviets had by then revealed they had captured not only Gary Powers but also intact sections of the top-secret aircraft; the CIA Director's arrogant claim that the pilot would die and the U-2 would disintegrate had now been proved completely wrong.

★ ★ ★

With Powers captured and the U-2 programme exposed, Eisenhower's administration was taking a public pounding. But the understanding of the missile gap was about to change dramatically. A special task force was created at National Security level to trawl over all the information available on Soviet long-range missile launch sites. It transpired the Air Force had made their own extensive list of potential Soviet missile sites, which, after some arm twisting, was handed over. The working group began with a potential ninety-five locations, but the more they investigated it, the stranger it seemed. There was only one confirmed launch site: the one in Kazakhstan that was first overflown in 1957. Of the rest, the team assessed four possible launch sites, twelve undetermined and the remainder doubtful. The Soviets were clearly testing long-range missiles, but, on the basis of the slim evidence available, they did not seem to be deploying them in any real numbers.

On 10 August 1960, the Discoverer XIII satellite was launched into space from Vandenberg in California. As with all satellite launches until the advent of the Space Shuttle, the rocket that propelled it beyond the earth's atmosphere had been originally designed as a missile. After the embarrassment of the Sputnik launch in 1957, the US satellite programme was now in fact significantly ahead of the Soviets'. The National Aeronautics and Space Administration (NASA) was carrying out a civilian programme under the title 'Pioneer', but 'Discoverer' was an entirely different project: even the name was a cover. The project's real title was 'Corona', and it was

President Eisenhower holds the Stars and Stripes carried in the Corona satellite capsule.

the first spy satellite programme in history. Discoverer XIII was the fifth test flight of the system. The satellite was successfully launched into orbit and then jettisoned a 120lb capsule back to earth, which splashed down 380 miles north-west of the Hawaiian island of Oahu. Five days after the launch, Eisenhower was presented with a US flag which had been to space and back. The next time a Discoverer launched into space, instead of carrying the Stars and Stripes, it carried a camera and 20lb of film. After a successful camera test, the 10 December flight returned the first satellite reconnaissance images of a Soviet ICBM missile site. The inaugural intelligence report from the new source, codenamed 'KEYHOLE', was entitled, 'An Assessment of an Installation at Plesetsk, USSR, as an ICBM Site'. From then on, the President would never be completely in the dark.

The same month as the successful Discoverer XIII launch, two US tourists hurrying back to their hotel through the rain after watching the Moscow ballet were approached by a local man on a bridge just off Red Square. The Russian asked them to light his cigarette, chatted for a few moments and then gave the Americans a letter to be delivered to the US Embassy. The two tourists were left clutching the confession note of a high-ranking Soviet military intelligence officer. In the letter, he wrote that he had already collected 'very important materials on many subjects of exceptionally great interest and importance to your government'. Colonel Oleg Vladimirovich Penkovsky was offering to be a spy. The 41-year-old former war veteran turned intelligence officer was deadly serious: he had already designated a dead drop to be used to communicate with him. He had also been truthful about the intelligence he had access to, and when the CIA recruited him, he immediately began supplying documentation which included details of the Soviet missile programme. Penkovsky's actions that day on the Moscow bridge would go on to cost him his life, but the information he began supplying confirmed the analysis by the National Security task force. When he finally had a face-to-face meeting with his handlers the following year, Penkovsky described the entire idea of the missile gap as 'a hoax'. By late 1960, it was beginning to become clear that the 'missile gap' was not the yawning chasm that had been feared. As Eisenhower would later phrase it in his memoirs, the missile gap was an 'imaginative creation of irresponsibility'. As far as the American public were concerned, however, the missile gap was still a problem, and a political as well as a military one.

★ ★ ★

Eisenhower had served his two terms as President, so in 1960 the contest would be between two new candidates. The Republicans selected Eisenhower's Vice President, Richard Nixon. Nixon was an experienced political operator and had been the obvious choice from the Republican field. In contrast, the Democrats selected a dynamic senator who was a war hero, a Pulitzer Prize-winning writer and the youngest man ever to run for the highest office. Ahead of his pitch for the White House, John Fitzgerald Kennedy castigated the Eisenhower administration, making the missile gap his weapon of choice. 'We are losing the satellite missile race with the Soviet Union,' he insisted in a speech in the Senate in February 1960. 'We are facing a gap on which we are gambling with our survival.' It was a theme he returned to in the now historic televised debates, where the vibrant Kennedy outshone Nixon, who appeared shifty and evasive. 'Mr Nixon talks about our being the strongest country in the world,' Kennedy told the viewers, '… [but] by nineteen sixty-one, two, and three, they [the Soviet Union] will be outnumbering us in missiles.' It was a simple message and it resonated with voters, but Kennedy's facts were wrong. The Democrat won the close-fought election, but he found out from the CIA before his inauguration that there was no missile gap of the kind he had claimed.

Once in office, the reality began to sink in. The missile gap which had so concerned Eisenhower, the CIA and the Pentagon, and which had been a key plank of Kennedy's election win, had never truly existed. As Kennedy's Defense Secretary phrased it to the new President in a conversation in the Oval Office that was secretly taped, 'There was created a myth in the country that did great harm to the nation. It was created by, I would say, emotionally misguided but nonetheless patriotic individuals.' Kennedy admitted he was 'One of those who put that myth around, a patriotic and misguided man', and the room descended into laughter.

The President the youthful senator from Massachusetts was replacing had never read his Daily Briefs, but Kennedy would come to rely on the CIA's special intelligence briefings. His close relationship with the Agency would trigger the most significant change in the Daily Brief since 1946 and the Briefs would bear witness to a crisis that brought the world to the brink of nuclear war.

Part III

A Path Full of Hazards: The Cuban Missile Crisis

10

'The CIA is the Place
I Have to Go'

On the night of 17 April 1961, an invasion fleet of antiquated Second World War-era cargo vessels prepared to disembark just over 1,000 soldiers into landing craft off the coast of the island of Cuba. The soldiers were going home. They had fled Cuba a few years before, but now the exiles were returning, with the aim of bringing down the government. The exiles had been trained in Guatemala and Florida by the CIA. At their backs, beyond the horizon, were ships from the US Navy. In the skies above they were expecting the support of US Air Force aircraft. But instead of landing secretly and unleashing a new revolution, their movements were broadcast to the whole population by a radio station on the beach, and within twenty-four hours more than a hundred had been killed by the Cuban Army and the remainder taken prisoner. To less invested observers, it was obvious that the odds of the supposedly secret Cuban operation being successful had always been rather slim: a week before, *The New York Times* front page had even carried a story reporting 'an army of 5,000 to 6,000 men, intent on deposing Mr. Castro, was massing in Florida, Louisiana and Guatemala'.

The island 90 miles from the tip of Florida had seen significant political changes in the previous three years. In 1959, Cuba's pro-USA dictator, Fulgencio Batista, was overthrown and replaced by a Communist revolutionary administration led by the bearded, cigar-chomping Fidel Castro. When Castro established formal diplomatic relations with the Soviet Union, the Eisenhower administration banned imports of Cuban-grown sugar, overnight removing the market for 80 per cent of the island's main export. But countering the newly Communist island in the USA's backyard was deemed to require more than economic sanctions. Many in the White House wanted Castro removed.

The plan for the invasion of Cuba by supposedly deniable exiles had been put in motion by Eisenhower, before Kennedy took office. It was an operation Kennedy inherited, but while the new President questioned elements of the plan, he was fully supportive of the intended outcome; during the 1960 election campaign, Kennedy had openly called for the USA to support the 'freedom fighters' who opposed Castro's government in Cuba. Two months before the invasion itself, at a White House meeting with CIA, State, Defense Department and National Security team aides, Kennedy pushed back against the idea of a mass, very public invasion: 'Could not such a force be landed gradually and quietly and make its first major military efforts from the mountains – then taking shape as a Cuban force within Cuba, not as an invasion force sent by the Yankees?' the President asked. In the end, Kennedy agreed to mounting the invasion, although the landing site was changed from Trinidad to the Bay of Pigs in an attempt to make the action less obtrusive. The proponents of the plan put forward the same argument that had been presented to Eisenhower over the U-2 flights: that if the worst happened, the USA could deny involvement. As his predecessor had, Kennedy naively believed it.

The embarrassing mess of the Bay of Pigs invasion did not turn Kennedy against the security services but hardened his determination to own any future such operations, rather than trusting the whole process to the 'experts'. As Kennedy confided in one aide, the Bay of Pigs had been 'the most excruciating period of my life'. He admitted he 'might make mistakes in the future, but they would be his mistakes, not someone else's'. The Bay of Pigs was the nadir of Kennedy's short presidency, but despite the abject failure of the mission, the CIA had acquired in Kennedy a Commander-in-Chief who was a staunch ally of the Agency.

★ ★ ★

Almost immediately after arriving in the White House, Kennedy took a shine to the CIA. He found pulling the stiff levers of government arduous and told one aide that posing a question to the State Department meant 'four or five days to get a simple yes or no'. In contrast, he found the CIA light on its feet and more in tune with the way he preferred to work. He told his National Security Advisor, McGeorge Bundy, 'I don't care what it is, [the] CIA is the place I have to go.' In a past life, Kennedy had worked as a journalist for the *Chicago Herald* and he liked documents to be short and to the point. The CIA was encouraged to ensure that anything destined for the eyes of the President was no more than two pages long and double-spaced. Kennedy liked the CIA, but initially he was harder to keep informed than Eisenhower had been. In short, Kennedy was easily distracted.

McGeorge Bundy had been a controversial choice for Kennedy's National Security Advisor. The Harvard professor had been an intelligence officer in the Second World War and, as a registered Republican, was seen to have double-crossed his own party and gone to work for his political enemies when he joined Kennedy's administration. He had a rapier-sharp mind and a low tolerance for fools. He was perfectly comfortable speaking what he perceived as truth to power and in May 1961 he penned a revealing note to the President. Kennedy was often not reading the papers he was sent, but he also refused to have an Eisenhower-style in-person presentation. Bundy passed on the note to Kennedy when the President was on the way back from a trip to Canada, his first official foreign visit.

'I hope you'll be in a good mood,' the note began, after which Bundy stated, 'We need some help from you so that we can serve you better.' The note covered a number of items, including the fact that Kennedy left the back door to the Oval Office open, meaning he was frequently door-stepped during meetings, and often let planned meetings he did have run late. 'When you start a big meeting half an hour late and let it go an hour overtime,' Bundy stated, 'you have not only disrupted the schedules of 30 men, but you have probably set 100 men under them to still greater trouble. This doesn't matter, except that it wastes executive energy, the most precious commodity you have brought to Washington.'

The National Security Advisor's first complaint with the President, however, was intelligence briefings. Kennedy had earlier asked Bundy to try giving him a morning intelligence briefing, but the idea had died a death. 'I have succeeded in catching you on three mornings,' Bundy noted, 'for a total of about eight minutes, and I conclude that this is not really how you like to start the day … we can't get you to sit still.' Even when the President did take an interest, he would shift his focus, with the result that 'Right now it is so hard to get to you with anything not urgent and immediate that about half the papers you personally ask for are never shown to you because by the time you are available you clearly have lost interest in them'. Bundy was open to Kennedy's wishes as to when he wanted his intelligence briefing, but was adamant it had to happen: 'maybe another time of day would be better for daily [intelligence] business. After lunch? Tea? You name it. But you have to mean it, and it really has to be every day.' The memo was a brutal evisceration of Kennedy's attitude toward intelligence, and it was clear that a dramatic change was needed, especially in the light of the Bay of Pigs fiasco, which Bundy described as 'a bad mistake', although he added, 'it was not a disgrace and there were reasons for it ... it must not throw us off balance'.

To help ensure there was balance would require a new approach to the written intelligence passed to the President, as well as someone making sure he set aside time to read and discuss it. On 15 June, two CIA analysts were summoned from their desks in Q-Building to the White House. Major General Chester Victor Clifton Jr, or Ted, as he was more commonly known in the West Wing, was the man responsible for the meeting. He was also supposed to be responsible for the President's regular intelligence briefings, which weren't happening. When the CIA analysts entered Clifton's office, he deposited a stack of papers on the desk in front of them. It was the Daily Brief (still officially titled the Central Intelligence Bulletin), along with papers from the Defense and State Departments. 'What I need,' the general told them, 'is something that will have everything in it that is worth the President's attention, everything that is worth his knowing in all these things, so I don't have to fuss with them.' In less than twenty-four hours, the CIA analysts from the OCI had created an entirely new version of their daily document. Instead of the previous six main items, the new Daily Brief (which the analysts named the President's Intelligence Checklist) had more than ten items, each with a succinct, single paragraph. Following the paragraphs were a series of bullet-point notes and then relevant maps. Clifton thought it was perfect.

The next day, a Saturday, the general got in a car and drove an hour west, out of Washington, to Middleburg, Virginia. Glen Ora was a 400-acre country estate far removed from the pressure of the capital. It was the Kennedys' bolt hole. Clifton found the President in the middle of his morning swim in the estate's outdoor pool, through a tree-lined path a couple of minutes' walk from the back of the grand, white-painted house. Kennedy was perched on a diving board, taking a break from swimming laps. Clifton presented him with the new version of the Daily Brief and Kennedy approved it straight away. From then on, he was a committed reader.

The contrast with Eisenhower could not have been starker. Kennedy's personal enthusiasm for his new Daily Brief was infectious and a huge boost to the morale of the intelligence officers who helped put the document together. As one later recalled, 'People were willing to work long hours and to come in at three o'clock in the morning because they knew damn well what they produced was read personally by the President immediately upon its delivery to the White House.' As with all the previous iterations of the Daily Brief, it was compiled the day before, although CIA analysts would get into the office for 5 a.m. to ensure it was up to date before the pages were delivered to the White House for 8.30, when the President was having his breakfast. If Kennedy was not able to read it straight away, he would look over the pages in the breaks between meetings and raise any questions he had. If he wanted more information than was contained in the short summary paragraphs, he would often get aides to call the CIA, or sometimes even call staff at the Agency himself.

The initial circulation for the new Daily Brief, outside of its authors, consisted of only the President himself and the CIA Director. For the first time since the original document Truman had commissioned in 1946, the President's Daily Brief really was for the President's eyes only. The Brief became the piece of paper the President always read and had to hand. When the archivists at the JFK Library were filing the President's papers years later, they found a hand-written note inside one Brief from Jackie Kennedy to her husband. 'Dear Jack,' she wrote, 'Could you please not play TV too loud as [I] am asleep.'

The very first of the new Daily Briefs, which Clifton handed to Kennedy at the poolside on 17 June 1961, was written in parallel to the existing version. There was significant overlap between the two. Both Briefs reported on an aborted ICBM launch at the Soviet testing site in Kazakhstan; both documents also covered political developments in the Congo and delays to the UK's efforts to join the European Common Market. However, the new version created specifically for the President had a number of unique items.

In the middle of the second page was a note that a Soviet ship had arrived in Havana, Cuba, two days before. The crates on its deck were of the type typically used to ship Soviet-made MiG-15 and MiG-17 fighter aircraft. It was evidence, the President's new Brief reported, of '[the] first Soviet jet fighters probably delivered to Cuba'. The Soviets were now actively arming their new ally, just a stone's throw from the USA.

11

Soviet Merchant Ships

The first inkling of the events that would bring the world to the brink of nuclear war appeared as a footnote in John F. Kennedy's 4 August 1962 Daily Brief. The item did not make the five main paragraphs but was included as the fourth note on the final page. It read: 'Eleven Soviet merchant ships are on their way to Havana and we strongly suspect they are carrying arms. Such a delivery would not be far short of the total amount of Arms delivered in the first half of 1962.' A few days later the authors added:

Soviet shipments to Cuba have been arriving on an unprecedented scale since mid-July. Some 32 vessels are involved; at least half of these we believe to be carrying arms. Five passenger ships with a total capacity of about 3,000 persons have already arrived. Some of the personnel are said to be Soviet technicians, and we have no reason to doubt this. We do not believe there are any combat troops among them.

The Soviets did not appear to be shipping soldiers to their Cuban ally; instead, they were shipping technical experts who could operate the weaponry hidden under the covered decks of the merchant vessels that were chugging into Havana on an almost daily basis.

★ ★ ★

Since the Bay of Pigs Invasion, Cuba had planted itself firmly in the Soviet camp. Six months after the exiles were pinned down and captured on a Cuban beach, Kennedy gave formal authorisation for a CIA programme that was intended to achieve what the invasion of the exiles had failed to do: bring down Castro's regime. Operation Mongoose was a wide-ranging covert operations programme that included espionage, sabotage, psychological warfare and attempted assassinations. The programme's phase one report, in July 1962, obliquely referenced the 'higher authority' who had in November the previous year desired a special effort 'in order to help Cuba overthrow the Communist regime'. The most obvious success was in Pinar del Río in western Cuba, where Cuban CIA agents had managed to create a guerrilla force 250 strong. The rest of the operation had not achieved similar demonstrable outcomes, but the psych-ops team had started radio broadcasts from US submarines 'appearing as broadcasts from Cuban guerrillas inside Cuba' to try and convince the Cuban population there was a sizeable internal resistance movement.

There was even an operation to treat a cargo of Cuban sugar being exported to the Soviet Union with chemical agents, in the hope that the Soviets would halt imports, leaving Cuba with no market for its main agricultural product; the Soviet Union had only stepped in to buy Cuban sugar when the USA banned imports overnight after Castro came to power. The Cuban sugar operation was eventually cancelled after strong objections from the State Department's legal advisor, who refused to believe the proposed chemical solution was harmless, noting in a memo to planners, 'ask how you would feel about the same thing happening to yourself or your family, if the action had been taken by the other side'.

The first offensive military operation took place on the night of 24 August 1962. A group of Cuban exiles who had been landed on the island by the CIA months after the Bay of Pigs took matters into their own hands. Cramming themselves into a speedboat, along with heavy machine guns, a 20mm canon and a lightweight artillery 'recoilless rifle', they cruised into Havana Harbor and opened fire on a waterside hotel known to be the home of Soviet and Czech advisors to Castro's regime. They fired for seven minutes from 11.30 p.m. and then disappeared into the night. The action was not officially CIA sanctioned, but those responsible were CIA trained and armed. It was not how events had meant to unfold, but the attack served its purpose. In Kennedy's Daily Brief a few days later, it was reported that 'the [Cuban] navy reacted quickly ... [but] subsequent search operations were badly handled, permitting the raiders to slip away'. The analysts added, with more than a hint of glee, that the incident had 'given Havana the jitters'.

The rationale frequently asserted by the Castro administration and Moscow for the massive build-up of weapons and material on the island, barely 100 miles from the US coast, was that the USA was threatening Cuba. It was an allegation always laughed off by Washington, but when the details of the efforts of Operation Mongoose came to light decades later, the apparent paranoia in Moscow and Havana at the time was clearly better founded than many had believed. In the early 1960s, Operation Mongoose was numerically the largest US intelligence operation inside the borders of a Communist state. There were more spies and covert operatives in Cuba than in the Soviet Union.

★ ★ ★

It was initially difficult for the US intelligence services to pin down the specific nature of the Soviet arms that had reached Cuba. Kennedy's 18 August Brief suggested that 'the large influx of Soviet military equipment and technicians into Cuba lately could be connected with the beginning of construction of surface-to-air missile sites', but the missiles angle was not confirmed until four days later. Most of the information in the Brief on the ground in Cuba had until that point come from Cuban sources, but that changed near the end of August. 'We now have several reports from the British Embassy whose people have been out looking,' the analysts reported. 'They have spotted at least one camp southwest of Havana ... Their information on the equipment coming in ... leads them to suggest that "an expert might consider the possibility of anti-aircraft rockets and radar."' At the end of August, the Daily Brief was reporting 'no sign of a let up in the movement of Soviet equipment and personnel into Cuba'.

From all the evidence available, it seemed the Soviets were shipping missiles to their Caribbean ally, although the Cubans themselves were not being allowed to operate them independently. The Kennedy administration needed more information, so it turned to the tool that Eisenhower had commissioned to fill the gaps in his information: the U-2 spy plane. On 6 September 1962, Kennedy's Daily Brief led with a map of Cuba on which suspected Soviet-made surface-to-air missile (SAM) sites were circled. The analysts confirmed, 'Nine SA-2 sites have now been firmly identified in the western one third of the island and it is highly probable that work on a similar installation is under at least one [other] site.' In case Kennedy might have had a hazy memory of past events, the following day's Brief reminded him precisely what the 'SA-2' SAM was: '[The] Soviets have provided Cuba with rockets of the same kind that shot down the U-2 [over the Soviet Union in 1960].'

The Cuban situation was now increasingly delicate. U-2 flights were giving Kennedy critical information on the weapons being supplied to Cuba, but the disconcerting news was that those very weapons were anti-aircraft missiles that could down another U-2, trigger another diplomatic incident and at the same time leave the White House again in the dark about the threats they faced. The spy plane flights were scaled back and the previous detailed sweeps up and down the long, thin island were reduced to sideways photography and shorter criss-crossing missions that did not linger over Cuban airspace.

In the weeks that followed, there was good news and bad news in the daily written intelligence that reached Kennedy. There were more convoys of merchant ships from the Soviet Union to Cuba, including one which, according to a US-flagged tug in the area, was being escorted by submarines. One of the SA-2 SAM sites turned out to be a smaller, simpler missile site, but that was counteracted four days later when the Brief noted, 'Latest photographic reconnaissance confirms two more surface-to-air missile sites.' The total number of anti-aircraft defensive missile sites in Cuba, according to the CIA, had reached thirteen. At the start of October more were added, taking the total to twenty, although it was unclear how many were operational. The problem, as the Brief noted, was that if any more missile sites came online, they would 'close one of the few remaining gaps in missile coverage of the island'. And the scaling back of the U-2 flights was reducing the flow of critical information.

On 9 October, the task force responsible for Operation Mongoose and Cuban strategy in general met at the White House. It included top-ranking CIA officials, NSA McGeorge Bundy, as well as the Secretaries of State and Defense. They needed an 'intrusive sweep' of Cuba, although the participants debated the risk, which the CIA assessed as a 'one in six' chance of losing a U-2. The SAM sites that could take out a U-2 were a serious concern, but the other worry was whether the construction of the large numbers of anti-aircraft missiles was intended to shield something more sinister. One 'in-and-out' flight over western Cuba was approved at the meeting, with the mission scheduled for as soon as possible.

In October, the skies above Cuba are often cloaked in heavy, rain-filled cloud, impenetrable to the eyes of cameras 70,000ft up. Given the risks of the flight, there was no desire to waste a U-2 mission, so the next U-2 flight over Cuba was delayed for three days until the weather forecast predicted less than 25 per cent cloud cover. Shortly after midnight on 14 October 1962, Major Richard Heyser guided his U-2 down the runway of Laughlin Air Force Base and took off into the humid Texas night. He gradually climbed to 72,500ft and passed over Cuba from south to north, just after dawn. He triggered his cameras and then watched the ground closely for a trail of smoke that might signal the launch of a surface-to-air missile. He crossed Cuba safely, gently banked his plane west, towards Florida, and landed at an Air Force base in Orlando. Immediately on landing, technicians whisked the film from the camera bays of his U-2 for processing. Years later, when interviewed about what he found on his flight, Heyser told journalists the experience had made him anxious, as he 'did not want to go down in history as the man who started World War Three'. When the negatives were developed, they revealed the cargo that had been shipped to Havana in the eleven Soviet merchant vessels mentioned in Kennedy's Daily Brief on 4 August. The CIA image interpreters spent most of the next day poring over the films to make sure they had not been mistaken.

At 8.30 p.m. on 15 October, the CIA Deputy Director telephoned McGeorge Bundy. Kennedy's National Security Advisor took the news calmly. Instead of immediately putting a call through to the President, he decided it would be best to wait. It was, as he would later describe it, 'big news' and 'its validity would need to be clearly demonstrated' before any action. More U-2s had been sent to overfly Cuba to get as much information as possible, and Bundy decided he would brief the President in the morning. As he justified it in a memo to Kennedy a year later:

> It was a hell of a secret, and it must remain one until you had a chance to deal with it ... I decided that a quiet evening and a night of sleep were the best preparation you could have in the light of what would face you in the next days. I would, I think, decide the same again.

12

Offensive Weapons

Just before 9 a.m. on Tuesday, 16 October 1962, the President's National Security Advisor was shown into the President's bedroom. Kennedy was sat up in bed in a dressing gown, reading *The New York Times*. He had only got back from a mid-term election campaign trip to New York at two o'clock that morning, and Bundy was the bearer of bad news. Bundy almost certainly had with him the President's Daily Brief for that day. The whole first page of that morning's intelligence report remains redacted, so it is not clear whether it contained the critical news from Cuba. The CIA analysts would definitely have had time to make it the first item, given Bundy had been informed early the previous evening. Sitting with Kennedy in his bedroom, Bundy said to him, 'Mr President, there is now hard photographic evidence that the Russians have offensive [nuclear] missiles in Cuba.'

Two-and-a-half hours later, Kennedy was in the Cabinet Room of the West Wing with his closest aides, staring at an enlarged version of one of the photographs. Helpfully, the CIA had applied some labels. 'There's a medium-range ballistic missile site,' said CIA Deputy Director General Marshall Carter. Kennedy seemed sceptical, and asked, 'How do you know it's a medium-range ballistic missile?' 'The length, Sir,' interjected the CIA imagery expert, who was at the meeting precisely to field that kind of question. The image analysts who had pored over the photographs for hours on end had assessed the missile types by the length of the transport vehicles, which they figured out by measuring the shadows cast by the dawn sunshine as the U-2 flew overhead. According to the available (incomplete) transcript of the meeting, the President did not speak much, inviting the thoughts of his inner circle first.

Kennedy's Secretary of State, Dean Rusk, seemed initially blindsided: 'Mr. President, this is of course, a serious development. It's one that we, all of us, had not really believed the Soviets could carry this far.' But as he warmed to his subject, he settled on what he thought were Kennedy's options. 'By and large there are these two broad alternatives: one, the quick strike; the other, to alert our allies and Mr. Khrushchev that there is [an] utterly serious crisis in the making here.'

At that morning meeting, Kennedy was all for a military response: 'I think we ought to, beginning right now, be preparing to [strike]. Because that's what we're going to do anyway ... we're going to take out these missiles.' The President was already acutely conscious of time pressure, admitting to his closest security advisors, 'I don't think we got much time on these missiles ... So it may be that we just have to [launch a strike], we can't wait two weeks.' The meeting had to wrap up, as Kennedy had an official lunch planned with Crown Prince of Libya, Hasan as-Senussi; at Bundy's recommendation, Kennedy was sticking to his pre-planned diary engagements, so as to alert as few people in Washington as possible that there was a crisis under way.

The same group reconvened at 6.30 p.m. that evening. The men around the table now had in front of them the first official CIA memorandum on the Cuban Missile Crisis. Each was marked 'TOP SECRET', with the copy number of the document stamped in the top-right corner. The first sentence read, 'Photography of 14 October 1962 has disclosed two areas in the Sierra del Rosario mountains about 50 n.m. west southwest of Havana which appear to contain Soviet MRBMs [medium-range ballistic missiles] in the early stages of deployment.' Attached to the memo was a black and white sketch map, with Cuba in the centre, ringed by a series of concentric circles. The circles showed the range of Soviet ballistic missiles. Inside the circles were the cities of Miami, New Orleans, Atlanta and Dallas; at the edge of the outermost was Washington DC.

Kennedy was obsessed with the circles and the map. 'When was this drawn?' he asked the Deputy Director. When the President was told the map had existed for some time, he demanded, 'Well, how many of these have been printed out?' Kennedy was hugely concerned the news of the missiles would leak; perhaps he was imagining the map and its deadly circles on the front page of the newspapers.

However, Bundy reassured him by replying, 'the circle is drawn in red ink on the map, Mr. President'. Critically, the CIA report noted, 'No facility to store nuclear warheads can be identified at any of these installations.' The missiles were there, the launchers were there, but it seemed that the deadly nuclear warheads might not yet have been readied. But time was short: 'Assuming … that warheads are in Cuba or en route, an operational MRBM capability could probably exist in Cuba within the next few weeks.'

The discussion moved back and forth, the men in the room trying to get their heads around the threat the USA faced, why the Soviets were taking such a seemingly provocative action and what a response might look like. Kennedy's Secretary of Defense, the smooth Californian Robert McNamara, whom Kennedy once described as 'the smartest man he had ever met', proposed an ocean blockade of Cuba. The plan would be to halt the arrival of more nuclear missiles, with US Navy vessels stopping and searching every ship. He also suggested:

a statement to the world … that we have located these offensive weapons; we're maintaining a constant surveillance over them; if there is ever any indication that they're to be launched against this country, we will respond not only against Cuba, but we will respond directly against the Soviet Union, with a full nuclear strike.

McNamara admitted, 'Now this alternative [a full nuclear strike] doesn't seem to be a very acceptable one, but wait until you work on the others', at which the room descended into nervous laughter. The other alternatives were less acceptable. The first option was an immediate strike against the bases, which Kennedy had favoured that morning, while the second was a full-scale amphibious and air invasion of Cuba. Both options had the potential to plunge the world instantly into conflict.

The suggestion of a statement was also already one that had crossed Kennedy's mind: 'There isn't any doubt that if we announced that there were MRBM sites going up,' he had remarked a few moments before, 'that would secure a good deal of political support … the fact that we indicated our desire to restrain, this really would put the burden on the Soviet[s].' Alongside the statement, Kennedy also liked the idea of communicating directly with the Soviet leadership and side-stepping Castro in Cuba. 'If we did a note, a message to Khrushchev,' the President mused aloud, 'I don't think, uh, that Castro has to know … He's initiated the danger really, hasn't he? He's the one that's playing his card, not us.'

★ ★ ★

The Soviet premier Nikita Khrushchev was not an unknown quantity. The First Secretary of the Communist Party of the Soviet Union had met the President of the United States in Vienna in the summer of 1961, not long after the botched Bay of Pigs Invasion. Kennedy had gone in underprepared, expecting his legendary charm to work its usual magic. Instead, he hit a wall. Born in what is now Ukraine, Khrushchev grew up in a mining town and had trained as a metalworker when he was a teenager. He had lived through the rise of the proletariat, losing his first wife to typhus in the years before he ascended the Communist Party ranks under Stalin. In contrast, the privileged Kennedy had grown up in the knowledge there was a trust fund with his name on it and had married a fashionable young woman from elite social circles who had studied at the Sorbonne in Paris. The Soviet leader's volatile personality and thundering debating technique were the opposite of Kennedy's suave, polished demeanour, and at their meeting in Vienna the young President had done badly, even by his own admission.

As the Soviet leader left their first meeting at the 1961 summit, he turned to his interpreter and said, 'This man [Kennedy] is very inexperienced … Compared to him, Eisenhower is a man of intelligence and vision' – and Khrushchev was not complimenting Eisenhower, either. But the fact remained that the two men had met, shaken hands and experienced a personal connection. The enemy had more than a name and a face. Kennedy's experience of meeting Khrushchev, and his knowledge that behind the Soviet leader's violent moods and strong opinions was a rational, clever man, would prove a critical factor over the fortnight that followed.

★ ★ ★

On the evening of 22 October 1962, after several days of closeted deliberation with his key advisors and yet more studying of high-altitude photographs, a calm, sombrely dressed Kennedy sat at his desk in the Oval Office. The curtains were drawn and the desk had been cleared save for a notes stand with two microphones. The President stared straight ahead. Just as someone in front of him gave the signal he was live, he glanced down at his speech one more time and shifted uncomfortably. He began with the words, 'Good evening, my fellow citizens.'

Eisenhower had revealed to the general public bit-pieces of intelligence in the wake of the U-2 incident, but this time it was different. Here was a President seeking to get ahead of the narrative, to slow the march of events. Intelligence normally reserved for a handful of decision makers – precisely the sort of information which had been included in President's Daily Briefs for the previous fifteen years – was being given to the uninitiated. Kennedy told the American people that their government had been maintaining a close surveillance of the Soviet military build-up on the island of Cuba. He informed them, 'Within the past week, unmistakable evidence has established the fact that a series of offensive missile sites is now in preparation ... The purpose of these bases can be none other than to provide a nuclear strike capability against the Western Hemisphere.'

He spoke openly of the consequences of the red circles on the map: 'Each of these missiles, in short, is capable of striking Washington, DC, the Panama Canal, Cape Canaveral, Mexico City, or any other city in the south-eastern part of the United States'. The nuclear missiles were, he said, a 'clear and present danger', and, 'a deliberately provocative and unjustified change in the status quo which cannot be accepted by this country'. Announcing the blockade, which he described as a 'quarantine' of ships going to Cuba, Kennedy also opened the door for Khrushchev to 'move the world back from the abyss ... [by] withdrawing these weapons from Cuba'. He ended his address with the admission to his 'fellow citizens' that 'The path we have chosen for the present is full of hazards'. The late city edition of *The New York Times* described Kennedy's 'quarantine' for what it was – a blockade – and led with 'Kennedy Ready For Soviet Showdown'.

The same day as Kennedy made his speech to the nation, he dispatched a letter to Khrushchev via the US Ambassador in Moscow. He began by stating, 'I have not assumed that you or any other sane man would, in this nuclear age, deliberately plunge the world into war which it is crystal clear no country could win and which could only result in catastrophic consequences to the whole world.' He noted the USA could not tolerate any action 'which in a major way disturbed the existing ... balance of power' and would 'do whatever must be done to protect its own security'. But he also expressed his 'desire to find through peaceful negotiation, a solution to the problems that divide us' to end 'this already grave crisis'. The President had made his decision and now played his own hand. There was to be no swift air strike on the missile bases and no mass invasion of Cuba. Instead, the world would wait for one of the superpowers to back down.

13

Men of Letters

The President's Daily Brief the morning after Kennedy's televised address included a round-up of the international response to the President's speech, along with the comment that 'The most recent analysis of photography (from mission flown on 20 October) does not alter our count on missile sites'. The news the following day was much the same, although there was now a belated effort to hide what was happening from the watchers in the sky: 'Latest photographic intelligence does not change our figures on missile sites, missiles and launchers. It pushes the estimated readiness date at two MRBM sites back from 22 to 25 October. Photography also shows erection of some camouflage nets under way at some sites.'

The same day as the Soviet missile crews started trying to cover up what was happening in Cuba, Khrushchev replied to Kennedy's letter. The Soviet leader was unapologetic, calling Kennedy's 'quarantine' of Cuba a threat and insisting, 'No, Mr. President, I cannot agree to this … I am convinced that in my place you would act the same way.' He flung Kennedy's concern over an atomic conflict back at the President, claiming the Cuban blockade's 'violation of the freedom to use international waters … is an act of aggression which pushes mankind toward the abyss of a world nuclear-missile war'. He told Kennedy that Soviet ships had been ordered 'not to retreat one step'.

★ ★ ★

For the men and women of the CIA who were involved in the Cuban Missile Crisis, it was a moment of high tension, but one which demonstrated how the processes and the personnel that had been put in place over the preceding decade and a half could be of immense value. The CIA had eyes in the sky and eyes on the ground and, while the 'offensive missiles' had already been in Cuba several weeks before they were discovered, they were still photographed and verified before their nuclear warheads had been mounted and the missile systems readied to fire. The Soviet hope had been that the nuclear missiles would be set up undetected, and the world would only learn of them when Khrushchev flew to Cuba to sign a formal defence agreement with Castro, the two men standing proudly as Havana hosted a military parade of loaned Soviet weaponry. Instead, the missiles were not ready and the Americans were now blockading Cuba. 'We didn't want to unleash a war,' Khrushchev told his key aides, 'we just wanted to frighten them, to restrain the United States in regard to Cuba.'

The CIA man who had briefed Kennedy in detail a few hours after Bundy spoiled the President's lie-in with the newspapers was Deputy Director General Marshall Carter. Carter was a military man, the son of a brigadier general, who had run clandestine operations in China in 1945 and who was a solid, safe pair of hands. As one of the senators at Carter's appointment hearing summarised it, 'Obviously you are a man that people trust and people have confidence in your intelligence and your ability to keep things to yourself.' Carter briefed the President on 16 October because Director John McCone, who had replaced Allen Dulles in November 1961, was unavailable. McCone had not even been in the country when news of the discovery of Soviet SAM sites broke: the 66-year-old was in the south of France, on honeymoon with his newly acquired second wife. McCone was firmly of the opinion that the SAMs were in place to deter reconnaissance flights, or even 'for [the] purpose of ensuring secrecy of some offensive capability such as MRBMs to be installed', as he said in one of the several messages he dispatched back to Washington from his now very interrupted holiday. The flurry of communiqués from the Riviera led one CIA analyst to joke, 'I have some doubts that the old man knows what to do on honeymoon.'

McCone had arrived at the CIA sideways, from the US Atomic Energy Commission, and was a political and business operator rather than a former serviceman. The often genial, white-haired Californian was a different

*John McCone (centre) is sworn in as Director of the CIA on 29 November 1961,
with President Kennedy at his side.*

character to many in the CIA, but knew the importance of being in the room, so by the time Kennedy briefed the nation on the situation in Cuba he had been back in Washington for four weeks. He was instrumental in pushing for the restarting of U-2 flights and he was also strongly against a pre-emptive strike, writing a memo to Kennedy insisting that 'the United States should not act without warning and thus be forced to live with a "Pearl Harbor indictment" for the indefinite future'. His suggestion was to notify the Soviets and the Cubans and 'give them twenty-four hours to commence dismantling and removal of MRBMs'.

Kennedy's speech to the nation that announced the blockade of Cuba presented a clear decision, but behind closed doors, the President had been under pressure from a number of generals to opt instead for an air strike, or even an invasion of Cuba. At a meeting with the Joint Chiefs on 19 October, Kennedy found himself in a room full of men who wanted to start a fight. They had been informed of developments, but until that point, all of Kennedy's deliberations had been with his close aides at the White House (the same group which had gathered in hushed circumstances on the morning of 16 October when discovery of the nuclear missiles was revealed). Air Force Chief of Staff General Curtis LeMay, who had overseen strategic bombing in the Pacific theatre in the war, including the firebombing of Japanese cities, was disdainful of the idea of just quarantining Cuba. 'If we do not do anything to Cuba … they [the Soviets] have got us on the run,' he claimed. A blockade was 'almost as bad as the appeasement at Munich', LeMay added, chiding Kennedy, 'You are in a pretty bad fix.' The deliberate parallel to Munich, which had encouraged Hitler to start the Second World War, sounded like an insult because it was. Neville Chamberlain, the UK Prime Minister at the time of the 1938 Munich agreement with Hitler, was regarded as an appeaser and weak leader. LeMay was tarring Kennedy with the same brush.

The President shot back, 'What did you say?', forcing LeMay to repeat himself. Then Kennedy chuckled, 'You are in there [a pretty bad fix] with me.' With the prospect of starting a nuclear war unpalatable, the blockade option won the day, but there were some in the Kennedy administration, and a number of leaders in the military, who would have been more than happy to respond to Khrushchev's placing of missiles on Cuba with significant force.

★ ★ ★

A close watch was now being kept not only on the missile sites but on every ship headed towards the Cuban quarantine zone. The 'zone' was in fact a 500-mile circle around Cuba drawn on a map, which was a vast area of sea to try and monitor. Although the USA had photographic satellites in operation, they could not be manoeuvred into different orbits and had to return their film canisters to earth, at which point they became useless space junk; they were an outrageously expensive and slow method of collecting intelligence. There were no Global Positioning System monitoring vessel locations, so the only way of finding a ship on the high seas was either by physically spotting it, or by triangulating its position from radio broadcasts. The result was that, for the blockade to be effective, US Navy ships or aircraft had to sight vessels nearing Cuban waters. The blockade was a huge naval search operation.

CIA Director McCone was exasperated at the speed of some of the information coming from the Navy. On one occasion when viewing photographs of a Soviet ship that had taken almost a week to reach Washington, he burst out, 'How the hell did the Navy get them to Washington – by row boat?' The Agency prided itself on the speed with which it could put information into the hands of decision makers. Dated information, as McCone remarked at the time, was 'history, not intelligence'. Events were moving fast, and it was proving a daily struggle to keep pace and ensure the Commander-in-Chief knew what was really going on.

For all Khrushchev's bombast in his reply to Kennedy's first letter, the Soviet leader had been pragmatic enough to immediately order three Soviet freighters carrying more missiles to Cuba to turn around. An oil tanker, the *Bucharest*, was given the all-clear to carry on as it did not have military cargo. Kennedy and his close aides, officially the Executive Committee of the National Security Council, reconvened again on 25 October. That morning, the Daily Brief had reported no new missile sites had been discovered, but that was hardly the main worry: within days, the ones that did exist would be fully operational. Meanwhile, the *Bucharest* was clearly not turning around. McCone gave the presentation on events for the morning meeting, which included the status of the Soviet oil tanker that would shortly cross the imaginary 500-mile border that the President had drawn around Cuba. The *Bucharest* had already been flagged down by a US Navy destroyer and had responded to radio messages, insisting that it was only carrying a cargo of petroleum. Bundy's minutes of the meeting are matter-of-fact: 'The President directed that the tanker *Bucharest* not be intercepted at present.' It was a moment of calm rationality.

The next morning, Kennedy's Brief contained a map of the missile sites in Cuba, an image he was by that time rather familiar with. The analysts noted, 'Photographs taken yesterday indicate there has been no slackening in the pace of construction work at the missile sites. They also now show what looks like missile check-out operations in progress at two San Cristobal MRBM sites.' The Brief noted, 'Havana remains quiet, but the prevailing atmosphere is one of slowly rising tension.' It felt like the world was one miscalculation away from all-out nuclear war.

At 4.43 p.m. Moscow time that afternoon, the US Embassy in the Soviet capital received a letter. Officially it was a message from a high-ranking Soviet official for the US Ambassador, but that was simply a cover. Inside was a second letter, from Khrushchev to Kennedy. The Embassy staff translated it into English as fast as they could and transmitted it in a coded telegram to Washington while stuffing the original in the next diplomatic air-mail pouch headed home. The tone of the message was completely different to Khrushchev's rant in response to the blockade of Cuba. The Soviet leader was calm, measured and open. 'I see, Mr. President, that you too are not devoid of a sense of anxiety for the fate of the world,' he began. Khrushchev warned of the perils of war and then moved on to a proposal, adding, 'My conversation with you in Vienna gives me the right to talk to you this way.' The Soviet leader suggested:

> Let us therefore show statesmanlike wisdom. I propose: We, for our part, will declare that our ships, bound for Cuba, will not carry any kind of armaments. You would declare that the United States will not invade Cuba with its forces and will not support any sort of forces which might intend to carry out an invasion of Cuba. Then the necessity for the presence of our military specialists in Cuba would disappear.

It was a remarkable admission. Khrushchev was suggesting to Kennedy that if the President would publicly commit to leaving Cuba alone, the need for the 'military specialists' (and presumably their missiles) would end. The Soviet leader concluded his letter, 'There, Mr. President, are my thoughts, which, if you agreed with them, could put an end to that tense situation which is disturbing all peoples.'

The following morning, Kennedy and his close circle met again just after 10 a.m. McCone began proceedings with a short intelligence briefing and then McNamara, the Secretary of Defense, outlined a plan of twenty-four-hour reconnaissance over the missile sites in Cuba, which would necessitate night flights by US Navy jets, using flares to illuminate the ground and taking low-altitude photographs. Eight minutes into the meeting, the President was handed a flash news broadcast that had been printed straight off the ticker tape from the Associated Press (AP) news agency. Kennedy read it aloud to the room: 'Moscow, October 27th. Premier Khrushchev told President Kennedy in a message today he would withdraw offensive weapons from Cuba if the United States withdrew its rockets from Turkey.'

Bundy was the first to react, flat out contradicting the news flash. 'No,' he told the room, 'he [Khrushchev] didn't.' The Soviet leader had just changed the stakes. The USA had deployed nuclear missiles in Turkey – first generation, liquid-fuelled designs that took hours to fuel ahead of launch and were practically obsolete – which Kennedy had previously requested be withdrawn, only to discover that the Turks were extremely proud to be hosting them and did not want to hand them back. Khrushchev's demand, not mentioned in the letter the day before, was not entirely illogical. The US missiles were effectively in his own backyard.

The President wondered aloud, 'He [Khrushchev] may be putting out another letter … let's just sit tight on it.' The night before there had been an offer, and now there appeared to be a deal on the table that could bring the world back from the brink. But first, Kennedy needed to know if it was genuine. He ended the meeting telling his aides they would have 'one more conversation' later that day, 'At about six o'clock, just in case during the day we get something important.'

Eight hundred miles south of Washington, Captain Roger Herman was waiting at the end of the runway of McCoy Air Force Base near Orlando. In Washington and the north-east it was unseasonably cold that week, with snow even falling in Cleveland, Ohio, but in the balmy Florida late morning, Herman was just in shirtsleeves. He alternately scanned the southern sky and glanced at his watch. The U-2 he was waiting for was overdue, and it had been flying a mission over Cuba. Herman had grown up obsessed with planes, earning his pilot's licence before his driving licence and enlisting in the Air Force straight out of high school. The Air Force was his life, and he was one of an elite group of eleven pilots who flew the U-2 over Cuba that autumn. Four and a half hours before, he had helped his friend, Major Rudolf Anderson, into the cockpit of a U-2, checked the pilot's oxygen system and then slammed the canopy shut. Herman's parting words were 'Okay, Rudy, here we go. Have a good trip. See you when you get back.' Now, Anderson was missing, and even if he was still airborne, he would by now have run out of fuel; there had also been no short, coded message to say the U-2 had re-entered US airspace. Herman's commander waved him in from his vigil and put in a call up the chain: a U-2 was missing over Cuba.

14

A Missile Misadventure

In the late afternoon of 27 October 1962, President Kennedy and his team reconvened in the Cabinet Room of the White House. Khrushchev's suggestion of a missile swap had proved genuine: AP had picked up the broadcast of a public letter to Kennedy that had materialised later in the day. Many of the men in the room were opposed to the optics of the deal. The day before, the Soviet leader had requested a commitment that the USA would not invade Cuba, but now he was demanding a missile exchange. As Bundy phrased it, 'we appear to be trading the defence of Turkey for a threat to Cuba'. There were multiple drafts of a reply to Khrushchev's latest letter and Kennedy hated them all. They spent a while writing by committee: reading each line aloud, with the President, Bundy or someone else then tearing it apart.

Eventually, Kennedy's brother Bobby, whom Kennedy had made Attorney General in the administration, suggested he and one other member leave the room and re-write the reply: 'Why don't we try to work it out for you, without you being there to pick it apart?'

While he was gone, an aide entered with a note, which was handed to McNamara. Above the chatter, the Defense Secretary told the room, 'The U-2 was shot down.' Anderson's body had been discovered in the plane.

Kennedy was quiet and then said, 'We can't very well send a U-2 over there, can we now, and have a guy killed again tomorrow.' In case of that eventuality, Kennedy had already drafted a letter of condolence for Major Anderson's wife, 'on behalf of a grateful nation', in which he stated that Anderson had been 'on a mission of most vital national urgency'. The 'sacrifice of brave and patriotic men,' the President added, had been 'in time of crisis the source of our freedom since the founding days of our country'.

The CIA correctly assumed that the SAM sites in Cuba were being manned by Soviet soldiers, not the Cubans. The downing of Anderson's U-2 therefore seemed a massive escalation. US military units were already on high alert and had been for a week. The Strategic Air Command, which was the umbrella for the entire US nuclear arsenal, had 912 nuclear-capable bombers on alert and 134 ballistic missiles in preparation to launch. Bombers carrying armed atomic bombs were constantly airborne and, the day before Kennedy's quarantine of Cuba was implemented, the system had gone to defence readiness condition (DEFCON) two, one level short of active nuclear war. A total of 220 targets for nuclear strikes had been selected in the Soviet Union, including Moscow. The much-analysed plan for a 'first strike' was one phone call away. The U-2 shootdown triggered a visceral reaction in the room. There were calls to bomb the SAM site responsible – to bomb all the SAM sites. While the aides argued, the President left the room. The mood of the moment was well summarised by the Chairman of Joint Chiefs of Staff, who, when he went to update the other heads of the US military on the progress in the Cabinet Room, told them, 'The President has been seized by the idea of trading Turkish missiles for Cuban missiles. He seems to be the only one in favour of it. He has a feeling that time is running out.'

Kennedy wrapped up the meeting, which had dragged on into the evening, once the group had finally agreed on the wording of a reply to Khrushchev. The letter effectively ignored the demand for a missile swap and focused on the original suggestion. It called for a commitment from Khrushchev to 'remove these weapons systems from Cuba', stating, 'We, on our part, would agree … to give assurances against an invasion of Cuba.' When most of the men who had been in the Cabinet Room for the hours of debate had headed home, the President called a small group into the Oval Office. It included Bundy, McNamara, Secretary of State Dean Rusk and Bobby Kennedy. Bobby would hand over the letter to the Soviet Ambassador. At the same time, he would also promise that the

JFK with his brother Bobby Kennedy outside the Oval Office. Bobby was the go-between for the secret deal with the Soviets to remove missiles from Turkey.

USA would remove the missiles from Turkey. The second communication was to be a secret between the men in the room, the Soviet Ambassador and Khrushchev.

Half an hour later, Ambassador Anatoly Dobrynin entered Bobby Kennedy's office. The 43-year-old was outwardly unassuming: he was short and bald with thick gasses, and he came from similar stock to the Soviet leader, having grown up in a village outside Moscow as the son of the local locksmith. But he was a considered, intelligent operator who went on to be the Soviet Ambassador to the USA under six different presidents. On seeing the Attorney General, Dobrynin thought, 'one could see from his eyes he had not slept for days'.

The American got straight to the point. In the coded, top-secret message Dobrynin dispatched back to Moscow for Khrushchev that evening, the Ambassador related how Bobby Kennedy told him:

> Because of the plane that was shot down [Anderson's U-2], there is now strong pressure on the President to give an order to respond with fire if fired upon when American reconnaissance planes are flying over Cuba ... But if we start to fire in response – a chain reaction will quickly start that will be very hard to stop.

He also narrated the promise from Kennedy to remove the nuclear missiles from Turkey, although it would take several months, and 'the President can't say anything in public in this regard about Turkey'. Before Bobby Kennedy left, he asked Dobrynin to get an answer the following day and gave him a direct telephone number for the White House.

That Saturday night, the Soviet leadership were ensconced in Khrushchev's *dacha* outside of Moscow. Soviet intelligence had received reports that US strikes on the missile bases in Cuba were in preparation for early the following week and the crisis was gathering a momentum that it seemed would be difficult to stop. When Khrushchev received the message from Dobrynin, he told the Politburo meeting at his house, 'Comrades, we now have to look for a dignified way out of this conflict.'

In Washington, Kennedy sent most of the staff home and stayed up late in the White House movie theatre to watch Audrey Hepburn's 1953 romantic comedy *Roman Holiday*. Before he went to bed, the President reminded an aide it was Sunday the following day and he would be attending church: 'We'll be going to the ten o'clock mass at Saint Stephen's … We'll have plenty of hard praying to do, so don't be late.'

★ ★ ★

The first sentence of the President's Daily Brief on the morning of Sunday 28 October 1962 was not good news. 'On the basis of aerial photographs obtained from missions flown on Friday and Saturday, we estimate that all 24 MRBM missile launchers are now fully operational.' They also noted that 'camouflage against aerial photography is becoming more effective'.

But soon, it all seemed irrelevant. Just as the Daily Brief was on its way to the White House, Dobrynin had received an urgent telegram from Moscow. It read:

> Get in touch with Robert Kennedy at once and tell him that you have conveyed the contents of your conversation with him to N.S. Khrushchev. Khrushchev herewith gives the following urgent reply: 'The suggestions made by Robert Kennedy on the president's instructions are appreciated in Moscow. The president's message of October 27 will be answered on the radio today, and the answer will be highly positive.'

The Soviet Ambassador later wrote in his memoirs, 'I have to admit that upon reading this cable I breathed a sigh of great relief. The prospect of a military showdown receded, and the strain of the last days somehow just vanished. It became clear that the critical point of the conflict had been safely passed.' Dobrynin picked up the phone and called the number Bobby Kennedy had given him the night before. They met within an hour, and Bobby took the reply straight to his brother.

The informal message was made official at 9.30 a.m., when Khrushchev gave a public address on Radio Moscow. He said, 'the Soviet Government … has given a new order to dismantle the arms which you described as offensive, and to crate and return them to the Soviet Union'.

The relief at the end of the crisis was palpable. *The New York Times* interviewed tens of people on the streets, describing how a 'wave of relief' was rolling over New York City. McCone heard the news on his car radio while driving back from an early church service; the Washington cold snap had turned crisply autumnal, and the trees were showcasing their seasonal splendour in the morning sunshine. Kennedy was getting dressed for church when he received the official confirmation of the Moscow message. He turned to an aide and said, 'I feel like a new man,' adding, 'Thank God it's all over.'

The CIA analysts who penned the President's Brief were also jubilant: 'We see Khrushchev's Cuban missile misadventure as a major set-back for him personally,' they wrote at the top of Kennedy's Brief the next day. They added:

> The decision to put the missiles in Cuba, as well as the decision to pull them out, was almost certainly his alone ... There are no scapegoats for this one and he will be blamed by just about everyone. Many of those whom he has bullied are probably secretly pleased.

However, every one of the analysts at the CIA Office of Current Intelligence who curated the President's Briefs, and even the CIA's Director, McCone, were completely unaware of the private deal Kennedy had made with Khrushchev; McCone had been in the room when the missile swap was on the table and it was clear Kennedy had been supportive of the notion, but to all concerned, it seemed the Soviets had caved anyway. Politically, the Cuban Missile Crisis seemed over, but words needed to be followed by actions.

The reports in Kennedy's Briefs were initially concerning. On 30 October it was noted that the analysts could not verify that the missiles had begun to be dismantled, but the following day there seemed to be progress. 'Though disappointing in quality, Monday's photography shows that as of mid-afternoon that day no definite steps towards dismantling or vacating the sites had been taken ... In several instances, however, the missile erectors have been moved away from the launch area.'

The news the White House had been waiting for came on the morning of 2 November. The Brief reported, 'Yesterday's photography shows the offensive missile sites being closed down and the equipment removed. ... The missiles and basic launching equipment have been removed from all of the MRBM launch areas; camouflage has been taken down, and support vehicles are being assembled for movement.'

Four days later, the President's breakfast reading was all good news: 'The Soviets are obviously in a hurry to get their missiles out [of Cuba] … photography shows that at least half the number of missile transporters and launchers previously seen at the MRBM sites and all six known IRBM [intermediate-range ballistic missile] launch rings are now at the dockside'.

Finally, on 9 November, a further message brought formal confirmation from the Soviets of what the photographs were demonstrating. The Brief that day stated, 'In New York [at the United Nations], the Soviets told us that nine of their ships had left Cuba carrying all 42 missiles the USSR admits to having sent there.' It was added that the nuclear warheads '[had] been taken out of Cuba some time ago'. The Cuban Missile Crisis was officially over.

★ ★ ★

For the duration of the crisis, the President's Daily Briefs provided crucial information. But the urgency of events and the need for immediate decision making meant the Briefs were not necessarily the first source of information for Kennedy, although they gave context and a timely summary. At times during the crisis, the Briefs were bypassed, and in the end, the entire CIA was left unaware of the secret deal that resolved the fortnight of tension. The style of Kennedy's Daily Briefs, which had been reworked to be more exclusive, with a significantly reduced circulation and succinct summary, fed into the President's own preferences.

Kennedy was used to having privileged and personal access to intelligence through his Daily Briefs and exclusivity of information and decision making was a hallmark of the crisis: the generals were often not in the room, as Kennedy did not wish to hear their frantic beating of the drums of war. For the most important decision of all (on the Turkish missiles), Kennedy even excluded most of his trusted aides on the Executive Committee of the National Security Council (ExComm). The existence of the Daily Briefs did not make Kennedy any more inclined to make decisions with a tight-knit group of advisors, which was his own preference and personality, but it supported the notion of an elite group 'in the know'. For the events that transpired in Cuba, it was probably the best option and perhaps the only one that would have resulted in such a safe and speedy resolution. But it was also exclusive and exclusionary. A similar decision-making process led to the actions of Operation Mongoose and, although Kennedy closed down the covert-ops effort in Cuba, he was more than willing to project US power in the shadows in other countries. That willingness was something Kennedy shared with his predecessor, Eisenhower. Both presidents saw the CIA not just as a source of information, but as a tool for changing the world.

Part IV

Friends Like These: Covert Operations

Part IV

Friends Like These:
Covert Operations

15

A More Reliable Government

Dwight D. Eisenhower's first official Daily Brief concerned a foreign leader whom the CIA were about to overthrow. Iran's new Prime Minister, Mohammad Mosaddeq, had told the US Ambassador in Tehran that the Iranian population were angry at the 'Western conspiracy to prevent Iran selling its oil' and that Iran would sell its natural resource 'to Stalin himself if he would buy it'. It was troubling news for Eisenhower on his first day in the job, given that Iran was not a country that the Eisenhower administration wished to see 'turn Communist'.

★ ★ ★

Iran's capital, Tehran, is 6,500 miles east of Washington. The country bridges the Caspian and the Arabian seas and borders Pakistan and Afghanistan, while the north-eastern corner sits next to what, in 1953, were the southern-central reaches of the Soviet Union. The nation, which had been known as Persia for most of its history, had become indebted, stripped of its past glories, although not its pride, and reliant for its future prosperity on a recently discovered natural resource: oil.

In the early twentieth century, imperial Britain and Russia had tussled over access to Iran, and in the First World War, the nation was invaded by the British, the Russians and the Ottoman Turks. It was of little consequence to the fighting forces that Iran's rulers had declared official neutrality. The British were determined to safeguard their pre-war oil agreement that granted the Anglo-Persian Oil Company a monopoly on oil extraction – an agreement which was still in place after the Second World War. A renegotiation in 1933 had still only left the Iranians with a 25 per cent share in the company and a paltry annual revenue. Having been occupied again in the Second World War, nationalist sentiment in Iran was growing, while the Soviets, who had taken control of parts of the north, simply refused to leave.

Just four weeks into the creation of the first President's Daily Briefs in 1946, Iran cropped up on the page in front of Truman. The President was warned about Soviet troop movements. As the US Ambassador in Iran at the time phrased it, the Soviet objective was 'complete control ... including all oil-producing regions'. Iran's King, the Shah, it was stated the following day, was 'apprehensive of a Soviet blitzkrieg sweeping through the whole Near East'. Towards the end of Truman's time in office, the concern of growing Soviet influence in Iran was a topic discussed with some trepidation. Truman's 14 March 1950 Daily Brief cautioned that the situation in Iran was 'especially dangerous' and that the Soviets would be quick to exploit it. 'The fall of Iran to the USSR,' it was noted, 'would have an especially depressing effect on the entire Middle East.'

By the time Eisenhower arrived in the Oval Office, Iran had transformed from a potential problem to a full-blown crisis. In 1951, Mohammad Mosaddeq's new government voted to nationalise the country's oil industry: four decades of British exploitation of Iran's natural resources were coming to an end. In September, when foreign workers at the world's largest oil refinery at Abadan were ordered to leave the country in a week, there was outrage in the UK. Prime Minister Clement Attlee's Labour government threatened military action, deployed troops to neighbouring Iraq and assembled a naval armada, but the Truman administration strongly cautioned the UK against going to war. Attlee, who was already in the middle of a general election campaign, backed down. After the foreign oil workers had gone, all British diplomats were expelled too. It was an embarrassing and swift end to the UK's influence. The move was costly for Iran, as it obliterated the country's oil export market, but the nationalists in Iran did not care. As Truman's Secretary of State, Dean Acheson, later phrased it: the White House was slow to realise that Mosaddeq was 'essentially a rich, reactionary, feudal-minded Persian inspired by a fanatical hatred of the British and a desire to expel them and all their works from the country regardless of cost'.

Mohammad Mosaddeq was certainly well off and well connected, but he was not feudal-minded. The 73-year-old was a Western-educated, veteran political operator. Slender, with thinning white hair and an aquiline nose, Mosaddeq often resembled a hunched bird in photographs, as suit jackets and coats flapped off his narrow-shouldered frame. But he was a dynamic personality and powerful force in Iranian politics. He initially courted the Americans, writing to Eisenhower to try and encourage him to intervene with the British, who were stymying Iran's every effort to sell their product: 'purchasers of Iranian oil have been dragged from one court to another', Mosaddeq lamented, 'and all means of propaganda and diplomacy have been employed in order to place illegal obstacles in the way of the sale of Iranian oil. Although the Italian and Japanese courts have declared Iranian oil to be free and unencumbered, the British have not as yet abandoned their unjust and unprincipled activities.'

The US government was already involved in propping up Iran: the country had received $1.6 million a year in aid before Mosaddeq was elected Prime Minister, and in 1953 that had been upped to $23.4 million. The situation had been articulated simply in Eisenhower's 22 January Daily Brief, in which the US Ambassador in Tehran reported how Mosaddeq had told him directly that, if Iran could simply sell oil to the highest bidder, it would prosper and no longer need US aid. But while Mosaddeq was writing letters asking for Eisenhower's help, the President was mulling the idea of supporting a covert operation to bring down the Iranian Prime Minister.

★ ★ ★

The idea of removing Mosaddeq and making it look like an inside job had been circulating for some time. In October 1952, the UK Foreign Office first proposed the idea to the State Department in Washington. The Assistant Secretary for Near Eastern, South Asian and African Affairs, who recorded the conversations in a memo, noted, 'The British Foreign Office has informed us that it would be disposed to bring about a coup d'état in Iran, replacing the Mosaddeq Government by one which would be more "reliable", if the American Government agreed to cooperate.'

In the twilight of Truman's time in office, the response was polite rejection. The proposal, it was noted, 'seems to be full of dangers and uncertainties … while we do not dismiss it entirely, we would prefer not to enter into combined planning on this course of action at this time.' But three months later, the wind had changed. Two primary factors created a fertile soil for the plan to oust Mosaddeq: the arrival of Eisenhower in the White House and his appointment of John Foster Dulles as Secretary of State, whose brother, Allen, was CIA Deputy Director.

New administrations in Washington seek to launch their agenda as swiftly as possible; in modern times they face being judged by their 'first 100 days'. When it came to Iran, the change in political leadership did not itself result in a new direction; it simply allowed officials who had been pursuing their own agenda to get the new administration onboard with pre-existing plans. Kermit 'Kim' Roosevelt Jr, a CIA operative and grandson of the twenty-sixth President of the United States, was the 'point man' on the ground in Iran in the months that followed. He later recalled, 'we had, I felt sure, no chance to win approval from the outgoing administration of Truman … The new Republicans, however, [we felt] might be quite different.'

The British also saw the opportunity and as soon as Eisenhower had won the election, a senior agent of the Secret Intelligence Service (now MI6) travelled to Washington for meetings with the CIA. The narrative pushed by the British was also changed. Gone was the harping complaint about the loss of UK economic interest in Iran. Instead, the idea of a coup was couched in the language of the Cold War: 'Not wishing to be accused of trying to use the Americans to pull British chestnuts out of the fire,' the MI6 agent who was Chief of Station in Tehran admitted afterwards, 'I decided to emphasise the Communist threat to Iran rather than the need to recover control of the oil industry.' John Foster Dulles was hugely supportive, and with the help of his brother Allen, now promoted to CIA Director, they swayed Eisenhower's mind.

The Dulles brothers appear to have carefully considered their use of intelligence in convincing Eisenhower. The Daily Brief on 4 March warned of the elimination of 'conservative pro-Western supporters as an effective political influence in Iran'. Eisenhower did not personally read his Daily Briefs but was told basically the same thing when Allen Dulles gave the pre-National

Security Council meeting briefing later that day. In the weeks that followed, Iran was a regular topic in NSC meetings, and the CIA prepared memorandums on the capacity of covert operations in Iran and the prospect of a tribal revolt ousting Mosaddeq, although Dulles did not use them in the discussions. Hints that Eisenhower was moving in the desired direction came in the 11 March NSC meeting, when the President stated that he had 'very real doubts whether, even if we [the USA] tried unliterally, we could make a successful deal with Mosaddeq'.

The political situation in Iran was extremely volatile. The country had a vocal Communist Party, which had strongly supported Mosaddeq's nationalisation of the oil industry, although the party and its leaders had been targeted in sporadic crackdowns for organising anti-government protests. Mosaddeq faced his own opposition, from political groups within Parliament and elements in the military with whom he had previously crossed swords, while Islamic religious political groups enjoyed strong support in rural areas. Above the political fray sat Iran's comparatively pro-Western monarch, Shah Mohammad Reza Pahlavi. In the assessment of one US Embassy report, the handsome 39-year-old Shah was 'confused, frustrated, suspicious, proud, and stubborn, a young man who lives in the shadow of his father. His fears, questionings, and indecisiveness are permanent instabilities of character. Yet, he has great personal courage, many Western ideals, and a sincere, though often wavering, desire to raise and preserve his country.' He was also still secretly meeting the US Ambassador, who was dropped off at the palace gardens for private conversations with the Shah. As they wandered the verdant, tranquil gardens for an hour and a half on the last Saturday in May, the Shah spoke of his concerns that, without foreign financial and economic aid, any change of government 'would merely be preparing Iran for its ruin'.

Under Mosaddeq, it seemed the country was destined for collapse. And, as Allen Dulles had gravely intoned in one NSC meeting, 'if Iran succumbed to the Communists there was little doubt that in short order the other areas of the Middle East, with some 60% of the world's oil reserves, would fall into Communist control'. Eisenhower was being groomed to find covert action favourable when the option was openly presented to him. In one State Department memo, a collection of dispatches from the US Ambassador in Tehran specifically curated for and sent directly to the President, it was ominously noted, 'Most Iranian politicians friendly to the West would welcome secret American intervention which might assist them ... Only those sympathetic to the Soviet Union and to international Communism have reason to be pleased at what is taking place.'

16

Counter-Coup

On 11 July 1953, President Eisenhower approved Operation Ajax, following a personal briefing by Allen Dulles that was deliberately light on detail. By then, the wheels had already long been in motion. Back in April, Allen Dulles had green-lighted the transfer of $1 million to the CIA Station in Tehran to help bring down Mosaddeq, and the money was already being spent. The plan was that Eisenhower would publicly announce an end to all aid to Iran, damning Mosaddeq for his association with Communists, while the CIA would approach one of the generals of the Iranian Army with a view to becoming Prime Minister. Mosaddeq would be arrested, and official decrees, signed by the Shah, proclaiming the general as head of a new government, would be circulated among the population. Meanwhile, local groups, funded by the CIA, would help get pro-Shah demonstrators out in the streets. When the actual coup happened, it was planned that both the Shah and the US Ambassador to Tehran would conveniently be out of the country.

In June, a month before Eisenhower signed off on the plot, the Daily Brief had noted, 'The Shah still appears to be the determining factor in any plan to remove Mosaddeq. If he lends his support and helps unite some of Mosaddeq's opposition, there is a possibility the Prime Minister could be ousted.' What was not mentioned was that the Shah had already agreed whom he would lend his support to during one of his ambles around the hedgerows with US Ambassador Loy Henderson. The Ambassador had pitched the name of General Fazlollah Zahedi as potential Prime Minister and asked for a 'frank

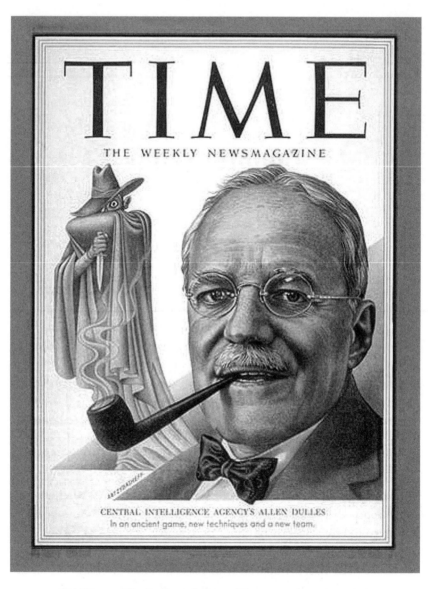

CIA Director Allen Dulles on the cover of Time *magazine, August 1953, six months after his appointment.*

statement' from the Shah regarding his attitude to the idea. The Shah had replied, 'he did not consider General Zahedi an intellectual giant', but that he would be acceptable. He added, however, if General Zahedi should come in as a result of a coup d'état, he would hesitate to support him 'unless he could become convinced that the General had behind him a strong array of political leaders as well as a considerable popular support'. The challenge for the CIA was now to coordinate all the moving parts.

The Shah was seen as the weak point of the operation. For Zahedi to have any shred of legitimacy, he would need to be in possession of official decrees from the Shah, making him Prime Minister. There was serious concern that the Shah would lose confidence and refuse to sign the documents. The CIA needed a reliable intermediary and settled on Princess Ashraf Pahlavi, the Shah's sister. The Princess and the Shah were twins, but diametrically opposite characters. Where the Shah was timid, his sister was forceful; where he prevaricated, she was decisive. The striking, elegant Ashraf lived in Paris, where her love of fashion, casinos and nightclubs could be indulged without criticism. The CIA put her on a plane home to Tehran to encourage her brother's compliance. While the active stage of the operation got under way, negative briefing against Mosaddeq was kept up in the President's daily intelligence reports. The 2 August Brief warned that Mosaddeq was 'accepting support' from the Iranian Communist Party. Two days later, it was reported that Mosaddeq had made a 'violent attack on US policy' over the refusal to give more aid, claiming the Americans were 'brazenly behind the British'. However, Mosaddeq had no idea of the true extent to which US and UK foreign policy was now 'brazenly' aligned against him personally.

After dithering for several days, the Shah finally signed the *firmans* (decrees), departing for his palace on the Caspian Sea in northern Iran, so as to be far away from Tehran. The operation was supposed to go ahead the following day, with the chief of the Shah's bodyguard leading a small force of soldiers to arrest Mosaddeq, but the Iranians insisted the plan be delayed until 15 August, after the Iranian weekend. The only thing left to do for the CIA operatives and the White House was to wait.

Kim Roosevelt stayed up sipping vodka and limes and waiting for the telephone to ring, confirming the plot had been a success. He heard the sound of tanks rumbling through the streets and, as the hours wore on, he grew increasingly concerned. At dawn he turned on the radio. At 7 a.m. Iranian time on 16 August, Radio Tehran broadcast an official announcement: a coup attempt against the Mosaddeq government had been foiled the night before. The Prime Minister himself came on air and declared that 'foreign elements' had encouraged the Shah to displace him as Prime Minister. The plot had failed. Roosevelt rushed to pick up Zahedi from the house he was staying in and bundled him into the back seat of a car. Covering the general with a blanket, he headed for the safety of the US Embassy.

The time difference gave the CIA analysts enough hours to make a 'Comment on the Iranian situation' the first item in the Daily Brief that day:

> The failure of the attempt to remove Mosaddeq and the flight of the Shah ... emphasise Mosaddeq's continued mastery of the situation ... [The] involvement of the commander of the imperial guards, and the royal decrees to remove Mosaddeq and appoint General Zahedi prime minister present Mosaddeq with the opportunity of reducing the Shah's position still further or attempting to eliminate the monarchy altogether.

The analysts added that there were some in Iran 'charging American involvement'.

Later that day, the Shah left his palace on the Caspian Sea and arrived in Baghdad aboard his small twin-engined Beechcraft plane. He was accompanied by his wife, one aide and the pilot. Only the Shah had a passport, and newspapers reported that piles of clothes belonging to the royal couple were 'strewn inside the plane'. The following evening, the Shah was visited by a US State Department Official, who wrote an account of his meeting with the monarch: 'I found the Shah worn from three sleepless nights, puzzled by turn of events, but with no bitterness toward Americans.'

The note on the meeting with the Shah in Baghdad was attached to a personal summary memo for Eisenhower on the failure of the coup. The 'turn of events' was explained in a single paragraph: 'The move failed because of three days of delay and vacillation by the Iranian generals concerned, during which time Mosaddeq apparently found out all that was happening ... The old boy wouldn't accept this and arrested the messenger and everybody else involved that he could get his hands on.' The final sentence was a blunt assessment of the seeming reality: 'We now have to take a whole new look at the Iranian situation and probably have to snuggle up to Mosaddeq if we're going to save anything there. I daresay this means a little added difficulty with the British.'

In Tehran, the US Embassy had contacted all the Americans in the city and told them to stay in their homes. Having originally planned to be out of the country so as not to arouse suspicion, Ambassador Loy Henderson now flew back to find out what had gone wrong. On the day the Shah landed in Baghdad, the Ambassador, CIA operative Kim Roosevelt and his Iranian allies, along with General Zahedi himself, were holed up in the US Embassy, trying to navigate a way out of the mess. It transpired that a soldier in the Shah's bodyguard had given away the plan to arrest Mosaddeq, so when the chief of the Shah's bodyguard arrived at the Prime Minister's residence clutching the decrees from the Shah, he was met by a loyal military colonel and several tanks. He had delivered the *firmans* and had then been promptly arrested.

The one positive aspect of the situation was that news of the Shah's flight had galvanised the population. Communist protestors had taken to the streets celebrating, in the process looting shops in downtown Tehran. The CIA still had enough agents on the ground who could encourage pro-Shah protestors onto the streets by handing out money and distributing photographs of the Shah's *firmans* appointing Zahedi. The Shah's supporters needed little encouragement: to many it genuinely looked like Mosaddeq was moving Iran towards a dictatorship; at the start of August, he had announced the dissolution of the Iranian Parliament. Throughout 19 August, protests grew as crowds swelled in the capital. Soldiers loyal to the Shah went onto the streets. In the afternoon, Kim Roosevelt extracted Zahedi from the basement of the US Embassy. The general waded into the crowds and was lifted onto a tank, which drove towards Mosaddeq's house. By the evening, Zahedi was in power.

The following morning, the Daily Brief led with the good news: 'The unexpectedly strong upsurge of popular and military reaction … has enabled the Shah's supporters to take over Tehran.' The coup had officially failed and, at the same time, succeeded. Popular opposition to violent Communist protests had given the military the cover that was needed to take control of government buildings, removing Mosaddeq's administration and replacing it with a junta that was supportive of the Shah. But even though Mosaddeq was gone and the hand-picked Zahedi was now in charge, the situation in Iran was still volatile and difficult. The CIA analysts cautioned straight away that 'The success of the new government will depend to a great extent on its ability to improve rapidly Iran's financial and economic position'.

The explanation for the sudden turnaround in Tehran was given in the Brief the next day. The 'royalist movement' of 19 August was 'a spontaneous mass demonstration'. The analysts noted, 'This information confirms … the successful countermove against Mosaddeq was unplanned and completely unexpected.' The scale of the pro-Shah protests was unexpected, but they were certainly not unplanned. Political action assets from CIA station in Tehran 'contributed to the beginnings of the pro-Shah demonstrations', as one CIA report later phrased it, and Zahedi's emergence onto the streets was carefully choreographed. With the help of a lot of good fortune, the outcome of events in Iran transpired to be exactly what the CIA had hoped for.

Zahedi settled into his administration and very quickly grasped the need to boost his country's economic prospects. The Soviets allegedly offered monetary aid, a report that made its way into the Daily Brief a week after the coup. The analysts noted, 'Zahedi and the Shah would not be averse to using an alleged or actual offer of Soviet help to stimulate American aid.' The British, meanwhile, were pushing to get back 'their' oil. In the first week of September, the Brief outlined that 'The British Foreign Office recognises that the Zahedi regime will probably need financial assistance to survive, but hopes the United States will limit such aid in order to maintain pressure on Iran to settle the oil question.' But however much the British wanted it, there was not going to be any movement on oil. As a subsequent Brief remarked, Iran's new Prime Minister was 'totally unacquainted' with the details of the country's oil woes, although he had a vague understanding of 'the difficulties of establishing markets for Iran's oil'. The analysts added, 'considerable time will probably elapse before oil talks can begin'.

Overall, though, Washington had reason to be pleased with the new man in power in Persia. When Zahedi signed a trade deal with the Soviets, he clarified with US officials what items they wanted excluded, and he also warned the Soviet Union against 'interfering' in Iranian internal affairs, after checking with Ambassador Henderson what he planned to say. For the writers of the President's Brief, it was 'a good indication of his [Zahedi's] desire to cooperate with the United States'. It seemed the least he could do. After all, the Americans had helped make him Prime Minister.

In his memoirs, Eisenhower made no mention of the covert operations in Iran, although he did not hide his disdain for Mosaddeq, referring to the Iranian Prime Minister as 'a semi-invalid ... often clad in pyjamas in public'. Between the lines, however, there are subtle hints that more was going on. Eisenhower wrote that during the crisis in Iran he 'conferred daily with officials of the State and Defense Departments and the Central Intelligence Agency and saw reports from our representatives on the spot who were working actively with the Shah's supporters'. He also openly admitted, 'Throughout this crisis, the United States had done everything it possibly could to back up the Shah.' The full extent of 'everything possible' would not be revealed until decades later. It was hardly a coincidence that a month after Eisenhower's Daily Brief had warned that the success of Iran's new government would depend on rapidly improving the country's financial position, the USA granted Iran $45 million in official 'assistance'. Secretly, the CIA had also handed Zahedi $5 million within two days of his taking office, so he could meet the end-of-month payrolls of government employees.

When it came to Iran, the US government was hiding secrets from itself, even in its secret documents. The writers of the Daily Briefs throughout August 1953 made no mention of US efforts on the ground, with the only comment on foreign interference being that others were 'charging American involvement'. The CIA was gleeful, but Kim Roosevelt had his own reservations. On 4 September 1953, he visited the White House and gave an account of the operation to Eisenhower, as well as John and Allen Dulles. Roosevelt had maps and charts, many with 'generally irrelevant information', which he displayed to the pleased President on an easel. In his closing summary, he insisted that the only reason deposing Mosaddeq had worked was the CIA's correct assessment that much of the population was not pro-Communist and still supported the Shah. 'If we, the CIA, are ever going to try something like this again,' he insisted, 'we must be absolutely sure that [the] people and army [of the country] want what we want.'

17

Banana Republic

It was the sixteenth and final item on that day's President's Daily Brief, almost buried at the bottom of the fifth page presented to Truman on 6 May 1946. The US Embassy in the Central American country of Guatemala reported it had been approached by a 'revolutionary group which plans to overthrow the ... Government by a bloodless coup'. It was noted, 'The emissary received no encouragement.' Eight years later, however, following the success of the CIA's covert operation in Iran, quietly manipulating the arc of history from the shadows was to become a fashionable and seemingly risk-free enterprise.

Eisenhower authorised covert action in Guatemala on 12 August 1953, in the heady days before the curtain raising on the Iran operation. Nothing that took place 6,500 miles away in the Middle East in the week that followed dissuaded the plotters and planners from trying to topple Guatemala's President. In fact, Iran seemed to show that the CIA had the Midas touch: even when it all went wrong, after the smoke cleared the result was still in the USA's interest. Kim Roosevelt was invited to lead the Guatemala operation but turned it down, claiming later in his memoirs that he had done so because it failed the acid test he himself had suggested: that 'the people and the army want what we want'. What the people of Guatemala wanted was hardly a consideration. What seemingly concerned the White House more were the wishes and interests of a US-owned corporation that owned half of Guatemala.

★ ★ ★

The United Fruit Company was founded at the turn of the nineteenth century out of banana-producing companies that operated across the Caribbean, the largest of which was the Boston Fruit Company. By 1930 it was the largest employer in Central America; it financed government debt in exchange for vast tracts of tax-free farmland and owned the rail and shipyards that transported bananas to North America and Europe. In Guatemala, the company monopolised the country's export of bananas, and by the early twentieth century, company annual revenue in Guatemala comfortably exceeded that of the country's government. As one company executive later put it, 'Guatemala was chosen as the site for the company's earliest development activities, because at the time we entered Central America, Guatemala's government was the region's weakest, most corrupt and most pliable.'

The Guatemalan government's pliability ended abruptly in 1944, when Juan José Arévalo became the country's first democratically elected president. Arévalo instituted labour reforms and a sweeping programme of economic development along socialist lines, which immediately provoked the ire of the company and its backers. Arévalo was acutely aware of the impact of his actions, years later penning an allegorical short story of US involvement in Latin America, in which he compared the USA to a shark, 'looking out of filmed eyes without seeing, lazily and soundlessly opening its gullet, grotesquely spewing out whirlpools of acid water'.

Arévalo was succeeded by Jacobo Árbenz, an intelligent, astute 41-year-old former Guatemalan military officer who had served as a minister in Arévalo's administration. Árbenz carried further the trajectory begun by his predecessor, enacting an agrarian reform law which appropriated unused farmland and gave it to impoverished peasant farmers. In March 1953, the Guatemalan government appropriated 209,842 unused acres from the United Fruit Company, the largest landowner in Guatemala. Landowners whose uncultivated land was redistributed were paid in government bonds to the same amount that they themselves had valued their land for tax purposes. Unsurprisingly, the United Fruit Company had been deliberately undervaluing its holdings, so painted a picture in which a successful US business enterprise had been both cheated and robbed by Communists.

The company began an eye-wateringly expensive but incredibly successful public relations campaign within the USA, lobbying in the press and in all corners of Washington to try and get the US government to intervene in Guatemala. The company even commissioned a special short report that alleged Communism had gained a foothold across Latin America, but critically in Guatemala, and that the next move of Árbenz and his cronies would be to engineer the seizure of the Panama Canal. It was largely hokum, but the report was sent to key figures in Washington and was even picked up and further circulated by the CIA.

The company's agents were pushing at an open door, and the PR campaign worked wonders. The United Fruit Company had connections across government. Secretary of State John Foster Dulles, like so many in Washington, had entered politics via law. As a young attorney, Dulles had personally negotiated the company's monopoly on the main railway system that led directly from the company's plantations to the country's only significant port. The Assistant Secretary of State for inter-American Affairs had family stock in United Fruit, while the company's public relations director was the husband of President Eisenhower's personal secretary. In his allegorical short story, Guatemalan leader Arévalo compared United Fruit to an octopus, with tentacles everywhere. It was an apt metaphor. The CIA-sponsored coup in Guatemala was launched within seventeen months of Eisenhower taking office. In hindsight, it is remarkable it took that long.

★ ★ ★

Like the CIA-backed coup in Iran, the Guatemala operation had been in the planning for some time, but unlike with Iran, even Truman's administration had shown an interest. In 1952, Truman gave the go-ahead for the CIA to provide arms to Carlos Castillo Armas, a dissident Guatemalan military officer in exile in Honduras, with the aim of removing Árbenz's government by outside forces. But the Truman administration's plot was thrown into disarray when it was discovered that the Nicaraguan leader Anastasio Somoza Garcia, whom the CIA had been trying to encourage to aid its proxy, was openly broadcasting the CIA's involvement to government officials across Central America. The panicked State Department then shut down the entire operation.

A year later, with Eisenhower now in the White House, there was renewed enthusiasm for the Guatemala operation, and CIA plans were already well advanced. The Guatemala playbook was far more heavy-handed than the action the CIA had prepared in Iran. Instead of utilising almost entirely local assets, the CIA funded, armed and trained its own invasion force. For the second time of asking, Castillo Armas was invited to invade Guatemala with a small army of revolutionaries, only this time the invasion would be a better-kept secret. Castillo Armas was the illegitimate son of a landowner who had risen through the ranks of the Guatemalan military before his attempt to mount a coup to bring down Arévalo's government led to his forced exile. He seemed the perfect man to lead a coup, not least because he had tried it before, even without the aid and assistance of the CIA, and had spent three years kicking his heels with a group of similarly minded ex-Guatemalan Army soldiers across the border in Nicaragua.

A month after Eisenhower had given his approval to the Guatemala operation, a short item appeared in the Daily Brief. There was almost no attempt to hide US support for the expected effort to overthrow Árbenz: 'some arms have been smuggled into northern Guatemala, but financial assistance is needed before more can be sent in. It is also planned to obtain three fighter planes from the United States by having a "friendly country", possibly El Salvador, request them through diplomatic channels for "training purposes".'

By December, the coup air force had managed to acquire thirty aircraft, as CIA Director Dulles himself had persuaded a rich friend to create a charitable medical institute running out of Miami, which provided a useful front operation. War-surplus fighter-bombers, including P–47 Thunderbolts, were purchased and donated to the medical institute, which then sold them on, tax-free, to CIA front corporations in the Caribbean, which shipped them to Guatemala. In the absence of any exiled Guatemalan air force, the aircraft were flown by Americans, with the 'Liberation Air Force' combining a motley crew of ex-US servicemen who had found their way to Latin America and pilots already on the CIA's payroll. As 1954 rolled around, preparations were almost complete, and Castillo Armas could call on a CIA-trained force nearly 500 strong, as well as his own private air force. The plan was that the Guatemalan Army, many of whose high-ranking officers were suspicious of Árbenz and his socialist policies, would only need a nudge to align behind the invading exiles.

In early June, the Guatemalan government was reportedly planning to 'take [the] diplomatic offensive', according to the President's daily intelligence summary. It noted, 'the Guatemalans have "planted" caches of American arms and intend to announce their "discovery" within "two or three days" as "evidence" of American plotting to overthrow the Árbenz regime'. Unlike Truman's State Department, Eisenhower was unfazed by the suggestions that the invasion plan was becoming less than secret. The CIA was spending nearly $3 million on the project, three times as much as it had initially directly funded in Iran, and there was now an expectation of a return on investment. Besides, the start of the coup was scheduled for the following week.

On 19 June 1954, the last headline in the President's Daily Brief read, 'Anti-Communist forces reported invading Guatemala'. Even in the now-declassified document, the text of the main item is redacted, and with good reason. News that the CIA-sponsored invasion was under way reached Washington in the middle of the night of 18 June. It was clearly relevant and important news for the Daily Brief, but there was uncertainty about how it should be included. The Central American Section Chief and the Western Division Chief were called out to meet with the Agency's Deputy Director of Plans, Frank Wisner, in L-building at the CIA's headquarters in DC.

Wisner was a former operative of the Office of Strategic Services (OSS), the USA's wartime intelligence agency, and the 44-year-old Virginian had spent time in Egypt, Turkey and Romania before returning to the USA and being brought into the newly formed CIA. As Deputy Director of Plans, he held the most senior role in the CIA's clandestine operations.

After discussing the Guatemala news, Wisner personally wrote the item for the Brief the next morning, but the staff at the Office of Current Intelligence in Q-Building insisted they could not just insert it into the next day's pages. Instead, the dictated note was treated like an 'incoming cable' and was processed and included in the Brief, as if it had arrived overnight from a source in Central America. Where necessary, when it came to covert operations, the CIA adopted a policy of embracing its own fictionalised narrative to hide its secrets. As an internal official CIA history of the Daily Brief observed:

In 1954, the Clandestine Services had an interest in the rebellion of Carlos Castillo Armas against the leftist regime of Jacobo Árbenz … [In] situations in which [the] CIA is involved, it has usually been felt advisable to run a careful item, rather than draw attention by omitting coverage. Obviously, such items have to be coordinated thoroughly with the Clandestine Services.

The day after the note on the invasion had been quietly slipped into the Daily Brief, the first item was an extended 'Comment on Guatemalan situation'. The news was not good: 'the outcome of the efforts to overthrow the regime ... remains very much in doubt'. The critical factor was which way the majority of the Army would swing. As the analysts noted: 'if it remains loyal [to Árbenz] ... [then Castillo Armas] will be defeated'. Castillo Armas' forces were achieving almost nothing, but his air force had bombed a few Guatemalan military bases and caused terror in the capital by dropping bombs on some of the slum areas. The actions of the 'Liberation Air Force' were discredited in the Briefs, with the analysts writing, 'There is thus far no evidence to confirm the charges and propaganda of the Guatemalan regime of bombing attacks', although the swift paint jobs of clearly US-made aircraft were not fooling many eyewitnesses. The CIA was also mounting a huge disinformation campaign of air-dropped leaflets and concocted radio broadcasts with Guatemalan voice actors, who announced to anyone listening that the country's liberation from Communism was at hand.

For the next five days, the Guatemala situation remained on a knife edge. Castillo Armas' tiny ground force of 500 was inadequate for dealing with any sustained military opposition and, although some Guatemalan Army soldiers had spontaneously joined Castillo Armas, if President Árbenz could convince his military to go on the offensive, the invasion would be very quickly over. Meanwhile, the American Embassy shared a concerning rumour that Communist groups were planning an attack on the building. The legation warned, 'They reportedly expect to seize documents in the American Embassy proving collaboration between the United States government and Castillo Armas, leader of the opposition forces.' The attack did not materialise, but there was clearly written evidence at the Embassy, as the CIA Station in Guatemala City was ordered to destroy all documents relating to the operation a week later. On 25 June, the Daily Brief did not make easy reading for the Washington architects of what was unfolding in Guatemala. 'Only limited and relatively unimportant territory has thus far been occupied by the rebel forces', it was noted, while the US Ambassador was 'not too confident' that Castillo Armas would succeed.

Unknown to those in the White House, the increasingly obvious involvement of the USA in the coup was its salvation. Guatemalan military commanders were concerned that Castillo Armas' tiny army was a precursor to a full US invasion; they feared the next fighters they would face would be US Marines. When Árbenz sent a trusted officer to talk to field commanders, the message he returned was devastating: '[They] think the Americans are threatening Guatemala just because of you and your Communist friends. If you don't resign, the Army will march on the capital to depose you.' On 27 June, President Árbenz went on public radio to announce the transfer of power to a colonel in the military. He condemned 'US ruling circles' for unleashing a 'cruel war' against Guatemala by 'commanding barbarous mercenaries' and said he was stepping down to 'do away with our powerful enemies' pretext', otherwise, 'Guatemala might be destroyed'. After the broadcast, Guatemala's legitimately elected leader quietly fled the country. Just as in Iran, the CIA's coup had been a spectacularly successful operational failure.

The success in Guatemala made the Daily Brief as a late item. It was claimed that 'pressure from Guatemalan army leaders forced President Árbenz' resignation'. The Brief also noted that Colonel Carlos Enrique Díaz, who had assumed control of government, had immediately met with the US Ambassador and told him that 'he was prepared to take over the presidency and clean out the Communists from the government'. A few days later, the Daily Brief carried the cheery news that the new Guatemalan government had outlawed the Communist Party. There were still wranglings within the military over who would be in charge – Díaz was replaced by another colonel named Elfego Monzón – but it was already reported that 'Although Colonel Monzón temporarily heads the new junta ... Castillo Armas ... appears to be in the stronger position.' And so it proved.

On 7 July 1954, Castillo Armas became President of Guatemala. By the end of the month, he had reversed the land reform law, forcing the peasants who had been granted land under Árbenz to hand it back. The United Fruit Company had regained its holdings. The rationale for the action in Guatemala had always seemed to be more about the threat to commerce than the threat of Communism, although the latter provided useful cover. One of the President's friends, Texas newspaperman William Prescott Allen, happened to be in Guatemala as the coup unfolded. Just three days before Árbenz resigned, the publisher, who prided himself on his paper's record of speaking truth to power, had messaged Eisenhower: 'Yes, Guatemala has a very small minority of Communists, but not as many as San Francisco.'

In mid-July, the President received his second post-CIA-coup special briefing. This time there were movies, as well as charts, and no Kim Roosevelt to dampen the mood. Eisenhower was delighted, remarking it was 'incredible' that Castillo Armas' forces had only lost one man, shaking Director Dulles' hand and telling the intelligence officers, 'Thanks to all of you. You have averted a Soviet beachhead in our hemisphere.' He did, however, have one question for the CIA planners. 'Why the hell didn't you catch Árbenz?'

One of the men in the room laughed at the idea of targeting a foreign leader and replied, 'Mr President, that would have set a very dangerous precedent for you.'

18

One Man

Patrice Lumumba faced an unenviable situation. The newborn country he had been appointed Prime Minister of less than two months before was falling apart. At more than 900,000 square miles, the Congo is the largest non-desert country in Africa. It would cover two-thirds of Western Europe, although it appears to be a great deal smaller on a map. The Mercator projection that makes our round world fit neatly on a page stretches countries further from the equator and squashes those near it. Due to a trick of the map and a colonial mindset, the Congo would forever be made less significant to Western eyes.

In June 1960, the 'Belgian' Congo had ceased to exist as a century of colonial rule ended, and the Republic of the Congo came into being. By August, the new nation was already tottering as it attempted to stand on its own feet; a United Nations peace-keeping force was unable to keep a lid on internal violence in the face of fractious political and ethnic divisions. Slim, with studious-looking eyes that lived behind black-rimmed glasses, the 35-year-old Lumumba was not new to politics – he had founded and led a nationalist political party – but he was new to governing. In a country where politics and ethnicity often intertwined, his lack of a strong ethnic association was a blessing and a curse. Because he did not come from a major group, he did not have a ready-made support base, but the young, charismatic leader was also able to promote a new, national ideal: that he and his countrymen were not simply Bantu, Ngbandi or Tetela, but Congolese.

Support for that ideal had propelled his party, the *Mouvement National Congolais*, to near-victory in elections, but to create a government, Lumumba had been forced to compromise. While he held the office of Prime Minister, his political rival Joseph Kasavubu (leader of the *Alliance des Bakongo,* which had come second in the vote) was President. The two men had a fractious relationship and were effectively building their own rival administrations.

In the middle of the political strife, the Congo's wealthiest region, mineral-rich Katanga in the south, was breaking away. Another powerful figure in Congolese politics, Moïse Tshombe, had huge regional ethnic support in Katanga and took advantage of the chaos to announce his region's independence; Tshombe was also being aided by European mercenaries, as Belgian mining companies based in Katanga sought to secure their interests. Lumumba, as the Congo's Prime Minister, had appealed for international assistance to stop the cessation of Katanga province, but neither the USA nor the United Nations was immediately willing to act militarily to suppress the rebellion in Katanga. Lumumba then requested Soviet assistance, and Moscow agreed to provide transport aircraft, vehicles and military advisers, so Lumumba could ship his army south to put down Tshombe's rebels.

The call for Soviet support was not well received. To a number of Western observers, it seemed the Congo's new leader was already running into the arms of the Cold War enemy. The Chief of the CIA Station in the Congo's capital, Leopoldville, sent an urgent message to his superiors: 'Embassy and [CIA] Station believe Congo experiencing classic Communist effort [to] takeover government. Anti-West forces rapidly increasing power [in] Congo and therefore may be little time left.'

★ ★ ★

Six and a half thousand miles away, President Dwight D. Eisenhower was taking a summer break from the claustrophobic heat of Washington, vacationing at Newport, Rhode Island. Eisenhower, along with his wife Mary – known to everyone as 'Mamie' – regularly retreated to the same white-painted, three-storey, clapboard house off the New England coast. The President would spend time golfing and painting, a hobby he had taken up in his late fifties, while he and his wife still entertained in the evenings. Mamie and 'Ike' had always had a reputation for socialising, and Mamie embraced public holidays as times to decorate wherever they were staying and have guests over. But some work always went with them. At 9 a.m. Eastern Standard Time on 18 August 1960, the President headed into his weekly National Security Council meeting. The situation in the Congo was the first item on the agenda; it had also been mentioned in the Briefs every day for the whole of August.

Eisenhower was in an uncompromising mood that morning. When it was suggested that the UN soldiers deployed to try and hold the fragile new country together might be forced out, he said it was 'simply inconceivable', asserting, 'We should keep the UN in the Congo even if we had to ask for European troops to do it. We should do so even if such action was used by the Soviets as the basis for starting a fight.' Eisenhower placed the blame at the feet of a single individual, telling the NSC, 'we are talking of one man forcing us out of the Congo; of Lumumba supported by the Soviets'. He then turned to Allen Dulles and said simply that Lumumba 'should be eliminated'. The staff member taking the minutes later recalled, 'there was a stunned silence for about fifteen seconds and [then] the meeting continued'.

The official President-approved minutes of the 456th meeting of the NSC do not contain Eisenhower's comment, and when asked years later as part of a Senate investigation, a number of those present would suggest there was 'no clear-cut order' for an assassination. But nine days after the NSC meeting at Rhode Island, the CIA Station in Leopoldville received a telegram from headquarters in Washington. The text had been drafted by Dulles himself. It read:

> In high quarters here it is the clear-cut conclusion that if Lumumba continues to hold high office, the inevitable result will at best be chaos and at worst pave the way to Communist takeover of the Congo ... Consequently we conclude that his removal must be an urgent and prime objective and ... a high priority of our covert action.

But the instruction, which included the release of additional funds, also seemed to go further. It gave the green light to earlier proposed plans to support youth groups and trade unions opposed to Lumumba, with the additional comment that there was 'wider authority' for 'even more aggressive action, if it can remain covert'. Dulles also added, 'To the extent the [US] Ambassador [in Congo] may desire to be consulted you should seek his concurrence. If in any particular case he does not wish to be consulted you can act on your own authority.' The Director of the CIA was giving his assets on the ground in the Congo permission to undertake covert operations to remove Lumumba and, if necessary, to keep the whole thing secret from their Ambassador.

At the start of September, the political crisis in the Congo escalated, when President Kasavubu dismissed Lumumba from his post as Prime Minister. Lumumba immediately rejected the move as unconstitutional and announced that he was dismissing Kasavubu from his post. For the US diplomats stationed in the Congo, it seemed yet another moment of madness in a country that was descending into chaos.

★ ★ ★

Larry Devlin bribed his way past the guards on the gates of the presidential palace in Leopoldville with packs of cigarettes and found himself waiting in a small, windowless room. He was there in the hope of seeing the President and ascertaining whether it was likely to be him, or Lumumba, who would most likely cling to power. Devlin was a confident, energetic Californian and former US Army captain who was in the Congo as a pretend diplomat: in reality, he was Chief of Station for the CIA. When he was given the Congo posting in 1959, a colleague told him to take two dinner jackets for the endless stream of fancy evening meals and to look forward to being on the golf course 'by two o'clock every afternoon'. Instead, Devlin found himself running CIA operations in a newly independent country that Washington was worried would turn Communist: he was on the front line of the covert Cold War.

Into the stuffy waiting room came not the Congolese President, but the young Army Chief of Staff. 'I'm anxious to talk to you', he said:

The president and prime minister have dismissed each other. Political games! ... The Soviets are pouring into the country ... I know we don't have enough educated Congolese to fill the shoes of all the Belgian civil servants who've left the country. But that doesn't mean I want Soviet technicians to take their place. We didn't fight for independence to have another country re-colonize us.

Devlin nodded.

'Here is the situation,' the Chief of Staff continued:

The army is prepared to overthrow Lumumba. But only on the condition that the United States will recognise the government that would replace Lumumba's. The government we would establish would be temporary and would stay in power only so long as necessary to get the Soviets out of the Congo and to create a democratic regime.

Devlin listened calmly and then asked, 'And Lumumba and Kasavubu, what happens to them?'

'They'll both have to be neutralised,' the soldier replied. The Chief of Staff told Devlin he needed to know on the spot if he had US support, and that he would need $5,000 as security money for the families of himself and his military co-conspirators in case the plot failed. The CIA man shook the soldier's hand, and the tall young man in uniform fixed his eyes impassively on the American. 'The coup will take place within a week,' he said.

On 14 September 1960, Mobutu Sese Seko staged a military coup in the Congo. He was described in one of the President's Daily Briefs as of '30 years of age ... considered reasonably intelligent but narrow minded and somewhat suspicious of white persons'. The US Embassy in Leopoldville's description was more charitable. Mobutu was, it said, 'an honest and dedicated man who is appalled by the magnitude of the Congo's problems'. His arrival in office was good news for Washington: two days after taking power he gave Soviet diplomats forty-eight hours to depart the country. The Daily Brief was very clear where the CIA stood on the rise of Mobutu and the fall of Lumumba. The day after the coup, in an update 'as of 0430 EDT', it was noted, 'if successful, his [Mobutu's] action may save the country from becoming virtually a Communist satellite'. The CIA immediately began funnelling money to Mobutu's administration, on top of the cash in hand from Devlin.

On 21 September 1960, the week after Mobutu had taken power, the NSC convened again. Lumumba was deposed but still at large and retained a devoted popular following. In the view of a number of the men around the table, being out of government was insufficient to keep him silenced. Allen Dulles told the President and key security advisors, 'Mobutu appeared to be the effective power in the Congo for the moment, but Lumumba was not yet disposed of and remained a grave danger as long as he was not disposed of.'

Dulles' macabre turn of phrase when he mentioned Lumumba at the 21 September NSC meeting was not an accident. Two days before, CIA Station Chief Larry Devlin had received a cryptic communiqué. Marked 'eyes only', it was from the head of the CIA's clandestine operations, the Deputy Director of Plans. The 'DDP' during the Guatemala coup, Frank Wisner, had departed his position after a deterioration of his mental health, leaving the role to a man he had recruited. Wisner, it later came out, had been living with manic depression for years. His CIA colleagues had often seen him 'flying', as some called it, but after more than half a decade as DDP, he had stepped down. While Wisner underwent electroshock therapy – a treatment that would leave him 'sad and diminished' – the figure now at the sharp end of CIA operations was a former economist, Richard Bissell. His instructions to the CIA's main man in the Congo were mysterious: Devlin was told he would shortly be contacted in person by a senior CIA officer, who would identify himself as 'Joe from Paris'.

A week later, the suited figure of Larry Devlin walked out of the gates of the US Embassy in Leopoldville, just a few hundred yards from where the wide Congo River curves lazily past the city's main shipyard. As the CIA's Chief of Station made his way towards his car, a balding, spectacled white man got up from a table at a café across the road and came towards him.

'I'm Joe from Paris,' he said. 'I've come to give you instructions about a highly sensitive operation.' Shortly afterwards, the two men sat face to face in the stiflingly hot sitting room of a CIA safe house. The visitor explained to Devlin that he had come to the Congo bringing with him poison to assassinate Lumumba, and Devlin was going to be the man to deliver it.

The CIA Station Chief was gobsmacked. 'Jesus H. Christ,' he said. 'Isn't this unusual?' Devlin demanded to know who had authorised the operation.

'President Eisenhower,' his visitor said calmly. 'I wasn't there when he approved it, but ... Bissell said that Eisenhower wanted Lumumba removed.' He added, 'It's your responsibility to carry out the operation, you alone ... it's got to be clean – nothing that can be traced back to the US government.' The visitor then handed over a selection of different poisons, including one that could be injected into a tube of toothpaste.

Shortly after Larry Devlin had received his 'eyes only' telegram, some of Mobutu's men had tracked down and detained Lumumba. To avoid a political spectacle, he was now under house arrest in his own home in Leopoldville. Outside the compound were Congolese Army soldiers making sure he did not escape, and inside were UN troops to make sure the deposed leader was not attacked. Meanwhile, across town, Devlin was making plans for how to get past all the armed guards and take out Lumumba. Devlin later claimed in his memoirs that, from the start, he believed the assassination plan to be 'morally wrong', but he still 'followed orders'. In doing so, he ruptured his relationship with his deputy at the Station in Leopoldville because he would often be leaving to attend secret meetings and 'could not explain … why I seemed to be paying less attention than formerly to matters that were important'. The CIA Station Chief was one of only a handful of people who knew an uncomfortable fact: that the US President had put out a kill order on the Congo's democratically elected Prime Minister. Once again, the intelligence services were hiding secrets from themselves.

19

Allies Overseas

On 8 November 1960, Eisenhower's two terms were officially bookended and the Republican began marking time until he relinquished the Oval Office to Kennedy. Lumumba was still a prisoner in his residence in Leopoldville, and the CIA was still trying to get to him. The problem was that he had not been seen outside the UN-protected compound and had fired most of the servants. Devlin had had 'exploratory conversations' with a number of local individuals who it was felt might be open to the job, but had drawn a blank. In early October, he cabled back to CIA headquarters using the special communication channel set up for the operation, stating the 'necessity [CIA] provide [Congo] Station with [a] qualified third country national'. Getting anyone close enough to Lumumba to poison him was proving a tall order, so Devlin had changed tack. His follow-up to the request for a dedicated assassin was that headquarters send in the untouchable diplomatic pouch '[a] high-powered, foreign make rifle with telescopic scope and silencer'. The assassination plot was becoming less discreet by the day.

On 21 November, the foreign assassin arrived in the Congo. In communications he was referred to only by the codename 'QJWIN'. When he had been invited to join the operation, he had not been told the details, only that he would go to Leopoldville and that it would 'involve a large element of personal risk'. For taking on the risk, he was being paid $1,000 a month.

Five days later, QJWIN and the CIA team in Leopoldville finally agreed on a plan. A local asset would supply four UN vehicles and six Congolese soldiers, who would be wearing blue UN armbands and berets; getting hold of UN vehicles was not hard, as fifty-five of them had been stolen. QJWIN would pose as an officer to enter the target's home and, after he had killed Lumumba, the 'UN' soldiers and vehicles would then escort the assassin out. With the jigsaw pieces finally falling into place, they just had to wait for the right moment.

The following night, a violent thunderstorm deluged the Congolese capital. As the soldiers around Lumumba's house ran for cover, the Prime Minister slipped into a black car and was driven away; later retellings of the story would claim he had calmly marched out of his own house dressed up as a Ghanaian UN officer. After spending two months encircled, Lumumba had slipped the net. It seemed most likely he was headed to the town of Stanleyville, where his most loyal support base might keep him safe.

Lumumba's escape wrecked the CIA's best-laid murder plans, although QJWIN volunteered to travel to Stanleyville using German business credentials and his own passport 'to execute [the] plan by himself'. In the event, he was not needed. On 1 December, Mobutu's soldiers picked up Lumumba in the town of Lodi, 1,000km east of Leopoldville. He was filmed calmly emerging from a DC-3 in a plain, open-necked white shirt, surrounded by guards, his hands roped behind his back. After landing, Lumumba was loaded onto an open-top lorry with a group of other prisoners and driven away to a military base.

★ ★ ★

When Kennedy entered the Oval Office on 21 January 1961, he found problems in Africa at the top of his in-tray. The very first Daily Brief prepared for Kennedy the day after his inauguration featured the Congo. The 3,000 Moroccan soldiers who were part of the UN force had reportedly been ordered not to fight by their home government, which was also apparently looking to 'dissociate itself from the UN Congo operation' and begin the withdrawal of their troops 'by 5 February'. The situation, in the words of the CIA analysts, was 'explosive'.

Events in the Congo had taken a dangerous turn after Lumumba's arrest. His incarceration at a military camp had become a problem. There were still soldiers in the Army loyal to him and the deposed Prime Minister remained a popular political figure; meanwhile, soldiers and police were not being paid due to a lack of government funds. The CIA Station in Leopoldville dispatched a despairing message to the CIA Director, warning that Mobutu's government could fall and that the result 'would almost certainly be chaos and return [Lumumba] to power'. Mobutu was acutely aware of the threat posed to his government by Lumumba's popularity and there seemed a simple solution: transfer him far from the capital, somewhere where he would be out of the way.

With assistance from the Belgian government, whose advisors were working closely with Tshombe's breakaway region in the south, Mobutu arranged for Lumumba to be flown to Katanga, despite the fact that the Leopoldville government and Katanga were practically at war. On 14 January, six days before Kennedy entered office, Devlin was told of the plan by a government official in Leopoldville. There is no evidence he made any protest. On 25 January, the new US President was the recipient of a seventy-seven-page 'Analytical Chronology of the Congo Crisis'. On the final page it was noted, 'on January 17, Lumumba was taken from the military camp at Thysville where he had been imprisoned since the beginning of December, and flown to Elisabethville, where he was turned over to the tender mercies of his archenemy, Moïse Tshombe'. No other details were given, as Lumumba was by then already missing.

Kennedy did not share Allen Dulles' supremely critical view of Lumumba. In 1959 and 1960, Kennedy, then a senator, had chaired the African Subcommittee. He held to a more charitable analysis of the anti-Western sentiments of many of Africa's independent leaders, including Lumumba, which he insisted resulted from their past experience of colonialism, rather than a natural pro-Soviet bias. Rumours were rife that Kennedy might try to work with Lumumba once in office, and when President-elect, he had spoken with a US diplomat who had met the Congo's Prime Minister and enquired, 'Should we save Lumumba?' The diplomat had poured cold water on the idea, suggesting it was impossible, even if Kennedy wanted to. By the time Kennedy was receiving his first Daily Briefs, QJWIN had left the Congo and

Larry Devlin had chucked the poisons he had received from 'Joe from Paris' in the Congo River. The operation was not officially 'off', but unofficially it was being wound down. Had Kennedy ever gotten wind of it, it would have severely dented his early, positive impressions of the CIA.

For nearly a month, there was no further news on the whereabouts or possible fate of the Congo's elected leader. At the UN, there were ongoing efforts to avert an all-out war in the Congo between the Leopoldville government and the southern secessionists, but as the Daily Brief noted on 13 February 1961, 'uncertainty regarding Lumumba has ... interrupted at least some of the efforts which had been under way at the UN to formulate a new Security Council resolution aimed at promoting a Congolese settlement'. The writers of the Brief added that Security Council members were calling for the UN to act 'for the release of Lumumba', with the added caveat, 'if still alive'. No news, they assumed, was bad news.

Later that day, the US Ambassador to the UN, Adlai Stevenson, put a call through to the White House. He spoke briefly with the President. The only other person in the Oval Office was the White House photographer, who recalled Kennedy saying, 'Oh no.' The photographer snapped a frame as Kennedy raised his hand to his furrowed forehead in despair. He had caught the moment the President was told Lumumba had been beaten, tortured and then shot by a firing squad the very afternoon he arrived in Katanga. The following day, Lumumba's death was the first item in Kennedy's Daily Brief. As it transpired, the CIA had absolutely nothing to do with the murder of the Congo's Prime Minister, although it was not for lack of trying; two days after Lumumba's transfer, CIA officers in Elisabethville had sent a jovial but sinister message to Washington: 'Thanks for Patrice. If we had known he was coming, we would have baked a snake.'

★ ★ ★

The newly arrived Democrat in the White House soon demonstrated few inhibitions when it came to deploying covert support to further US foreign policy interest in Africa. Kennedy was not about to order a hit on a foreign leader, but he was entirely comfortable with attempting to ensure the USA had friends in the right places. Mobutu's administration retained Kasavubu as President, but the country was still in disarray. The same month as Kennedy learned of

Lumumba's murder, the CIA approved another 'significant' request for funds from Mobutu, to stave off a mutiny in the unpaid army and police. Mobutu himself eschewed political office, so a UN-sponsored plan to select a new Prime Minister gained traction. A special parliamentary session would be held at Louvanium University, just outside Leopoldville, in July 1961, at which a new Prime Minister for the whole of the Congo would be elected. Tshombe immediately rejected the idea, as he would not have had sufficient support outside of Katanga, but the special session was planned to go ahead anyway.

On 16 June 1961, Kennedy received the first of his new, more exclusive Daily Briefs, reading the draft version as he sat on the diving board by the swimming pool at Glen Ora. His next five covered the Congo, and there was a problem. Lumumba's former Deputy Prime Minister had done what Lumumba had tried to do when he escaped house arrest: set up a rival administration in Stanleyville. Antoine Gizenga did not have Lumumba's charisma, but his 'government' had been formally recognised by Egypt, China and the Soviet Union. Gizenga was putting his name in the hat for the special session, and he would have strong support.

The Kennedy administration had already selected the horse they would back, a man Kennedy's Secretary of State had described as 'the strongest and most attractive of the moderate Congolese leaders'. Cyrille Adoula was also favoured by Mobutu and Kasavubu, and the 40-year-old, strong-set former labour leader had, crucially, disavowed the Soviets. In Kennedy's 21 June Daily Brief, however, there was a stark warning that at the upcoming special parliamentary session Adoula's support 'risks being outvoted by the Gizengists'. Kennedy's National Security Advisor, McGeorge Bundy, discussed the situation with the President that same day and Kennedy approved a 'substantial contingency fund', which the CIA were to use to make sure their man got elected. If necessary, Kennedy was comfortable with buying an ally in Africa's Congo.

The special parliamentary session opened in late July. The temple-like, white-fronted building of the Louvanium University was teeming with politicians and UN soldiers, who were supposedly there to preside over a fair vote. They were not just selecting a Prime Minister, but other key positions as well, and in the early voting Gizenga's allies scored important victories. Dean Rusk, Kennedy's Secretary of State, was given a dressing down by Kennedy when the news reached Washington and immediately authorised US agents in the Congo to 'use all means' to get Adoula elected. Meanwhile, the Embassy in Leopoldville was dispatching dire warnings to Washington that a 'bandwagon psychosis would take over [the delegates] and would result in a landslide for Gizenga'. A nine-strong Soviet delegation arrived in Leopoldville and Larry Devlin 'assumed the size of the delegation meant that the Soviet Union had decided once again to make a major effort in the Congo'. It seemed that the country might again be turning red. With approval from Washington, Congo Station officers became suddenly generous, making offers of cash and cars to voting Congolese politicians, some of whom would then openly go to the Soviets to try and get a better offer.

Finally, on 2 August, the parliamentary session approved Adoula as Prime Minister. In the words of one official, the Americans had 'simply outbid' the competition. It was deemed to be well worth it, with the Assistant National Security Advisor stating in a memo to Kennedy that the victory for Adoula in the Congo was 'the most encouraging development since you became President'. Afterwards, Adoula and his wife were frequent dinner guests at Larry Devlin's house. The following year, Adoula visited Washington and was photographed at the White House having a cosy fireside chat with Kennedy. Adoula's victory did not spare the Congo from strife, but for a short window, the Americans had their man in power. The CIA's actions, however, supported by two different occupants of the White House, had set a precedent for sponsored coups and rigged elections in the heart of Africa.

★ ★ ★

From 1952 and into the 1960s, the White House was occupied by presidents happy to project US power in the shadows and use the covert assets at their disposal to put favourable leaders in place in other parts of the world. Rationalised through the lens of the Cold War, it did not seem to matter if the men in the Oval Office were Democrats or Republicans, although Kennedy was less direct in his methods than Eisenhower.

The consequences of the operations mounted by the CIA between 1953 and 1961 shaped the course of history. The removal of Mosaddeq planted a seed of animosity among many Iranians that remains to this day and was pivotal in preparing the ground for the 1979 revolution, which placed an ardently anti-Western government in power in Tehran. Guatemala suffered under US-supported military rule, before tensions spilled over into an open conflict and decades-long civil war, while in the Congo, the wounds of division that marred the country in 1961 were never able to heal. The nation has suffered violence and unwelcome interventions from outsiders ever since.

Covert actions were almost always kept out of the Daily Briefs, to ensure an administration's right hand did not know what its left was doing. Operations in Iran and the Congo were barely hinted at, but the threads leading to the CIA's operations in Guatemala were more obvious. When it came to covert ops, it was the one time that US presidents were happy with appearing not to be fully informed.

By the time of Kennedy, the Daily Brief had once again become a document read assiduously by the President. In the nearly two decades of its existence, it had covered events in many nations, but there was one constant: concerning reports from a country in South East Asia.

Part V

Unfolding Tragedy: The War in Vietnam

20

A Situation

On the morning of 22 November 1963, Abraham Zapruder shut up shop at his dress manufacturer's on Elm Street in the heart of Dallas, and he and his employees made the short walk to Dealey Plaza park. The 58-year-old had forgotten his video camera, but one of his assistants persuaded him to pop home to pick it up; the Russian-born child of immigrants wanted to capture a historic moment in the country that had given him a new home and new life. For the first time, Zapruder was going to see the President of the United States in the flesh.

The rainy skies from the early morning had cleared and it was a balmy 19°C with a light breeze. Zapruder readied his 8mm movie camera and started recording just as Kennedy's motorcade turned onto Elm Street. Twenty-six seconds and 486 frames later, Zapruder turned his camera off. The short movie he had captured would make him rich but leave him haunted for life: Zapruder had filmed close up the shooting of the President. Kennedy was rushed to a nearby hospital, but the gunshot wounds to his back and head were fatal. Half an hour after Zapruder had started his camera rolling, the President was pronounced dead.

Two cars behind the sleek, open-top Lincoln Continental limousine which carried John and Jackie Kennedy, Vice President Lyndon Johnson and his wife could only watch as the President's car sped away after the gunshots. At the hospital, among the frenetic Secret Service agents and harried doctors, Johnson's wife Claudia, known to everyone as 'Lady Bird', hugged Jackie Kennedy, who stood alone in a small hallway. Her dress and the white gloves she wore were stained red: 'Somehow that was one of the most poignant sights [of that day],' Lady Bird recorded in her diary, '– that immaculate woman exquisitely dressed, and caked in blood.' The entourage, with what was now the President's body, rushed to Dallas' Love Field Airport to fly back to Washington.

Johnson himself was in a state of shock. 'I found it hard to believe that this nightmare had actually happened,' he wrote later in his memoirs. 'A few hours earlier I had been having breakfast with John Kennedy – alive, young, strong and vigorous. I was bewildered and distraught.' On the plane, as the jet's engines started up to take off, Johnson was sworn in as the thirty-sixth President of the United States. Remarkably, he was not aware that the Daily Brief Kennedy had received every day even existed.

Since its earliest days during the time of Truman, 'the President's Secret Newspaper' had become considerably less secret. First, the press heard about it, then its circulation had massively increased when Eisenhower was in the White House. It had changed names a number of times, from the 'Daily Summary' to the 'Current Intelligence Bulletin' and then the 'Central Intelligence Bulletin', but the newer, more secret version commissioned for Kennedy in June 1961 had been kept under wraps. The Daily Brief that Kennedy received, titled 'The President's Intelligence Checklist', came out of the CIA Office of Current Intelligence the same as all the previous versions had, but the Vice President had been deliberately kept out of the loop, seemingly at Kennedy's instigation.

On 23 November, Johnson's first morning in office, CIA Director John McCone – the man who had been on honeymoon in France at the start of the Cuban Missile Crisis – drove to the White House. The CIA had had precious few dealings with the Vice President, and everything was still up in the air. McCone had telephoned one of Johnson's staff first thing that morning to say he would 'take the regular 9 a.m. intelligence briefing', but that itself was a charade. Kennedy, despite all the efforts of McGeorge Bundy, had never had a regular, daily sit-down. The Director of the CIA and the new President of the United States met in Bundy's basement office on the lower floors of the West Wing, as the cleaners were still removing Kennedy's effects from the Oval Office. McCone told the President about the existence of Kennedy's special Daily Brief and talked him through the document. The analysts who wrote the Brief had even slightly modified it overnight. They began including more context and background, aware that there was much the new man did not know. As one of the Brief writers later admitted, they were 'trying to bridge the gap without having to talk down to him [Johnson], which was difficult'.

Lyndon Baines Johnson was a burly, stubborn Southerner who was nearly a decade older than Kennedy. He had grown up in rural Texas and gone to the local Southwest State Teachers College before running for Congress and working his way up the political ladder, becoming a senator in 1948 and Senate Majority Leader in 1954. He was a highly astute political operator with an enviable reputation for getting bills over the line, but after bolstering Kennedy's ticket as a Vice President with legislative know-how and political nous, he was left out in the cold. Kennedy did not like Johnson, and the feeling was mutual. The President made sure his Vice President was not furnished with the same information he was and often excluded him completely from decision making. That exclusion included intelligence.

Johnson himself did not fit with Kennedy's style. Kennedy had a celebrity wife and had brought in advisors like Bundy for his White House team: men who were academics by nature and who oozed confident expertise. For the grafting Johnson with his state college background, they were 'damn smart men', and he did not mean it as a compliment. But Johnson was inheriting a White House staff not of his own choosing, and he desperately needed to appear to be bringing continuity and stability. In the eyes of much of the mourning American public, Johnson was literally stepping into a dead man's shoes, and his predecessor had been a popular colossus. Johnson would have to contend not only with the man Kennedy was but also the President most would remember him as: the ever-youthful victor of the Cuban Missile Crisis, whose flaws were forgotten because it served a nation well to deify the dead. And on top of it all, there were only eleven months until the next election. Johnson's first 100 days as President would leave him less than 250 days away from a vote that could put him out of office. The pressing concerns that faced 'LBJ' were arguably more pressing than they had been for any other President.

The first item on the first Daily Brief Johnson ever saw covered a country he already knew well. It was the item McCone led with that morning when he explained the Brief to Johnson in a downstairs office of the West Wing. Headed 'South Vietnam', it noted that attacks by Communist guerrillas were less frequent than the week before, but still '50% above the year's weekly average'. They were 'small-scale' and 'designed more for their psychological impact than for immediate military gain', but already it was a familiar pattern. Conflict in Vietnam had been going on intermittently since 1946 and showed no signs of stopping. US soldiers had been deployed as 'advisors' to try and help anti-Communist forces, but their advice did not seem to be helping and already some saw them as unwelcome visitors. As Johnson's Brief the following day noted, 'The North Vietnamese ... believe that sentiment is growing in the US for the withdrawal of US forces. They reportedly plan to keep the heat on to encourage it.'

★ ★ ★

Nearly two decades before Johnson, President Truman had found his own Daily Briefs full of sobering news from 'Indochina', the name for the modern--day countries of Laos, Cambodia and Vietnam, which had been part of the French Empire before the outbreak of the Second World War. During the war, the area was occupied by the Japanese, but when Japanese forces surrendered in 1945, the French wanted their empire back. Many of their subjects, however, were considerably less keen. The result was war. In August 1946, Truman's Brief contained a report from the US Consul in Hanoi, who warned of rising tension between the French and Vietnamese after the ambushing of a French motor convoy on 3 August. The US diplomat cautioned there was 'danger of an open break, followed by anarchy'. He added, 'The French admit that ultimate pacification of the country would be a long, bitter operation.'

The resistance movement against the return of French rule was led by a 56-year-old Vietnamese-born political leader with many names and a colourful backstory. Born in a village, he had sailed the world working as a cook on a French ship, and had lived in London, Boston and Paris. In France, he found fellow Vietnamese who opposed French rule and, in the 1920s, he officially converted to Communism. He travelled to Moscow where he made a name for himself, returning to Vietnam to found an independence movement called the Viet Minh. After aiding the OSS – the forerunner to the CIA – in clandestine operations against the Japanese during the war, the Viet Minh marched on the northern city of Hanoi in the void left after the Japanese surrender. In front of adoring crowds, the villager who inspired the movement quoted the United States Declaration of Independence: that all people are created equal. Ho Chi Minh ended his short speech asserting, 'Vietnam has the right to be a free and independent country – and in fact is so already.' But the independence was short-lived, as the French first retook southern Vietnam and then pressed north. In Washington, Vietnam's independence movement was viewed as anything but, as one of Truman's November Briefs noted. There was, according to the French, irrefutable 'positive proof that Ho Chi Minh is in direct contact with Moscow and is receiving advice and instructions from the Soviets'. War began the following month.

The conflict that became known as the 'First Indochina War' ran from 1946 until 1954. The French had been correct back in '46: pacification was proving a long and bitter operation. Ho Chi Minh's forces melted into the jungle; his numerous men were badly equipped and poorly trained, but the French could not pin them down. The French government, bankrupted by the Second World War, was hardly in a position to finance an extended overseas campaign. The first three years of fighting achieved no real victory. In an attempt to outflank Ho Chi Minh politically, in 1949 the French set up a sympathetic southern Vietnamese government, officially under the leadership of a regional princeling named Bao Dai. South Vietnam was wealthier and more ethnically diverse than the north, and many southern Vietnamese were not especially fond of the Viet Minh, but it was soon obvious that Bao Dai was nothing more than a French puppet leader. After Bao Dai was installed in the south, the Soviet Union officially recognised Ho Chi Minh, while Communist China began supplying arms, munitions and training to Ho Chi Minh's fighters.

The change in the dynamic of the conflict pushed the French into seeking their own allies. Truman's 1 February 1950 Daily Brief noted, 'The US may soon be faced in Indochina with a situation … In resisting the Communist advance, France can now turn for assistance only to the US.' CIA analysts appended their own two-page assessment in an annexe to the Brief. They added that the Soviet recognition had 'jeopardised the already uneasy position of the French'. If the French were forced out, they believed, Burma and Thailand would probably turn 'toward the Communist orbit'. Sixteen days later, the US Deputy Ambassador in Paris reported that the French Ambassador had been asked 'to request large-scale US assistance to Indochina on a long-term basis'. The tendrils of the conflict in South East Asia were already coiling themselves toward Washington.

In the Cold War context, which turned into open proxy conflict in Korea a few months later, there were many who saw Vietnam as a battle the USA should be fighting. Truman was supportive of the French, as a French-controlled Indochina was a bulwark against the further advance of Communism, and it simply became a question of how far the USA was willing to go to help. For some in government circles, it was an imperative. As the US Ambassador in Moscow assertively messaged Washington, in a note that made Truman's Brief in February 1950, 'everything possible short of [the] involvement of US fighting forces should be done to prop up Indochina'.

21

The Jungles of Indochina

When Eisenhower entered office in 1953, he discovered that the USA was paying for nearly half the cost of France's war. Chinese and Soviet assistance to the Viet Minh had dramatically altered the nature of the conflict. The Viet Minh had the numbers and the equipment to hold ground, and Vietnam itself had been effectively divided into two, with the north under the control of the Viet Minh and the south the territory of the French and their sympathetic South Vietnamese leader. The French also still clung to a northern enclave in the area of Tonkin, around Hanoi. The intelligence bulletin written for Eisenhower on his first day in the Oval Office featured an item on the ongoing war, noting the Viet Minh were now placing underwater mines in the central delta of Tonkin, effectively turning the waterways into traps for French military vessels. The analysts noted, 'Increasing success with mines in the north would seriously handicap the French Navy in maintaining the security of the river traffic and continuing its indispensable support to ground forces.'

To fight in Vietnam was to fight in another world. Outside of the cities, the vast majority of the population were subsistence rice farmers whose lives revolved around the seasonal weather changes that determined when their crop needed planting, weeding and harvesting. The impassability of the terrain – even today, nearly half of Vietnam is uncultivated forest – left foreign soldiers reliant on support from the air or from waterways. Firepower had the capacity to prove decisive, but for it to be successfully deployed the enemy had to be exposed, and the number of soldiers sent never seemed enough.

Although French forces only experienced a handful of military reversals in the first six years of the war, the decisive breakthrough seemed always to be over the next jungle-covered ridge.

In the snapshot from the Daily Briefs that can be included in this book, it is impossible to convey the sheer relentlessness of the bad news from Vietnam in the pages prepared for Truman and through to Eisenhower. Truman famously had on his desk a wooden sign which read 'The Buck stops here', a sentiment he proudly adhered to. But the metaphor applied more widely. Even though it was officially a French war, ultimate responsibility for what happened in Indochina was increasingly becoming a US problem. The USA was financing the fight against Communism, and once it was a battle of ideologies, losing was no longer an option.

In August 1953, Eisenhower gave a speech in Seattle in which he spoke as if to the common man:

> You have seen the war in Indochina described variously as an outgrowth of French colonialism, and its refusal to treat indigenous populations decently. You find it again described as a war between the Communists and the other elements in southeast Asia. But you have a confused idea of where it is located – Laos, or Cambodia, or Siam [Thailand], or any of the other countries that are involved. You don't know, really, why we are so concerned with the far-off southeast corner of Asia.

The President explained simply that:

> If Indochina goes [Communist], several things happen right away. The Malayan peninsula, the last little bit of the end hanging on down there, would be scarcely defensible ... So you see, somewhere along the line, this must be blocked. It must be blocked now. That is what the French are doing.

Eisenhower powerfully tried to justify the creeping US involvement:

> When the United States votes four-hundred-million Dollars to help that war, we're not voting for a giveaway program. We are voting for the cheapest way that we can prevent the occurrence of something that would of the most terrible significance to the United States of America.

What he did not admit to his listeners was that the hundreds of millions were making little impact. Two days previously, appended to a Daily Brief item on news that the French were sending a further nine battalions to Indochina, the CIA analysts had admitted, 'This policy of reinforcing Indochina … cannot be expected to survive in the long term unless the military situation undergoes a marked improvement in the coming months.' And soon, the Eisenhower administration sent even more money. Truman had started funding the French in 1950, when the USA had given $10 million to the war in Indochina, three years before Eisenhower spoke in Seattle. By 1954, the amount had sky-rocketed to $1,063 million, 78 per cent of the cost of the conflict.

Eisenhower spent Christmas 1953 with family at his and Mamie's New York home, although the television cameras were briefly permitted in on Christmas Day and captured the President playing with his grandson's new electric train set. He seemed jovial and relaxed despite being dressed in a three-piece suit. But, back at work in the New Year, there was more cautionary news from Vietnam. The 1 January 1954 Daily Brief noted 'a major Viet Minh attack on Dien Bien Phu, the French strongpoint in northwest Tonkin, to be "almost certain"'. The news was hardly surprising. Since the French had found it almost impossible to pin down the Viet Minh in a traditional extended engagement, they had adopted a new strategy: *le hérisson*. 'The hedgehog' involved deliberately taking ground in enemy territory, before constructing a defensive position that would draw the Viet Minh in to attack and hopefully suffer substantial losses.

Dien Bien Phu was in a valley 175 miles west of Hanoi and had been held by the French years before. It had many things going for it as a defensive position, not least its own airstrip, and the plan was that it would become an unassailable redoubt in the middle of Viet Minh territory. French paratroopers had jumped into battle on 20 November 1953 and forced off the Viet Minh, who were defending the cluster of hamlets and the deliberately damaged runway. After mending the strip, the French flew in equipment, vehicles and men, with the number at Dien Bien Phu reaching 12,000. The French then fortified their position and waited to be attacked.

Eisenhower's Brief on 1 January 1954 noted 'reported movement of enemy artillery to the area'. That in itself was remarkable: to transport guns to the hills above Dien Bien Phu, the Viet Minh had had to manoeuvre them by hand through the jungle. 'By sheer sweat and tears we hauled them into position one by one,' a Viet Minh officer later recalled; 'it became the work of a whole torchlit night to move a gun five hundred or a thousand yards'. The arrival of artillery was a dangerous development. As Eisenhower's Brief noted, there was concern 'about the expected use of artillery against Dien Bien Phu, where special terrain features make it impossible for the French completely to deny the enemy close-in observation'. It was a polite way of saying the French would be sitting ducks.

The battle of Dien Bien Phu was a disaster for the French. It lasted from March until May 1954 and resembled an attritional, defensive fight from the First World War. The Viet Minh artillery obliterated the runway, halting all but air-dropped supplies, and maintained a withering barrage on the defenders. As the causalities mounted, Eisenhower's administration came under growing pressure to intervene. One proposed scheme was for B-29s flying out of the Philippines to carpet bomb the Viet Minh artillery positions, with a number of voices even suggesting that the deployment of tactical nuclear weapons would be one way to swing the battle in favour of the French.

On 3 April, Secretary of State Dulles assembled Congressional leaders from both sides of the aisle and briefed them on the situation at Dien Bien Phu. Among those present was Lyndon Johnson, as the leader of the Democrats in the Senate. Dulles told the group that the President was requesting a joint resolution of Congress to endorse the deployment of US air and naval power in Indochina, effectively a predated declaration of war. The group made it clear to Dulles that there would be little support for the USA to go it alone, with Johnson reportedly 'pounding the desk' to emphasise his opposition. Eisenhower would need some allies. He wrote to UK Prime Minister Winston Churchill, then in his first post-war term, having returned the Conservatives to power in 1951. The reply was unflinching: 'The British people would not be easily influenced by what happened in the distant jungles of South East Asia.' Without the UK, Eisenhower did not feel the USA could become actively engaged.

On 8 May, the President's Daily Brief included a 'Comment on the fall of Dien Bin Phu'. 'The French have lost approximately 16,000 men', the writers began, noting that 'the end of the Dien Bien Phu crisis may reduce the emotional pressure for an immediate cease-fire, though not for a negotiated settlement'. As the fighting at Dien Bien Phu came to its bloody conclusion, the parties were already assembled around the negotiating table at Geneva. After twenty days of preliminaries, the French and Viet Minh delegations eventually sat down in the same room. The result of Geneva was an armistice which agreed an end to the fighting and the division of Vietnam along the 17th Parallel. Vietnam was left with a Communist north and a weak, pro-Western leadership in the south that was already propped up by US money and military aid. The French were forced to evacuate Tonkin and Hanoi, and departed Indochina having lost 93,000 men.

For years, there was a stream of cautionary tales from Indochina in the Daily Briefs. Eisenhower never read them, and, had he been able to find foreign friends, he might well have gone to war in Vietnam. In the view of a young US senator from Massachusetts, even considering the idea bordered on the insane. As John F. Kennedy insisted, 'to pour money, materiel, and men into the jungles of Indochina without at least a remote prospect of victory would be dangerously futile and self-destructive'. It would be impossible, he said, to 'conquer an enemy which is everywhere and at the same time nowhere … which has the sympathy and covert support of the people'.

22

Boots on the Ground

When Kennedy arrived in the Oval Office, he found it hard to practise what he had preached as a senator. Bao Dai had been succeeded as South Vietnamese leader by Ngo Diem. Diem came from a politically well-connected family and was decidedly not a man of the people: he was a Catholic who at one point had considered going to seminary in a country that was more than three-quarters Buddhist. Diem also had a taste for power, an intolerance of opponents and the proclivity to use heavy-handed methods to get his way. It was painfully ironic that, while the country he ruled was propped up by the USA, Diem refused to hold free and fair elections. Diem was an easy leader to dislike.

The Communists soon found that they could slip into South Vietnam and wage a clandestine war against Diem's regime, and there was little Diem could do to stop them. The fighters were known as the Viet Cong. Their life-support system was the 'Ho Chi Minh Trail', a network of routes that wound its way from North Vietnam, through Laos and Cambodia and into the south, along which they shipped supplies. Once there, the Viet Cong began a wave of political assassinations of pro-Diem local leaders, alongside guerrilla operations. The peace deal thrashed out at Geneva had officially stopped the war, but the fighting was still going on. With the French departed, Diem's main ally was the USA. Given the money and material already invested in the cause of saving South Vietnam from Communism, the new President followed the same path as his predecessors.

In May 1961, Kennedy ordered 400 Green Berets to Vietnam. Elite US Army Special Forces, the Green Berets had earned their name from their headgear and were trained in counterinsurgency. As Kennedy phrased it in a message to their commander, following a visit to the US Army Special Warfare Center at Fort Bragg, 'The challenge of this old but new form of operations is a real one ... I am sure that the Green Beret will be a mark of distinction in the trying times ahead.' The Green Berets were followed a few months later by forty helicopters. By mid-1962, the collective number of the soldiers themselves, the maintenance teams for their equipment, and advisors working with the South Vietnamese Army totalled more than 8,000 people.

In Vietnam there was a war for the hearts and minds of many peasant villagers, long before the Americans deployed en masse and with their thundering flocks of helicopters. Significant numbers did have sympathy for the Communist cause, but there were many more who simply sought an uninterrupted life. Forced to name a side as the Viet Cong infiltrated southern Vietnam, the choice between a despotic, brutal, foreign-supported regime and the ardently political and violent Communist guerrilla forces was hardly a simple one. Allegations of government informants in a village could lead to fighters emerging from the jungle to enforce allegiance with violence: the Viet Cong frequently executed 'informers' publicly and brutally, while demanding protection money. The Saigon security forces in the south were little better, hauling political prisoners into squalid jails and sometimes mounting summary executions during raids on villages. Outside of the cities, much of Vietnam was already a complex hinterland that, on a map, could quite comfortably have been marked as 'contested'.

On 21 October 1962, a 28-year-old journalist stationed in Saigon had a sobering dispatch published in *The New York Times*. David Halberstam would go on to win a Pulitzer Prize for his reporting from Vietnam and, by '62, he was already uncertain of how events would play out. In the article, titled 'US Deeply Involved in the Uncertain Struggle for Vietnam', he wrote:

This is a war fought in the presence of a largely uncommitted or unfriendly peasantry, by a government that has yet to demonstrate much appeal to large elements of its own people. The enemy is lean and hungry, experienced in this type of warfare, patient in his campaign ... above all, an enemy who has shown that he is willing to pay the price.

Sadly, Kennedy had little time to read *The New York Times* that week, as it was the middle of the Cuban Missile Crisis. For years, that had been the reality for what began as the 'situation' in Indochina; it festered away underneath other urgent issues, like an invisible tumour.

As 1963 dawned, Kennedy was still preoccupied with events in other places. His final Daily Brief of the previous year had led with an item on Cuba, reporting that tactical missile transporters were still on the pier at Mariel port. His first Brief of the new year headlined the Congo and problems with foreign mercenaries in Katanga. Vietnam appeared in his second daily intelligence briefing of 1963, where it was noted, 'Two more US casualties (and 29 South Vietnamese) were suffered early this morning in the Viet Cong attack on a special forces training centre in west-central South Vietnam.' In admission of how challenging it was ascertaining who was friend or foe, the report of the attack stated, 'A number of renegade village defenders undergoing training in the camp opened the gates to the Viet Cong.' For Kennedy's benefit, the analysts added that 'The fighting that led to three American casualties yesterday 45 miles South West of Saigon was continuing this morning. The Viet Cong, who usually fade away before superior forces, are showing stiff resistance.' Even at the start of 1963, US soldiers were dying in Vietnam. Kennedy was fully versed in the reality of what was going down in South East Asia, as it was covered in the Daily Briefs he read so carefully each day.

There is a popular perception that Kennedy was the President who refused to be embroiled in Vietnam. It is a myth. That the man who had so carefully avoided conflict with the Soviets in Cuba would allow himself to be lured into Vietnam seems a stain on his legacy. But Kennedy was the first US President to deploy US military units. The impression that Kennedy would not have gone to war in Vietnam hangs almost entirely on a single document. In the early autumn of 1963, McGeorge Bundy sent a memo to the Secretaries of State and Defense and the Chairman of the Joint Chiefs of Staff. A copy also went to the CIA. Six days previously, Kennedy had approved a suggestion in an earlier report from Defense Secretary McNamara and Chairman of the Joint Chiefs General Taylor. The 'military recommendation' was that the USA withdraw 1,000 military personnel by the end of the year, although Kennedy insisted that 'no formal announcement be made of the implementation'. The sentiment was that some progress was being made against the Viet

Cong, and there was hope that the bulk of US military personnel might be able to be pulled out by 1965 if training of the Vietnamese proved successful.

It has been suggested for decades by Kennedy supporters that NSAM-253 was a precursor to an evacuation of Vietnam, an idea Oliver Stone's 1991 Hollywood film *JFK* pitches as a reason for Kennedy's assassination. Alluring though it might be to claim Kennedy would never have allowed the country to be sucked into Vietnam, just two months before he was shot, Kennedy was adamant the USA would not be leaving. In a recorded television interview with leading anchorman Walter Cronkite, he calmly insisted that responsibility lay with the Vietnamese, but that the USA would not withdraw. 'In the final analysis, it is their war,' Kennedy said. However, he added, 'But I don't agree with those who say we should withdraw. That would be a great mistake ... We also have to participate – we may not like it – in the defence of Asia.' By the time Kennedy was assassinated, there were 16,000 Americans in Vietnam.

★ ★ ★

Vietnam was the first issue Lyndon Baines Johnson was presented with when he was dramatically elevated to office after Kennedy's death. But the new President soon showed a far less keen interest in the ins and outs of intelligence. The daily intelligence meetings that Director McCone had started on Johnson's first morning soon lapsed. By early December, they had shortened to a few minutes, and then they ceased altogether. At the start of 1964, Ted Clifton, the presidential aide who had pressed the revised Daily Brief into Kennedy's hands on the diving board at Glen Ora, reported to the Brief's writers at the CIA's Office of Current Intelligence. They recorded Clifton's concern at the 'meagre volume' of intelligence reaching Johnson, noting that:

> ... while the President does get up on situations demanding an immediate solution, he is not getting a steady feed of intelligence on world situations. He reads the papers and occasionally asks questions. He gets what Clifton and Bundy can tell him orally when they see him, which, Clifton says, isn't much.

Very quickly, the situation seemed to be regressing to the Eisenhower years, when the President cared little about the Briefs, but this time the man in the

White House did not have decades of experience in dealing with military intelligence. And that was a concern when there were problems around the world Johnson needed to be up to speed on.

The CIA did exactly what the CIA had done before and started dishing out the Daily Brief more widely. First, the Joint Chiefs started receiving it, and then the Assistant Secretaries at the State Department. The change riled the Executive Secretary of the NSC, Bromley Smith, who noted it was 'just another intelligence paper which has lost its value to the President'. He was also concerned about security: 'With this many fumbling with the Checklist [the official name of the Daily Brief] ... we might as well print it in the *New York Times*.'

Even CIA Director McCone was troubled. He met with Johnson just before 5 p.m. on one Wednesday in April 1964 and recorded afterwards:

> I said that I was concerned that the President was not getting sufficient and adequate intelligence briefings; that I was not seeing very much of him, and that this disturbed me. He said he was available any time that I wanted to see him. All I had to do was call up. I said that this had not been the case on several attempts ... He invited me to bring to his attention any matters of special and particular interest; however he did not wish to be briefed just for the purpose of being briefed.

When McCone asked, Johnson insisted that the Daily Brief was 'perfectly adequate'. The following morning, Johnson's Brief included a comment from the Secretary General of the United Nations. Speaking to the press in Paris, he had told them the 'problem' in South East Asia 'was not essentially a military one'. Instead, it was 'A political problem which can only be solved by political and diplomatic means.' He added, 'military means did not solve it ten years ago, [there is] no reason for them to succeed now'.

23

Wider War

On 2 August 1964, a US warship patrolling in the Gulf of Tonkin off the coast of North Vietnam came under attack. Three North Vietnamese torpedo boats targeted the US destroyer, which fired back, sinking one and damaging the others. As it was a Sunday, there was no Daily Brief that day. The report of the events appeared on 3 August. 'Yesterday's attack on USS *Maddox* was planned and directed by [North Vietnamese] naval authorities ashore. In recent weeks intercepts have shown Hanoi's Navy reacting with greater touchiness to US and South Vietnamese activities in the Tonkin Gulf.'

The 'touchiness' was not without reason. The *Maddox* had deliberately strayed into North Vietnamese waters to intercept communications, around the time South Vietnamese naval forces had been raiding naval installations along the coast. When Johnson put in a call to his Secretary of Defense a few hours after receiving his Brief, Robert McNamara openly admitted that four South Vietnamese torpedo boats had attacked a radar station and that this action, followed by the appearance of the US destroyer in the area, had 'undoubtedly' led the North Vietnamese 'to connect the two events'.

Johnson was already pulling his pistols: 'We're gonna be firm as hell,' he told McNamara. 'If you shoot at us, you're going to get hit.'

On 3 August, the *Maddox* returned to the area, along with another destroyer, in a statement of intent. They continued intercepting North Vietnamese radio traffic, which seemed to hint at another coming attack, although in fact it was commenting on the earlier incident. Johnson's

Daily Brief on the morning of 4 August contained a 'late item' on 'North Vietnam and the US', which the CIA archivists have decided to keep completely redacted, despite releasing to the public the Daily Brief for that day. Given the twelve-hour time difference between Vietnam and the US, it is entirely possible that the late item contained the warning of a second possible attack. The White House was certainly aware of the warning: 'This ship [the *Maddox*] is allegedly to be attacked [again] tonight,' McNamara told Johnson on the phone later that morning. The President was clearly already frustrated at the limited options for response. 'What I was thinking about when I was eating breakfast, but I couldn't talk it,' Johnson said, 'I was thinking that it looks to me like the weakness of our position is that we respond only to an action and we don't have any of our own.'

An hour later, the two spoke again. McNamara reported that the USS *Maddox* was being supported by aircraft from a nearby US carrier, telling Johnson, 'We have ample forces to respond not only to these attacks on the destroyers but also to retaliate should you wish to do so against targets on the land. And when I come over at noontime, I'll bring you a list of alternative target systems.' Before he popped to the Oval Office with the list of targets, he put in another call to inform the President he had received word that the *Maddox* – battling through rough weather on a stormy night in the Tonkin Gulf – was again under fire.

Johnson took a long lunch that day, following an emergency meeting of the National Security Council. Defense Secretary McNamara joined the President, along with McGeorge Bundy and CIA Director John McCone. Over lunch, Johnson agreed to a swift retaliatory air strike against North Vietnam. At 1.30 p.m. Washington time, a message was received from Captain Herrick, the commander of the *Maddox*. He cast doubt on the earlier reports of the second attack on the ships: 'Freak weather effects on radar and overeager sonar operators may have accounted for the reports,' he admitted. It is suggested McNamara received the message but did not inform Johnson.

Eight hours later, the President took to the airwaves to address the American people. He told them of 'hostile actions' against US ships in the sea off North Vietnam, asserting:

> repeated acts of violence ... must be met not only with alert defense, but with positive reply. That reply is being given as I speak to you tonight. Air

action is now in execution against gunboats and certain supporting facilities in North Vietnam which have been used in these hostile operations.

He added, 'our response, for the present, will be limited and fitting. We Americans know, although others appear to forget, the risks of spreading conflict. We still seek no wider war.' Within half an hour, US strike aircraft arrived over their targets in North Vietnam.

Three days later, on 7 August, Johnson secured the 'Gulf of Tonkin Resolution' from Congress. It authorised the President 'as Commander-in-Chief, to take all necessary measures to repel any armed attack against the forces of the United States and to prevent further aggression'. It would serve as the formal declaration of war for Vietnam. A decade before, Eisenhower had tried to secure a similar concession from Congress so the USA could support the French in Vietnam, but Johnson had been one of the senators most staunchly against. Ten years on and now President, he seemed comfortable ignoring his own past reservations.

In the month leading up to the Gulf of Tonkin incident, Johnson's Daily Briefs often covered Vietnam. On 4 July, the analysts noted, 'The Viet Cong in the central Highlands [of South Vietnam] have been especially active lately. In an attack at battalion strength on 4th July, the Communists killed 51 and 139 wounded, including four US personnel.' The following day, Johnson's Brief reported that a Viet Cong attack on a special forces camp had killed fifty-seven, including three US soldiers. The scale of the attacks was of significant concern, with large attacks at the 'highest level ever', while it was estimated that the Viet Cong force was now between 28,000 and 34,000 strong. Johnson's Briefs in July informed him of the deaths of six US soldiers, some killed at a base where they were training South Vietnamese, others in an ambush of a convoy.

Diem's government had fallen in a military coup in 1963, one which the USA happily supported, as the profoundly unpopular leader had been a cause of instability. South Vietnam's leader in 1964 was General Khanh, who as a younger man had fought for the Viet Minh, before joining the French anti-Communist efforts. One of Johnson's July Briefs noted that the South Vietnamese leader harboured a 'deep concern over evidence of popular passivity and war weariness'. The analysts added, 'He seems convinced the people need a stimulant like carrying the action north [into North Vietnam] in one way or another.' A day later, less than ten days ahead of the Gulf of Tonkin incident, the Daily Brief included a comment from the US Ambassador in Saigon that he had been assured by Khanh that 'he is not trying to manoeuvre the US into action against North Vietnam'. It was an assurance that was hardly required. Johnson and his administration were already willing for an escalation.

★ ★ ★

In November 1964, Johnson secured another term in office, this time with his own name at the top of the ticket. Four years before, Kennedy had won by a whisker, but Johnson turned all but six states blue. His win would always face the allegation that it was a 'sympathy vote' for the martyred President who had been in the car ahead of him in Dallas, but Johnson's skills as a politician had helped pass the much-contested Civil Rights Act; it was Johnson who had managed to force through Kennedy's stalled domestic agenda.

Winning an election seemed to give Johnson a personal confidence he had previously lacked. One of the first things to change was the Daily Brief. Bundy had already been privately racking his brains for a way to make the President more interested in intelligence and, taking a leaf out of what had been done before, he opted for a redesign of the document. He also applied his own knowledge of Johnson. The publication time was switched from the morning to the evening, as it had originally been for Truman; it was not in homage to history, but because that was when Johnson preferred to sit down with papers. The previous version's six to eight pages were replaced with only two pages of text, and the whole thing was given a new title. For Truman, the President's daily intelligence document had been called the Daily Summary, before it was changed to the Current Intelligence Bulletin and then the Central Intelligence Bulletin under Eisenhower. Kennedy's specially revised document was titled the President's Intelligence Checklist, but the version Bundy gave to Johnson on 1 December 1964 had a new name that stuck. A month after winning an election, the President sat down to read what was officially the very first 'President's Daily Brief'. His National Security Advisor had added his note on the inside: '[The] CIA and I,' Bundy wrote, 'have worked out this new form of a daily intelligence briefing on the premise that it is more useful to you if it comes in your evening reading.' He added he hoped it would be 'more nearly responsive to your own interests than the papers we have been sending heretofore'.

Overnight, Johnson became an avid reader. The timing, the brevity and, for a man with a sensitive ego, the knowledge that the CIA really had prepared it especially for him, all perhaps helped to encourage him to open it. In the words of one aide, 'the President likes this very much'. The authors of the new President's Daily Brief in the OCI were using the same information and writing very similar pieces: as an official CIA history later admitted, 'the contents of the Brief remained essentially the same as that of the Checklist [which had preceded it], the cover and format were different and the Brief was issued late in the afternoon instead of the early morning'. In one sense, that did not matter. The change had made the President feel special and they knew he was really reading it.

The President's Daily Brief of 1 December 1964 included three maps in the opening pages – one of the Congo, one of Laos and one that remains redacted – followed by a single page of six punchy paragraphs. On the final page was an 'annex' with four other short points. For the week before, the CIA had published the new President's Daily Brief alongside the Checklist, but from 1 December, it was the Brief that was placed in the President's hands every day.

As well as Johnson, one of the other recipients was NSC Executive Secretary Bromley Smith, who was also the go-between for the Daily Brief writers at the CIA and the White House. Smith had been at the White House since 1952, and the former journalist and State Department official had strong opinions about the President's daily intelligence document. He did not like the use of annexes, which he thought were at risk of being set aside by Johnson to read later and then forgotten about, and he also did not like some of the language the analysts used. Although he admitted that there should be some colour to the writing, he thought it should not be 'frivolous or light-hearted'. The shattered CIA analysts, pecking at their typewriters with bags under their eyes and hauling themselves through the coffee-fuelled early hours to cut down matters of national importance to a few choice sentences, were ordered not to use phrases like 'hopping mad'. They also received a telling off for one Brief item which included a mention of India as an 'unwilling bride'. The President, however, was happy with his intelligence.

President Johnson reads the President's Daily Brief as Lady Bird looks on,
cradling their first grandchild.

★ ★ ★

The LP cover showed the black and white portrait of a nonchalant-looking musician with foppish hair, smiling beneath the aggressively lettered song title. The single was officially released on 12 August 1965, but by then 'Eve of Destruction' was already playing on the radio and had become an instant hit. Barry McGuire's growly, earnest vocal articulated what many were quietly thinking: that the world was exploding. Johnson's insistence that 'we seek no wider war' had proved delusional, as 1965 saw the first mass bombing campaign across North Vietnam and, in March, the first public deployment of combat troops to South Vietnam. A war in the Far East was now regularly claiming American lives. The evening before McGuire's record hit the stores, Johnson's Daily Brief had noted the shooting down of a US bomber over North Vietnam, admitting 'the fate of the ... pilot is not yet known'. Not only were troop numbers increasing, but the existence of 'the draft' – a conscription policy introduced during the 1940s and still in force – meant men could find themselves compulsorily called up. Young men of the age of 18 in suitable health, who were not studying at university, could be drafted for twenty-one months, even though in almost every state they were still three years short of being allowed to take part in elections. McGuire's song was the first of many hits that millions of younger Americans adopted as their protest anthems against the war. In 1965, official US Military Fatal Casualty Statistics recorded 1,928 deaths in Vietnam, while troop numbers were up to 400,000 by the following year. The prosaic warning that Truman had read in his Daily Brief fifteen years before had come to pass: the US now faced a situation in Indochina.

24

America's Soul

The President's Daily Brief on 5 January 1967 began with a photograph taken from a low-earth-orbit spy satellite. Enlarged five times and labelled, it showed a missile launch facility. There were the familiar towers and bunkers and lines in the earth, except the image was not of Cuba or the Soviet Union, but of the arid Gobi Desert in northern China. Johnson's Brief noted, 'Mid-December photography of the Chinese missile test range shows that launch complex "B" is now complete. Construction of this site, which we have monitored for over a year, has been extremely rapid even by US or Soviet standards.' The Chinese had detonated their first atom bomb in October 1964 and successfully fired their first nuclear-equipped missile in 1966. Now, a few months later, they were rapidly developing their launch capabilities. The news from China bumped Vietnam to the second item in that day's Brief, where it was noted that Hanoi's 'price for peace negotiations' was unchanged: the North Vietnamese would consider talks only if the USA 'finally and unconditionally' halted its bombing campaign over North Vietnam.

The mass bombing of targets in North Vietnam by the US Air Force had started in March 1965 and never stopped. 'Operation Rolling Thunder' had rolled on, despite its initial eight-week planned campaign; by December 1967, the total volume of ordnance dropped on North Vietnamese targets had exceeded 800,000 tonnes, significantly more than had been dropped in the entire Pacific theatre in the Second World War. The Daily Briefs contained fewer details of the day-to-day conduct of the war, as since 1965 the CIA had begun creating a separate, daily Vietnam report for the President. Unlike the Daily Briefs, this has not been declassified. There were still updates and significant items in the Daily Brief, but the war was now not so much news as battle reports from a faraway frontline.

The sentiment expressed in Barry McGuire's hit song had found especially fertile ground in a younger generation of Americans who resented the risk of being called up to fight and die for a cause they did not believe in. On Saturday, 15 April 1967, there were mass anti-war demonstrations across cities in the USA. Half a million marched in New York, where the leaders delivered a petition to the United Nations that noted 'the imperative need for an immediate peaceful solution to an illegal and unjustifiable war'. Ten days before, Martin Luther King Jr, who had been a strong supporter of President Johnson because of the President's promotion of the Civil Rights Act, had for the first time reluctantly spoken up against the war and its consequences. It was, he said, 'incandescently clear that no one who has any concern for the integrity and life of America today can ignore the present war. If America's soul becomes totally poisoned, part of the autopsy must read: Vietnam.' The following month, the CIA analysts noted in Johnson's Daily Brief, 'The North Vietnamese seem to want a war of attrition ... we feel, the Communists hope to create the illusion of "a war no one can win."'

Johnson had always talked of peace, insisting in his 1966 State of the Union address that 'we will withdraw our soldiers once South Vietnam is securely guaranteed the right to shape its own future'. In his memoirs, he later wrote:

> At one time or another we were in touch with virtually every government or other diplomatic source that might have been able to make contact with the North Vietnamese. Time and time again we passed along our views: We are ready to talk in private or in public; we will meet quietly in any capital; we will stop the bombing if you will do something on your part to lower the level of fighting.

There were multiple pauses in Operation Rolling Thunder, but no successful negotiations. Johnson forever laid the blame on the North Vietnamese and Ho Chi Minh: 'Hanoi had slammed the door on peace,' he said. By the end of 1967, more than 20,000 US service personnel had died fighting in Vietnam.

★ ★ ★

The dynamic of the conflict shifted on 31 January 1968. Thirty-six of South Vietnam's forty-four provincial capitals and five of the six largest cities came under simultaneous attack, with Viet Cong fighters even reaching the inside of the US Embassy compound in Saigon. There was barely a whisper in the Daily Brief in the run-up. On 30 January, the Brief reported that some enemy units were 'completing battle preparations', but there was no inkling of what was to be printed the following day. On 31 January, the Daily Brief's South Vietnam item was updated 'as of 5.30am EST' and reported, 'Information is still sketchy on what is happening,' admitting that cities and bases had been 'hit by the well-coordinated and unprecedented Communist offensive'. The CIA's analysis was that the Tet Offensive – so called because it took place over the Tet holiday when there had traditionally been an unofficial ceasefire – was 'designed for maximum psychological impact, the Communists concentrated on showing they could shoot their way into major populated areas'.

The Tet Offensive was not a complete surprise, but the scale and success of the mass infiltration had a huge political impact. In Johnson's memoirs, he claimed that from October 1967 he was 'increasingly concerned by reports that the Communists were preparing a maximum military effort'. However, he admitted he had made a mistake by not saying more about Vietnam in his State of the Union address two weeks before, conceding, 'If I had forecast the possibilities, the American people would have been better prepared.' Johnson was deeply critical of the response of the US press to the Tet Offensive, which he described as 'a great deal of emotional and exaggerated reporting ... [a] daily barrage of bleakness and near panic'. Most of the urban areas were back in US/South Vietnamese hands by 2 February, with the Daily Brief noting that life was 'gradually returning to normal' in Saigon by 12 February.

But the Tet Offensive carried on far longer than is implied in Johnson's later recollections. The historic city of Hue was occupied for twenty-six days and, on 24 February, even though Saigon was 'relatively quiet', the Brief noted that 'firefights persist on all sides of the city'. The writers conceded, 'The Viet Cong have overrun many rural areas, while South Vietnamese [and US] forces remain tied down defending the cities.' The changed dynamic was revealed in another Brief a few days later, where it was noted that in one province 'stretches of the countryside [are left] completely to the Communists. A number of once pacified hamlets are no longer safe, and two major highways in the area which had been partially secure for more than two years are now insecure.' Vietnam held the top spot on the President's Daily Brief until 11 March.

The assault was a huge shock to the system for the Johnson administration but was felt even more strongly by the American public. While Johnson followed developments in Vietnam during the offensive 'on a daily, sometimes hourly, basis', for many Americans the events seemed to show the war as completely unwinnable. A Gallup poll in December had Americans split almost 50/50 on 'whether sending troops to fight in Vietnam was a mistake'. A few months after the Tet Offensive, 65 per cent believed the USA should not have sent soldiers.

In March 1968, President Johnson announced a unilateral end to the mass bombing campaign of North Vietnam and in a melancholy television address to the public conceded that the USA was 'a house divided'. To stop the office he held being caught up in 'partisan divisions', Johnson conceded, 'I shall not seek, and will not accept, the nomination of my party for another term as your President.' Johnson personally wanted his double decision, of the end of the bombing and his refusal to run, to be cathartic for the USA: 'I also hoped that the combined announcement would accomplish something else. The issue of Vietnam had created divisions in hostilities among Americans, as I had feared. I wanted to heal some of those wounds and restore unity to the nation.' Johnson would depart, leaving the problem of Vietnam to his successor and living only four more years before he died of a heart attack at the age of 64. The President who followed him would finally begin the withdrawal of US forces from Vietnam, although history would remember Richard Nixon for very different reasons.

25

A Healthy Interval

Before he even entered the Oval Office, Richard Nixon had made up his mind that he did not trust the CIA. He had stood opposite Kennedy and sweated under the television lights in the 1960 presidential election debates, knowing that Kennedy's claims about the 'missile gap' were lies: lies that Nixon forever felt cost him the presidency the first time around. Nixon had known what the NSC knew about the backwardness of the Soviet missile programme, but, for the sake of national security, he had not been able to let on to the youngster taking pieces out of him over the issue live on television. The CIA had also been cautious about what it told Kennedy. He was kept in the dark, not just about the 'missile gap' but also about covert operations in Cuba. Allen Dulles went down to Palm Beach in Florida to brief Kennedy while he was on the campaign trail but did not cover the active covert operation in the Caribbean. 'I have found that candidates don't generally want to be told too much,' he claimed in an interview years later, although he admitted, 'When the issue came up with Nixon, Nixon indicated that he thought he'd been double-crossed.'

For Nixon, there was no nuance. It seemed to him the CIA had preferred his opponent. As he told his appointee as National Security Advisor, Henry Kissinger, Nixon 'felt it imperative to exclude the CIA from the formulation of policy; it was staffed by Ivy League liberals who behind the facade of analytical objectivity were usually pushing their own preferences'. Growing up, the Nixon family had struggled to make ends meet, and as a teenager Nixon helped out at the family grocery store. He still excelled at school, but the family forced him to turn down a scholarship to Harvard in favour of going to a local college, so he could still assist at home. The man who had never made it to the Ivy League was suspicious of those who had.

The CIA staff could not control how they were perceived by their Commander-in-Chief, but if the Office of Current Intelligence at the Agency had learned anything by 1968, it was that presidents liked their intelligence personal. The CIA had tweaked the Brief for Truman and redesigned it for Kennedy and then for Johnson, and now, for the first time, they modified it ahead of the new arrival entering the White House. The Daily Brief had become part of the fabric of the President's day under Johnson, and the CIA wanted it to stay that way. Following feedback from a member of Nixon's campaign staff, the analysts re-drafted the Brief so it was longer, with three sections. The first was titled 'Major Developments', the second 'Other Important Developments', with a final section of annexes with additional commentary. It was bound at the top, like a legal brief, because they thought that was what the former lawyer who was to become the thirty-seventh President of the United States would appreciate. The special new version for Nixon started being sent to him in late November 1968, just after he won the election, while he was in New York with his transition team preparing for the move to Washington. Three days before Nixon's inauguration in January, the CIA received a parcel from New York. Inside the box were the 'Nixon special' Daily Briefs the team had been dispatching to the President-elect for the previous two months. All the envelopes were unopened.

In the new administration, the CIA hardly had access to the President. Everything relating to security went through Kissinger, Nixon's National Security Advisor. He even appropriated the Briefs. With Kennedy and Johnson, McGeorge Bundy had fought the fight to make intelligence assessments a regular part of the President's day, but with Kissinger in post, the occupant of the Oval Office only saw what his Security Advisor deemed of importance; Kissinger even added his own handwritten comments to the items in the Brief. From almost the moment of the 1968 election victory, Nixon's visceral hatred of the CIA had forged a situation which was unheard of for the intelligence community: the CIA effectively had a new 'First Customer', and it wasn't the man in the Oval Office.

*President Nixon and National Security Advisor Henry Kissinger in the
Oval Office, February 1971.*

When he read it, Kissinger was not impressed with the Brief. It seemed to him scatty and at the same time obsessed with particular locales. 'Why are you paying so much attention to Panama?' he enquired of two high-level Agency officers. When they explained their view of the importance of the country and its potential to the US national interest, Kissinger cut them short. 'Our attention, the attention of Mr. Nixon and myself,' he insisted, 'is going to be centred on the Soviet Union and Western Europe.' Once Nixon was in the White House, Kissinger changed everything around for the Brief. He cut the circulation completely to just himself and Nixon, and told the CIA to revert publication back to the evening – Johnson had switched back it to the morning in 1966 – so he could read it each night, before updating the President of anything relevant in the morning. When the analysts complained that this would create a seventeen-hour delay between the information being published and its potentially reaching the President, Kissinger simply told them they were welcome to add as many 'late items' as they liked in the morning, as long he saw them first.

For the CIA, it was a painful turn of events. As one intelligence officer later lamented, 'We had the impression as young analysts that basically Nixon and Kissinger didn't give a crap about the PDB [President's Daily Brief].'

Kissinger himself viewed it rather differently. It was simply the case that Nixon, as a former Vice President, and Kissinger, with his academic background and experience advising on foreign policy, were better informed than many who had trod the path before them. 'Nixon and I both really knew a lot about foreign policy – we were not novices,' he would later insist. 'We didn't need a daily newspaper ... Nixon and I probably thought our analysis was as good as the CIA's. The PDB was not a central document in our thinking.'

As one originally secret internal CIA assessment from 1970 later phrased it, 'The policymaker [Nixon] tends to take his intelligence for granted, like the paper at the door in the morning, unless he has specifically asked for something.'

For CIA Director Richard Helms, it was personally, as well as professionally, painful. The 56-year-old CIA traditionalist had been Director since 1966 and held his post after Nixon's election win; Johnson had personally commended him to Nixon. But the new President openly criticised the CIA. As the debonair, high-society-connected Helms later wrote, 'Whatever my faults and the possible shortcomings of the Agency's

President Johnson in the Oval Office with CIA Director Richard Helms.

senior officers, explanation for Nixon's persistent deriding of many who were in the best position to serve him and his administration must rest deep within the personality of Nixon himself.' Nowhere was the deriding more obvious than in the meetings of the National Security Council. Long gone were the days of Allen Dulles, who had had a seat at the table with Eisenhower and frequently driven the NSC in his desired direction. Instead, Nixon banished Helms from the room immediately after the opening intelligence briefing. Helms was reliant on sympathetic allies to keep him in the loop.

On one occasion, in the summer of 1969, he was sent a note from a friend titled, 'My reconstruction of the President's remarks at the NSC meeting this morning'. They were not complimentary. Nixon had slammed the Agency analysts for 'showing a tendency to use intelligence to support conclusions rather than arrive at conclusions', saying, 'I want you fellows to be very careful to separate facts from opinions in your briefings and intelligence papers'. Nor did Nixon rate the 'intelligence papers' he received, stating in one budget meeting, 'The CIA tells me nothing that I don't read three days earlier in *The New York Times*.'

★ ★ ★

When it came to Vietnam, Kissinger and Nixon also had strong opinions. By 1969, the USA had 536,000 troops in Vietnam and the war was costing $30 billion a year. Nixon had admitted to a speechwriter back in March 1968 – as Johnson was announcing he would not run in the election – 'There's no way to win this war. But we can't say that of course.' When he arrived in the White House, he told the Director of the Federal Bureau of Investigation (FBI), 'I'm not going to end up like LBJ ... I'm going to stop that war. Fast.'

Kissinger phrased it in less direct terms, writing in a widely lauded article in *Foreign Affairs* magazine in January 1969, 'The Tet Offensive marked the watershed of the American effort. Henceforth ... [the USA] could no longer achieve its objectives within a period or with force levels politically acceptable to the American people.' As far as the Nixon administration was concerned, they would end the Vietnam War, but extricating the USA would prove more problematic in practice.

Kissinger had a clear idea of how events would potentially unfold. The 46-year-old had been born into a Jewish family in Germany in 1923 and arrived in the USA at the age of 15 as his family fled the Nazis. Heinz changed his name to Henry, going from night school to Harvard, with a wartime stint in Army intelligence in-between. He became an academic and, in 1961, McGeorge Bundy hired him as a consultant. Eight years later, after initially courting several Republican presidential hopefuls, the wavy-haired, spectacled foreign policy theorist was National Security Advisor. On multiple occasions in 1968 he had suggested it would be an appropriate policy for the USA to withdraw American soldiers from Vietnam, leaving an 'interval' of two or three years before the probable collapse of the South Vietnamese government. He even went on to state the policy explicitly in a secret memo he penned for Nixon once he was in office: 'A peace settlement would end the war with an act of policy,' he wrote, 'and leave the future of South Vietnam to the historic process. We could heal the wounds in this country as our men left peace behind on the battlefield, and a healthy interval for South Vietnam's fate to unfold.' It was Kissinger's doctrine of *realpolitik* at its sharpest: get the troops out, declare the war over, and hope South Vietnam was not overrun too quickly.

Between 1969 and 1972, the number of US troops in Vietnam was reduced from 549,000 to 69,000. The Nixon administration adopted a policy of capacity building, with the intention of equipping and training the South Vietnamese sufficiently so that US forces were no longer needed. In the background there were peace talks, initially kept very secret. In August 1969, only seven months into Nixon's first term, Kissinger opened communication with the North Vietnamese. The official peace effort in Paris had stalled, so he began discreet discussions with a high-level representative from the North Vietnamese government. After each meeting, he sent a summary memo and the transcript direct to Nixon. The meetings were long and laborious, with Kissinger's words being translated from English into French and then Vietnamese, and translation going in the reverse for the other side. The negotiations excluded the US State Department, the CIA and the South Vietnamese.

The outcome, once the talks had been made public, was a draft treaty, which Kissinger revealed in October 1972. The day before, the Daily Brief noted 'widespread reports that a ceasefire may be imminent', but the analysts had no inside track on negotiations: throughout the entire process, the CIA had been left out in the cold. The treaty was immediately rejected by the South Vietnamese government, but Kissinger had pre-empted that happening, telling journalists at his announcement press conference that the fact the South Vietnamese government had not accepted the proposed terms was not 'any real barrier to working out a final settlement'. The timing of the announcement seemed suspicious: thirteen days after Kissinger had told the world that 'peace is at hand' in Vietnam, Americans went to the polls to decide whether or not to give Nixon a second term.

26

What Happens If?

On the morning of 20 November 1972, the Director of the CIA was summoned to the President's private retreat at Camp David. Helms had been in post for six years, for half of which he had had to carry the certain knowledge that the President did not like him, either personally or professionally. Helms was expecting to battle over the Agency's budget and filled his briefcase with documents proving why the CIA needed its cash, before going to the Pentagon heliport for the noisy flight up the Potomac River. That day's Daily Brief was still being worked on and would be delivered to Kissinger that evening, although, as with all the others, it was assumed Nixon had little intention of reading it.

Helms was escorted to the Aspen Lodge where he found the President seated on a small sofa. Helms sat on a chair in front of him. Nixon made bad small talk and then got to the point: he wanted 'new blood' in the Agency in his second term. Helms was being fired. He later learned that Nixon's Chief of Staff, Harry Haldeman, had made notes on Nixon's second-term plans for the CIA several months before the election. They were short and simple: 'Helms has got to go. Get rid of the clowns – cut [CIA] personnel 40 percent. Its info is worthless.' It was hardly a surprise for Helms, who had always known Nixon had no time for the CIA or its efforts to inform the President. The Director later admitted that neither he nor his deputy 'were ever sure how often Nixon ever glanced at the PDB'.

There was perhaps another reason for Helms' sudden forced departure. Five months before, on 17 June, he had been woken by a strange phone call from the CIA's Chief of Security, who informed him that five men, including a former CIA operative, had been arrested the night before trying to plant listening devices in the Democratic National Committee headquarters offices in downtown Washington DC. The Democratic National Committee coordinated election strategy for the Democrat Party and was the nerve centre of the operation to try and beat Nixon in that November's election. The concrete office block that had been broken into was called the Watergate Building.

Within days, Helms found himself under pressure from Nixon's Chief of Staff, Haldeman. He was asked to pay hush money to the burglars from CIA clandestine funds. When he refused, he was summoned to the White House, where Haldeman threatened to expose Agency assets in Mexico and added darkly, 'The President told me to tell you this entire affair may be connected to the Bay of Pigs.' Helms was outraged while also having no idea what on earth the President seemed to be threatening. He stood his ground. Soon after Nixon's resounding election victory and Helms' forced departure, the FBI's investigation into who might have tried to bug the Democrat election campaign office and why began closing in on the President himself.

★ ★ ★

Gerald Ford was the second man to find himself sitting in the Oval Office reading the Daily Briefs having not expected to be there. On 9 August 1974, Richard Nixon had caved in to the mountainous pressure over Watergate and resigned. The day Ford was sworn in, the Daily Brief had reported Communist gains in South Vietnam with the incongruously optimistic note that 'the situation is less ominous than a day ago', although it conceded, 'Communist forces north and west of Saigon also seemed to be preparing for more aggressive action … Communist units in the South are clearly capable of carrying out large attacks throughout much of the country.' US combat troops had by then been gone for a year, and it seemed that Kissinger's 'healthy interval' might turn out to be shorter than he had anticipated.

The first Daily Brief created for Ford was delivered the following day. It noted, 'The world in the past 24 hours has seemed to mark time as the US succession process worked itself out. None of the potential troublemakers – Vietnam, Korea, Cyprus, fedayeen – has produced even a rumble.' While Vietnam was still front and centre in many Briefs, Truman's conflict in Korea, which had never officially ended, was still dangerous, as North Korea continued to threaten the South. The island of Cyprus, off the coast of Greece, was in the middle of a war, as Turkey had invaded, claiming to be protecting Turkish Cypriots from Greek oppression; the war was wound up a week later, but Cyprus would stay permanently divided. Meanwhile, in the Middle East, Palestinian armed groups known as *fedayeen* were mounting cross-border attacks on Israel only a year after the end of the most recent Israeli–Arab conflict. As always, the President's Daily Brief was mostly bad news, and it was not confined to one part of the world.

The 10 August 1974 Brief was not the first Ford had read. Two months before, following a trip to the CIA's headquarters at Langley, Ford had requested access to the document. Kissinger had released his vice-like grip on the Daily Briefs, allowing several of the Joint Chiefs to have access, and from July, Ford also received the Daily Brief every day and had an in-person briefing on its contents from a CIA analyst. Given the President's continued lack of interest, the CIA was more than happy to share its prized intelligence product with someone who cared. Just over a month later, Ford was President.

Ford was 61 years old when he assumed the presidency. The former college football star and Navy lieutenant commander had a considerable weight to carry on his broad shoulders. He was entering the Oval Office in unique circumstances. Nixon was the first President in history to resign, but Ford himself had not even been elected as Vice President. He had been appointed to the position after Nixon's Vice President in the 1972 election, Spiro Agnew, had been caught up in a separate corruption scandal and forced to resign in October 1973. Ford owed his elevation to the Twenty-Fifth Amendment and to Congress, which had chosen the man who seemed to have the most unimpeachable character. As he stated in his first address to the American public as President: 'I am acutely aware that you have not elected me as your President by your ballots, and so I ask you to confirm me as your President with your prayers.'

★ ★ ★

As 1975 dawned, the news from South Vietnam was once more ominous. The Daily Brief on 2 January reported the capture of the town of Phuoc Binh by Communist forces, less than 100 miles north of Saigon. The analysts added, 'This was the fourth district town in the province to fall since early December and leaves only the provincial capital in [South Vietnamese] government hands.' Over the coming weeks, the situation rapidly deteriorated. On 28 March, the Brief noted, 'the collapse of the government's forces in the northern two thirds of South Vietnam has occurred with such speed that the full magnitude of the disaster has not yet registered in Saigon'. The analysts included a six-page annexe for Ford, in which they noted that Communist momentum 'will be hard to stop', predicting '[total] defeat by early 1976'. The CIA was hopelessly optimistic.

On 16 April, they modified their position, warning, 'An offensive by newly arrived divisions north of Saigon ... might lead to a rapid crumbling of the government's position.' They added that 'The most immediate concern of most South Vietnamese, especially those who have worked closely with the Americans, is "what happens if?" Reassurances that they will be evacuated are much sought after ... A sense of impending disaster also permeates the military.' Thirteen days later, the headline item on the President's Daily Brief reported, 'The emergency evacuation of Americans is underway.' US Marines shepherded American citizens to safety, while the President, along with millions of others, watched helplessly on television as Saigon was overrun and desperate civilians and 'collaborators' fought for places in helicopters departing to the last US ships. The Daily Brief the next day, 30 April 1975, noted:

> The flag of the Viet Cong's Provisional Revolutionary Government was hoisted over the presidential palace at 12:15 today Saigon time, marking the end of over 30 years of war in Vietnam ... Immediately after the US evacuation was completed ... the US Embassy and consular office were looted by South Vietnamese mobs.

As far back as Truman's time, the USA had faced 'a situation' in Indochina. What had begun as support for the French against Communists in Asia had, by the time of Eisenhower, become a costly commitment; and after the expenditure of money, it was only a matter of time before the USA

President Ford takes a call to update him on the evacuation from Saigon on 29 April 1975. His Daily Brief the next morning commented on the fall of the city as 'the end of over 30 years of war in Vietnam'.

counted the cost in men. Kennedy's avoidance rhetoric was not matched in his policy, but it was Johnson who exploited the Gulf of Tonkin incident to lead the USA into the abyss. Even Tonkin would not have been irreversible, but as the Daily Briefs make obvious, the conflict in Vietnam had been gradually ensnaring presidents for decades. In many ways, it was a wonder that it took until March 1965 for the USA openly to deploy combat troops to push back the march of Communism in Indochina. Gerald Ford was just the last in a long line of US presidents who received bad news from the region in their Briefs.

The CIA had correctly forecast that Saigon would fall, but its prediction was wrong by eight months. Ford, however, was not bitter with the CIA for what could have been perceived as an intelligence failure printed in black and white in his Brief. Unlike his predecessor, he appreciated his Daily Brief and was aware of the complex nature of intelligence. Speaking at the swearing-in of a new CIA Director in 1976 at the Agency's Langley headquarters, he told the CIA staff:

As every President since World War II, I depend on you as one of America's first lines of defense. Every morning, as a result of your efforts, an intelligence report is delivered to my desk which is complete, concise, perceptive, and responsible. As a result, I am fully aware of the tremendous effort, the tremendous teamwork that goes into it and all of the intelligence reports that I receive that are so vital to the making of sound policy decisions on national security.

★ ★ ★

The Daily Briefs that Ford so clearly valued are available for anyone to read. You can now sit and peruse the same pages of intelligence that Ford was presented with every morning and which coloured his view of world events and told of the goings-on behind the news. Ford's Daily Briefs, however, are the last collection to have been declassified. Subsequent Briefs are still locked away in red-marked folders and are likely to remain so. A former government declassification official admitted to me when I was researching for this book that it is highly unlikely any further Briefs will be declassified: the amount of work required is simply too great, and their contents would impinge significantly on the actions of current administrations. There have only been two exceptions to the blanket ban on access to items from the President's Daily Brief in the decades since Ford left office. Their unveiling was not out of a desire for transparency, but as part of an investigation into exactly the kind of intelligence failure the President's bespoke, top-secret daily briefing was supposed to prevent from happening.

Part VI

Known Unknowns: 9/11 and Afghanistan

27

Under Attack

On the morning of 11 September 2001, President George W. Bush was visiting a primary school in Sarasota, Florida. He was sitting at the front of the classroom listening to a reading exercise called *The Pet Goat* when an aide discreetly whispered something in his ear. He remained seated, calmly looking around the room, lips pursed together, and then picked up an exercise book and studied the page. The President stayed until the end of the reading, chatted to some students and then left to meet with his staff. Before he had sat down to read with the children, he had been informed an aircraft had crashed into one of the World Trade Center towers. The message from the aide was that a second plane had crashed into the iconic high-rise offices and that 'America is under attack'. Bush later claimed that he stayed where he was because he 'didn't want to rattle the kids', but when the video of the event later emerged it appeared to many viewers that their President looked frozen and powerless while Americans perished.

9/11 was not only a deadly act of terror: it also scarred the psyche of the American people. Not since 1941 had so many Americans died in an attack on US soil. The perception that there had been a failure of intelligence was palpable; the idea that such an orchestrated attack on civilians could come out of the blue, unthinkable. The system of presidential intelligence updates that Truman had put into motion with his creation of the first 'Daily Summary' in 1946 was supposed to ensure that the Commander-in-Chief was aware of all threats to the republic. Things were always going to be missed, but the

President should never be blind-sided. As one Assistant CIA Director phrased it in the early 1950s: 'In order to avoid another Pearl Harbor, we should see to it that the men who make the final decisions should have all the information ... and that without delay.'

The shattering truth, when it finally came to light, was that the President had not been completely in the dark. The 6 August 2001 President's Daily Brief, which Bush received just over a month before 9/11, included an item under the heading, 'Bin Laden determined to strike in US'. Beneath, the analysts noted:

> We have not been able to corroborate some of the more sensational threat reporting, such as ... that Bin Laden wanted to hijack US aircraft ... Nevertheless, FBI information since that time indicates a pattern of suspicious activity in this country consistent with preparations for hijackings or other types of attacks, including recent surveillance of federal buildings in New York.

Because it is the only item declassified from that day, it is easy to read it in isolation, forgetting that it would have been one of a page of listed potential problems, some deemed of greater concern than others. The general public have not been given access to any further information from the Briefs, although three members of the 9/11 Commission were permitted to read Daily Briefs relating to terrorism from the Clinton and Bush years as part of their investigations. What they discovered, we do not know, although it was reported that there were forty other mentions of al-Qaeda or bin Laden in the President's Daily Briefs before 9/11. Bush did not know the 9/11 attack was coming, though he had been warned. But in the maelstrom of anger and grief, there was only time for action, not introspection. What prior intelligence the President might have received was subordinate to the bigger question of how to respond.

Four days after the 9/11 attacks, the President met with his National Security team at the country retreat of Camp David in Maryland. Around the table that Saturday morning sat Vice President Dick Cheney, Secretary of State Colin Powell and Secretary of Defense Donald Rumsfeld. They were all dressed casually – Bush in a dark-green bomber jacket – and presented a strangely relaxed-looking audience for the Director of the CIA.

He briefed them on the situation in Afghanistan and the plan to remove the Islamic fundamentalist Taliban from power and thereby eradicate the 'safe haven' they had provided for al-Qaeda and its leader Osama bin Laden.

Unlike so many of his predecessors, George Tenet had not newly arrived in office along with the administration he served. The barnstorming New Yorker and son of a Greek diner owner from Queens had already been head of the CIA for four years. He had a presence and ability to chat that brought life to any room he entered and usefully masked his tireless work to master the details of his craft. He had worked for Senate Intelligence Committees and then on President Bill Clinton's National Security Council, moving sideways into the CIA. He had good Washington connections, a propensity to swear in meetings and also go 'walk-about', as his secretary phrased it, around the corridors of Langley. George W. Bush had not originally intended Tenet to retain his post. Bush's first choice for Director had been Donald Rumsfeld, but when Rumsfeld ended up at the Pentagon as Defense Secretary, the way was cleared for Tenet to stay. It helped that the new President and the head of the CIA had personally clicked. '[He] was just easy to be around,' Tenet later said. 'He was very direct, very focused, very clear … I liked him and he liked me.'

Bush had personal, daily CIA briefings of the kind that McGeorge Bundy had always hoped Kennedy would have – only Bush was interested and stuck to the schedule. Soon after they started, Bush immediately asked for Tenet to be present every day. From then on, the CIA Director was at the White House almost every morning, adding his comments and additional details to the items in the Brief. Tenet also saw the document ahead of the President: 'Most nights I would spend an hour or so reviewing the draft articles comprising the PDB, then call the PDB night editor with suggestions on needed changes and areas that required greater explanation. Sometimes, I spiked items that weren't ready for prime time.' At 6.15 a.m., Tenet would get into an armoured SUV on his driveway and a CIA briefer would hand him the completed Daily Brief in its leather binder, plus raw intelligence reports that had come in overnight. At 8 a.m., he would go to the West Wing and to the Oval Office for that day's intelligence briefing, where Bush would read the items carefully, often 'tossing out questions before getting to the bottom line'. Tenet was there to 'provide colour commentary and provide the larger context'.

*CIA Briefer Michael Morell (left) in conversation with President George W. Bush
in the White House Situation Room, three days after 9/11.
CIA Director George Tenet sits on the right.*

On the morning of 11 September, Tenet was having breakfast at a hotel
in Washington; with Bush out of town in Florida, he wasn't required at the
White House for the morning intelligence briefing. He later wrote in his
memoirs, 'I instantly thought this had to be Al Qaeda ... our safe American
world had been turned upside down. The War on Terror had come to our
shores.' At Camp David, Tenet expanded on the war plan: 'We were going
to strangle their safe haven in Afghanistan, seal the borders, go after the
leadership, shut off their money, and pursue Al Qaeda terrorists in ninety-
two countries around the world.'

Nearly 7,000 miles east of the congenial, quietly wooded surrounds of
Camp David, Osama bin Laden sheltered in a cave in Afghanistan's White
Mountains. The cave complex commandeered by al-Qaeda's leader was east
of Kabul, on the Afghan border, and known locally as Tora Bora: black
dust. The warrens in the rock had been hammered out through hard work
and blasted with dynamite; the fighters slept with their backs to walls of
streaked feldspar and glittering quartz. It was within a stone's throw of
the Khyber Pass, the ancient gateway between Afghanistan and its eastern

neighbour, through which multiple invading armies had marched since the fifth century BCE. Along the winding old silk road, through the gap in the forbidding mountains, lay Pakistan.

The son of a Saudi millionaire, bin Laden had first seen the mountains in his twenties, when he came to fight a war against a foreign army invading Afghanistan. In 1979, the Soviet Union militarily intervened to prop up Afghanistan's Communist government, which was facing armed insurrection in rural areas. Bin Laden arrived answering the call for *jihad* – holy war – in support of Afghan Muslim brothers taking on a godless invading power. He soon found himself working as a recruiter, persuading foreign nationals to join the cause of the *Mujahadeen*.

The porous eastern border of Afghanistan created an ideal opportunity for the USA to destabilise its Cold War enemy by supporting the armed groups fighting in Afghanistan. Recruits could be trained and armed in Pakistan's tribal areas and then simply slip across to wage war on Soviet soldiers in Afghanistan. The CIA provided funds to Pakistan's intelligence services and shipped vast quantities of weapons into Pakistan, including US-made anti-helicopter missiles known as Stingers. Afghanistan was the final proxy battleground of the Cold War, and it has even been claimed that bin Laden's recruitment operation was one of many that received CIA funds. The Arab fighters who bin Laden led into battle proved poorly trained and had no wider impact on the Afghan conflict, but in 1987 they did repel an attempt by the Soviets to evict them from Tora Bora. Bin Laden later claimed that a handful of Arab fighters had routed a hundred Soviet special forces, grandly asserting, 'The morale of the Mujahadeen soared, not only in our area, but in the whole of Afghanistan.' The Soviets were finally forced into an ignominious retreat and pulled out in 1989, leaving a gaping power vacuum that was eventually filled by the Taliban.

Bin Laden repurposed the network he had built into an organisation to fight *jihad* around the world. Under bin Laden's auspices, the secretive group (named al-Qaeda) first bombed a hotel in Aden, Yemen, in an attempt to target US troops on their way to deploying in Muslim-majority Somalia. A year later, an al-Qaeda-trained terrorist detonated a truck bomb in the basement of the World Trade Center in New York, killing six people and injuring over a thousand. Bombings of US embassies followed across Africa, and seventeen US Navy personnel died in an attack on the USS *Cole* as the warship refuelled in Aden harbour. By the end of 2000, bin Laden was already a wanted man. In the days before 9/11, bin Laden and his closest lieutenants were once again holed up in the mountains. He is said to have told his men that 'something great was going to happen, and soon Muslims from around the world would join them in Afghanistan to defeat the superpower'.

★ ★ ★

For Bush and his team around the Camp David table that September day, there needed to be a moment of decision. 'The morning session at Camp David was freewheeling, all over the place,' Tenet recalled. 'Sometime around noon, the President suggested we take a break. When we reassembled that afternoon, the discussion was much more directed, and the President was in full agreement with just about everything we had said during the day.' Four days later, Bush addressed Congress. He told the legislators and listeners around the world that al-Qaeda was responsible for the attack on the United States. Naming Osama bin Laden, he stated:

> The leadership of Al Qaeda has great influence in Afghanistan and supports the Taliban regime in controlling most of that country. In Afghanistan, we see Al Qaeda's vision for the world. Afghanistan's people have been brutalized – many are starving and many have fled. Women are not allowed to attend school. You can be jailed for owning a television ... we condemn the Taliban regime. It is not only repressing its own people, it is threatening people everywhere by sponsoring and sheltering and supplying terrorists.

He gave the Taliban an ultimatum: to hand over al-Qaeda, but added, 'Our war on terror begins with Al Qaeda, but it does not end there. It will not end until every terrorist group of global reach has been found, stopped and defeated.' The war that the USA was unleashing would touch much of the globe, dividing nations into 'those who are with us' and those 'who are with the terrorists'. And it would start in Afghanistan.

28

Failures

Between the end of Gerald Ford's presidency and the arrival of George W. Bush, there had been four presidents, alternately Democrat and Republican. Within that time, the Cold War that had defined the Truman, Eisenhower and Kennedy years had ended. The monolithic enemy had, it transpired, always possessed feet of clay. Institutional and economic weakness, the spread of more representative political reforms and a military disaster in Afghanistan all arguably contributed to what seemed like the overnight collapse of the Soviet Union. As cheering Berliners hacked down the wall that divided the East and West halves of the German capital, the hegemony of the USA seemed unquestioned; on 31 January 1990, the first McDonald's opened in Moscow. The challenges of the new age seemed subordinate to the victory achieved by Western liberal ideals. Writing in *The National Interest* journal, one political scientist, who was working in policy planning at the State Department, famously proposed 'The End of History'. Francis Fukuyama has been much misquoted since. In claiming that the world had arrived at 'the end point of mankind's ideological evolution', he also admitted that 'terrorism and wars of national liberation will continue to be an important item on the international agenda', but for the incoming occupants of the Oval Office, the USA seemed almost untouchable.

The Daily Briefs read by Jimmy Carter, Ronald Reagan, George H.W. Bush and Bill Clinton remain under lock and key, but we still know much about how they treated intelligence. Bush and Clinton faced the challenge of a 'new world order', but for Carter and Reagan there were echoes of the problems that had kept previous presidents avidly reading the paragraphs of their Briefs.

★ ★ ★

The helicopters thundered in low over the flat Georgian farmland, looking like crooked, angry insects through the heat haze. For the aircrafts' occupants, it was a rare visit to the 'real' USA, beyond the busy corridors of Langley and the high-octane schmoozing of Washington DC. They landed just outside the small town of Plains, the Army pilots having initially been confused by their instructions to land at 'Peterson Field', only to discover their destination was not an airfield but a field belonging to a farmer named Peterson. The only reason the CIA officers had arrived by helicopter was because they had not been able to find a nearby airport big enough to take the Agency's Gulfstream jet.

The most well-known CIA figure was Richard Lehman. The Missouri-born career officer had spent half his life in the Office of Current Intelligence that authored the Daily Briefs. He had sat at the back of the Cabinet Room swapping out the maps and images that Dulles used in his weekly NSC presentations to keep Eisenhower interested; he had been one of the analysts responsible for the redesigned Daily Brief that was first presented to Kennedy during his morning swim; and finally he had finished up as head of the OCI itself. Lehman had never intended to join the CIA but was recruited out of Harvard in 1948 as he spoke Russian. He had stayed with the Agency ever since. By 1976, he was no longer officially head of the OCI, but the officer known inside the CIA as 'Mr Current Intelligence' was along for the ride that day because he was the institutional memory. Next to him was the man President Ford had just appointed the CIA's new Director, George Herbert Walker Bush, whose then 30-year-old son would be President on 9/11.

Bush was partly brought in to rescue the CIA's reputation. In the fallout from the Watergate scandal that brought down Nixon, the American public's appetite for openness and demands to know the extent of what was being done clandestinely in their name led to investigations in both the Senate and House of Representatives. The committees unearthed some of the CIA's shadier activities when they reported in 1975, including programmes to assassinate foreign leaders. Top of the list in the report published in November 1975 was the targeting of Lumumba in the Congo. The public heard of Eisenhower's angry threats, Dulles' urging to Agency staff, and even read testimony from the Leopoldville Station Chief Larry Devlin about the intricacies of the plot, although Devlin's name was changed in the official report. Alongside the assassination operations, the newspapers dined out on the revelation that under Allen Dulles, the CIA had conducted illegal investigations into mind-control and psychological torture, even giving unwitting American citizens LSD simply to record what happened. In the context of the 'MK-ULTRA' programme, trying and failing to take out Lumumba seemed almost a footnote. The only saving grace was that, while the CIA was hugely embarrassed, Congress also went after the FBI, leaving the USA's domestic and foreign intelligence establishment licking its wounds.

Bush was a Massachusetts-born former Navy pilot who had gone from oil company work in Texas to being a representative for the state in Congress, later leading the Republican National Committee and serving as UN Ambassador and an envoy to China. Kissinger, who stayed on as NSA and Secretary of State after Nixon resigned, had personally asked Bush to head up the CIA on behalf of Ford. Even though it seemed a political dead end and a thankless assignment, Bush had seen it as his duty to 'serve his country'. Bush was considerate and unfailingly polite; though many later critiqued his politics, he was a thoroughly decent man. On 28 July 1976, the 52-year-old Bush was engaging in one of his more welcome and easier tasks: briefing a presidential candidate on matters of intelligence.

The man Lehman and Bush had travelled to meet had been born in the state and raised on a farm. He had a wiry build and sandy hair, and was down to earth, self-effacing, and a private but devout Baptist. One thing people often noted about James Earl Carter Jr was his broad grin and the way he put people at ease; it suited a man who preferred to be called 'Jimmy'. When he accepted the Democratic nomination, he told his party:

> It is time for America to move and to speak not with boasting and belliger-ence but with a quiet strength, to depend in world affairs not merely on the size of an arsenal but on the nobility of ideas ... The tragedy of Vietnam ... the disgrace of Watergate, and the embarrassment of the CIA revelations could have been avoided if our government had simply reflected the sound

judgement and good common sense and the high moral character of the American people.

Common sense and high moral character were to be watchwords of the Carter administration, but would prove high ideals to attain in a dangerous and difficult world.

The CIA men and their staff arrived at Carter's brick ranch and were ushered into his study, which was one of the few rooms with air conditioning. But the rattle of the unit drowned out conversation, so it was switched off, and for five hours they sat with 'clothes stuck to the back of the chairs'. Lehman remembered being 'hotter than hell', but he left with the impression that the Democrats' candidate cared. Carter, he later recalled, 'sat without getting up and very intent, totally concentrating and taking it all in'.

By the time he won in November, Carter had already scrawled his own notes across a series of Daily Briefs, giving personal feedback on what he would like in his – less of what was already covered in the newspapers and longer background – something no other incoming leader had taken the time to do. Instead of receiving a personal CIA briefing, Carter sat each morning with his National Security Advisor and the two read the Daily Brief. The Brief's circulation was cut back from the final days of Ford, so it now only went to the President, NSA, Vice President, and Secretaries of State and Defense. Carter shared his own copy (and notes) with his Vice President, Walter Mondale, and if he left the room while it was still on his desk, his secretary would lock it in the safe.

During Carter's presidency, the Daily Brief was printed with wide margins, so the President had plenty of space to jot down his own comments. The Brief was well regarded for much of Carter's time in office. Encouragingly for the analysts, they knew it was being read, but there was the slight rankle that the President discussed it daily with his National Security Advisor, rather than CIA staff. There was positive feedback – at one point, Carter himself visited Langley and thanked the Brief staff – but at the same time there were rumblings of discontent and criticism of the Daily Brief's political commentary. The problems were most acute when it came to a country that had featured in the Briefs many times before: Iran.

Carter visited Iran in December 1977, near the end of his first year in the White House. In a toast at a banquet at a palace in Tehran, Carter – looking more like a best-man than a President, as he grinned and raised his glass at the flower-covered table – complimented the Shah that his nation was 'an island of stability in one of the most troubled areas of the world'. The Shah had held power for the two-and-a-half decades since the CIA-supported coup that brought down Mosaddeq and cemented the monarch's rule. There was still opposition to his authoritarian and modernising agenda and the control he wielded over the country's parliament. And given how long he had been in power, it was easy to blame all the country's ills on one man. Opposing the Shah was, however, a risky undertaking: the secret police had also incarcerated more than 2,500 political prisoners.

Opposition to the Shah coalesced around the figure of Ayatollah Ruhollah Khomeini, an Islamic cleric whose denouncements of the king led to him being exiled to Paris in the year following Carter's visit. In 1978, strikes and protests crippled the country. By September, the Shah had declared martial law. The analysts at the CIA were unanimous: the Shah might be forced to make political compromises, but the discontent was not sufficient to depose him. Carter was aware of the problems, noting in his diary on 25 October, '[The] CIA gave me a definitive analysis of the economic and political problems of Iran. The Shah ... has alienated a lot of powerful groups, particularly the right-wing religious leaders.' In November, the Shah appeared on television and told the Iranian people, 'I [have] heard the voice of your revolution.' The attempt to assuage the protests failed and millions of Iranians took to the streets. In January 1979, the Shah fled, as he had before. This time, he did not return. The power vacuum he left behind was filled by those with the loudest voices, and Ayatollah Khomeini established the country as an Islamic Republic in the months that followed.

Carter's Defense Secretary, Harold Brown, later conceded, 'Our intelligence apparatus did not function in Iran – and that meant that neither the PDB nor the other intelligence entities were providing well-based knowledge, let alone an ability to anticipate what was going to happen.' The CIA, and everybody else, had dropped the ball. Alongside efforts to improve the quality of information and sources in the Middle East, CIA analysts completely redesigned the Daily Brief. They still kept it at under ten pages, but it was reformatted to include graphics, photographs and maps on a daily basis. It covered more of the world, with short, punchy news that was routinely updated as late as 4 a.m. on the morning of publication. They also included a couple of longer, more analytical pieces in each publication.

When it was presented to Carter in March 1980, the President was pleased. But the changes came too late. In November 1979, a revolutionary mob had overrun the US Embassy in Tehran, taking fifty-two Americans hostage. Securing their release was an arduous and very public process, remembered today as the Iran Hostage Crisis. By the time the next presidential election rolled around in November of the following year, the Americans were still imprisoned. Their fate kept Carter up at night. In his memoirs, he recalls walking the White House gardens at dawn and lying awake, 'Trying to think of additional steps I could take to gain their freedom'; angst that only worsened when the Delta Force rescue operation he personally approved to try and break the deadlock had to be aborted, and when its failure became public knowledge. It was not just the Iran Hostage Crisis that led to Carter losing by a landslide in November 1980 – there were domestic economic issues too – but the failure of intelligence had been a significant factor. It raises the tantalising question of what might have happened if Carter's Daily Brief had correctly called how events would unfold in Iran.

29

Freedom Fighters

The first change the 69-year-old Ronald Reagan asked for in the Daily Brief was for the print to be made larger. For the CIA, it was another reorganisation at the top and a new 'First Customer'. The attitude of many of the staff is well summarised in a 1998 article by two former CIA officers, including the Deputy Director from the Reagan years, who wrote, 'we faced another new administration, another foreign policy team, another group to which we had to prove ourselves all over again'. Providing daily intelligence to the President was not a thankless task, but it was one that could easily be misunderstood: new presidents 'started with the expectation that intelligence could solve every problem, or that it could not do anything right, and then moved to the opposite view. Then they settled down and vacillated from one extreme to the other.'

At least the new man in had agreed to sit down with the CIA for twenty minutes each morning, and in Regan's Vice President, the CIA had an ally and a man already well versed in intelligence. Reagan gladly allowed his second-in-command access to the Daily Brief, although he had already read many hundreds of them; George H.W. Bush had departed the CIA soon after Carter arrived in office and, after a stint in the non-political world, returned to run in the 1980 election, missing out on the nomination, but getting a place on the ticket as Vice President. For many in the CIA, it was a joy to have a familiar face in the midst of many new ones. Bush also supported the Agency's cause, encouraging the idea of daily, in-person presidential briefings and regular feedback.

Bush need not have worried too much: President Reagan proved to be 'studious' in the reading of his Daily Brief. Reagan listened keenly to the CIA's perspective, but knew where he stood. During an in-flight briefing in mid-January 1981, alongside that day's Daily Brief, the CIA presented a special report on the Palestinian Liberation Organization (PLO) and the factions in the organisation that were involved in the long-running Israel–Palestine conflict. After spending nearly a quarter of an hour poring over it, the President turned to the CIA representatives and said, 'But they are all terrorists, aren't they?' The Californian had strong views and strong politics, but he liked the redesign of the Brief that had been undertaken in early 1980 after the Iran 'failure' and specifically asked the CIA to keep it that way.

Reagan was the first President to receive what might be described as multimedia briefings. In his youth, he had been a Hollywood actor, before moving into politics and later becoming governor of California. He had never lost his love for the movies, and someone at the CIA decided to supplement the Daily Brief with the occasional short film, typically on a foreign leader. Reagan always wanted the personal details – how many children they had, their upbringing – and therefore biographical films seemed an excellent way of keeping the President informed. One short movie, on Soviet leader Mikhail Gorbachev, led Reagan to call the CIA Director to tell him it 'was a great film', while the President noted in his diary in June 1985 that a biopic of Indian leader Rajiv Gandhi was 'good preparation for his visit' and left Reagan feeling 'a sense of having met him before'.

Although they were classified, the films made the news, with *The New York Times* running a special piece in December 1981 on how Reagan was watching 'a White House version of "This Is Your Life" … put together by the Central Intelligence Agency'. The journalist added that 'White House sources' had revealed the President 'prefers the film briefing to the heavy reading'. The reports in the press played into a perception among some of the public, exploited wherever possible by Reagan's opponents, that the ageing actor-President didn't do books, or reading in general. However, it was a complete fabrication, particularly when it came to intelligence. Reagan not only read his Daily Briefs but carefully annotated many of them. Sometimes he would write queries – 'and?' – other times he would fill the margins with additional information he knew, labelling a particular Soviet missile that was pictured, or noting other information he was aware of that related to the item. Receiving current intelligence through his Daily Briefs was so regular for Reagan that he described it in one diary entry as 'the usual Presidential chores', along with having things to sign and making phone calls.

There was a particular Eisenhower echo to the Reagan years. Like Eisenhower, Reagan had a 'doctrine' when it came to foreign policy and it was similarly designed to roll back the reach of Communism. In his 1985 State of the Union address, after securing his second term in office the previous November, Reagan asserted that freedom was 'not the sole prerogative of the chosen few' and openly aligned the USA to the anti-Communist side in two conflicts. 'We must not break faith with those who are risking their lives – on every continent, from Afghanistan to Nicaragua – to defy Soviet supported aggression and secure rights which have been ours from birth.'

Citing Nicaragua would prove problematic for Reagan. The Central American country had been ruled by the Somoza family until 1979, when they were overthrown by the Sandinista National Liberation Front. The socialist-leaning group quickly turned to Cuba and the Soviet Union for assistance and, in response, Reagan authorised CIA support for the counter-revolutionaries, or 'Contras'. The Republicans held a slender majority in the Senate, but the House of Representatives had been Democrat since the early days of Eisenhower. Conscious of past history and determined to derail any efforts to support regime change in Central America, the Democrats passed a series of remarkable amendments, tagging them on to other legislation as 'riders'. The Boland Amendments specifically and legally prohibited the CIA and Department of Defense from using money 'for the purposes of overthrowing the Government of Nicaragua'. There would be no second Guatemala, no CIA-trained army; besides, a significant chunk of Contra funding came from the distasteful cocaine trade.

What should have proved a roadblock in fact seemed to be taken as a challenge by a number of key figures in the Reagan administration. First, they tried funding anti-Sandinista guerrillas through the National Security Council, which they insisted was excluded from the prohibition on defence spending that tied the hands of the CIA and Department of Defense. Then, when that failed, they went covert. Through secret arms deals with Iran, which was under US sanctions following the revolution, the Reagan administration acquired funds to pass on to the Contras. 'The Iran–Contra Affair' led to criminal investigation and brought down senior figures, including a

National Security Advisor. However, there was enough distance between Reagan and the events for him to escape impeachment, even though it was clear that the whole operation was a hustle he supported in principle, if not explicitly. In November 1986, as the story began to break in the foreign press, George H.W. Bush recorded in his diary, 'I am one of the few people that know fully the details. This is one operation that has been held very, very tight, and I hope it will not leak.'

We have no idea to what extent Reagan's Daily Briefs mentioned Nicaragua, or the efforts to fund the Contras, but it is likely that any references would have been carefully managed. It had been the same for all the previous covert operations. In addition, under Reagan, the circulation of the Daily Brief had been kept relatively tight, but the document was not perceived as being especially secure compared to previous versions. The main issue in the Reagan era was how his administration cycled through a disturbingly high number of National Security Advisors. One of the unintended consequences was that Daily Brief circulation informally increased: Daily Briefs were copied, in breach of protocol, and sometimes left 'lying around the West Wing'; Deputy National Security Advisor John Poindexter even later admitted photocopying the Daily Brief for his own files. The Iran–Contra paper trail that eventually became public in 1993 includes White House memos and minutes of meetings, but there were no Daily Briefs. If they hold any secrets, they are still well hidden.

The other conflict Reagan mentioned in his 1985 State of the Union address was Afghanistan. The Soviet invasion in 1979 drew in thousands of individuals seeking a cause to fight for, among them bin Laden who was working as a recruiter, moving between Pakistan and Afghanistan. The *Mujahadeen* were, in Reagan's words, 'freedom fighters ... defying Soviet aggression' and, working on that simple assumption, it was an easy decision for the USA to provide extensive support. Afghanistan became the last proxy conflict of the Cold War, ending when the Soviets exited in 1989, leaving the country in the throes of a civil war. As Reagan prepared to depart office, the Soviet Union was on the verge of collapse, and the defeat and embarrassing withdrawal in Afghanistan contributed to the disintegration of the myth of the all-powerful Moscow leadership. The next President would face a very different world, but for the CIA and the writers of the Daily Brief, it would be the easiest transition in history.

★ ★ ★

George H.W. Bush was the first former CIA Director to become President. He later recalled, 'One of my favourite times of day was when I would sit down with a briefer and read through the PDB.' He read it every single day, 'religiously, without fail'. George H.W. Bush would start at the first page of his Brief at his first meeting every morning and ask for extra detail as he went. The main items were called 'snowflakes', just two or three lines long; officers submitting items were in some cases asked to cut them down to thirty-two words. Writing for a former Director had its perks: Bush was knowledge-able, appreciative of the analysts' efforts and aware of the complexities they faced. On occasions he would call them directly, and he was, in the words of one former Deputy Director of Intelligence, 'a serious and avid consumer of intelligence ... the easiest to brief in the world'.

After he left office, Bush conceded that he 'wouldn't have wanted to try tackling any of the many issues we confronted without the input from the intelligence community ... I hope they all know how much I have appreciated them, and the excellent product they produced.' On one occasion, how-ever, he did disagree with the Brief, and with the analysts. Nicaragua's first monitored, free election was scheduled for April 1990, and the CIA analysts forecast that Daniel Ortega, who had been President of the Central American nation since 1975, would remain in power. The US President turned to the CIA briefer as they read through the Daily Brief and said, 'I'll bet you an ice cream cone that you're wrong.' After Ortega was voted out, the CIA briefer sheepishly delivered an ice cream to the Oval Office the following day.

Alongside the camaraderie he built with CIA staff, George H.W. Bush treated his own Vice President very differently from how Kennedy had treated Johnson. Vice President Dan Quayle remembers George H.W. Bush coming into his office early in their term and inviting him to attend any intel-ligence briefings he wanted. 'You need to know exactly what I know,' the President told him, and it stayed that way. Quayle got the Daily Brief around 7.30 a.m. each morning and chatted about its contents with a CIA officer for around half an hour. The document itself was carefully safeguarded. Each of the handful of copies in circulation was delivered personally and then taken back to Langley, something George H.W. Bush had himself requested; unlike

Jackie Kennedy, Bush's wife, Barbara, would never have the opportunity to scrawl a late-night note for her husband on the carefully classified folder.

In the summer of 1991, one of the regular items in the Daily Brief concerned the Middle East. Iraq's ruler, Saddam Hussein, was threatening neighbouring Kuwait, but the prospect of the war of words and the dispute over oil escalating was discounted by almost everyone. Dick Cheney, who was George H.W. Bush's Secretary of Defense before later being Vice President for George W., recalled being 'assured by everybody over there … that Saddam would never invade', but on the night of 1 August, the staff at Langley found themselves making last-minute changes to the next day's Brief.

The Brief on the morning of 2 August warned of an imminent invasion. George H.W. Bush considered calling Saddam to try and dissuade him, but before the President was able to initiate a phone call, there were reports from the US Embassy in Kuwait City that there was shooting in the capital. Saddam had misread the situation and an international coalition combined to expel Iraqi forces from Kuwait. Not since the Korean War had the UN backed a multinational military campaign of that scope and scale.

During the 1991 Gulf War, the Daily Brief was modified to include tactical details of the conflict, battle-damage assessments and satellite images, effectively serving as a daily battlefield, as well as intelligence, report. The war was over so quickly that there was no need ever to create a separate document, as presidents had received during previous conflicts. In his 1991 State of the Union address, Bush called on his listeners to 'prepare for the next American century' following the end of the Cold War. The intervention in the Gulf was part, he insisted, of a 'new world order'. It was an order that would require a new focus in intelligence too, one the CIA would struggle to adapt to, with devastating consequences.

30

'A Jungle Full of Poisonous Snakes'

For the CIA, the end of the Cold War was the end of the gravy train. When George Tenet became acting Director in 1996, three years after Republican George H.W. Bush had been succeeded by Democrat Bill Clinton, he found the Agency a shell of its former self. 'We had lost twenty-five percent of our people. We had lost billions of investment … I was the fourth director in seven years,' he later recalled. For all the camaraderie and understanding of the George H.W. Bush years, the Agency was struggling to reorientate itself in a simultaneously budgetarily-austere and multi-threat world. Overseas stations in Africa and Latin America were shut down as a raft of old spies from the Cold War era retired, taking their practical espionage expertise with them. In addition to all the internal and budgetary issues, the CIA also had another President who, it seemed, did not have much time for the Daily Brief.

Bill Clinton had trodden the now well-worn path from law to politics, becoming Arkansas' Attorney General and then its Governor before bidding for the White House. Clinton was good-looking, young and charming; *The Washington Post* even ran an article ahead of the poll titled 'Comparing Clinton and Kennedy'. George H.W. Bush had won the Gulf War, but foreign policy was no longer a priority for the majority of Americans. With the economy in recession and Bush having broken a pledge not to raise taxes, Clinton secured enough votes to make the White House Democrat for the first time in twelve years. He would later acquire the dubious distinction of becoming only the second President to be impeached, but when he arrived in office, the embarrassment of the Clinton–Lewinsky scandal and his forever famous lie – 'I did not have sexual relations with that woman' – were problems for the future.

Clinton's first CIA Director, Jim Woolsey, was a well-regarded government official who spent two years in post without once having a one-to-one meeting with the President. Intelligence briefings were regular, but they were tightly held by Clinton's National Security Advisor, Tony Lake. 'We just sat outside the Oval Office waiting to get in,' Woolsey later recalled, '[then] Tony Lake would say, "I'm sorry, he's just not going to have time today."' Part of the problem, the CIA Director decided, was that Clinton was domestically focused and after winning the Cold War there was a perception that the USA was almost untouchable overseas. After a while, it became common for a member of Clinton's staff to ask the waiting CIA officers just to hand over the Daily Brief document, at which point Woolsey stopped trying to attend any regular intelligence briefings and only saw the President at the weekly NSA meetings. He would later insist, 'I didn't have a *bad* relationship with President Clinton. I just didn't have one at all.'

The CIA felt shut out, although Clinton himself insisted he was a careful reader of the Brief:

> I found it more fruitful and practical on most days to read it myself early in the morning – and then to make, as I almost invariably did, a set of notes actually on the PDB for what further information I wanted ... I really tried to read the PDB carefully, seriously, and thoroughly.

The pattern that George H. W. Bush had pioneered of a close involvement for the Vice President in intelligence was continued under Clinton. Woolsey felt shut out of the Oval, but Al Gore, Clinton's Vice President, got all the Daily Briefs and Clinton would often ask him to make further investigations on topics that interested him. The Vice President therefore developed a stronger relationship with the Agency, and certainly its staff, than Clinton ever managed. On one birthday, the briefers who met Al Gore each day mocked up a fake Daily Brief, which Al Gore did not notice until he came to a farcical article about penguins; the Vice President loved it. At the CIA, however, there was a sense that intelligence was a very long way down Clinton's list of priorities.

★ ★ ★

After he became Director, Tenet set about rebuilding morale and realigning the Agency towards one of the very concerns that Fukuyama's famous essay had highlighted would remain a problem in the 'post-history' world: terrorist threats. As Tenet's predecessor, Woolsey, phrased it, 'We fought with a huge dragon for forty-five years, finally killed him and then found ourselves in a jungle full of poisonous snakes.' The Agency's main targets were Hezbollah in Lebanon and al-Qaeda, now resident in Afghanistan. The twin embassy attacks in August 1998 and the first World Trade Center bombing in 1993 had gained the organisation notoriety and made assessing the al-Qaeda threat a priority for the CIA.

On 4 December 1998, Clinton received a Daily Brief item entitled 'Bin Laden Preparing to Hijack US Aircraft and Other Attacks'. The short piece warned of reports that 'Bin Laden and his allies are preparing for attacks in the US, including an aircraft hijacking to obtain the release of Shaykh 'Umar 'Abd al-Rahman, Ramzi Yousef, and Muhammad Sadiq 'Awda', who were imprisoned for involvement in the 1993 bombing of the World Trade Center. The item also noted that some members of the al-Qaeda network had 'received hijack training'. It was admitted, however, that the organisation had not carried out any previous hijackings and, even though terrorists were thought to be 'moving closer' to implementing attacks, the analysts were forced to concede, 'we do not know whether they are related to [the planned] attacks on aircraft'. This is the only one of Clinton's Daily Briefs ever to be made public.

Al-Qaeda remained active and, in October 2000, seventeen US Navy personnel died in the attack on the destroyer USS *Cole* when it moored in the Port of Aden in Yemen. Afterwards, the CIA directly informed President Clinton, 'This is obviously an Al Qaeda attack.' But there was no question of intervening in Afghanistan. Al-Qaeda was one of the most threatening 'poisonous snakes' hiding in a jungle no one had any desire to set foot in. The CIA continued to monitor the organisation's activities, which escalated from early 2001. By the time George W. Bush and his staff settled into the White House, there was an entire, dedicated CIA al-Qaeda team. It was difficult to pin down specific threats, but the 'noise' was deafening. 'The system was blinking red', Tenet would later admit. 'Something was being ordered from Afghanistan out. But it was very difficult for us to figure out what it was.'

★ ★ ★

On 10 July 2001, less than six months after George W. Bush had been inaugurated, the situation came to a head. The leader of the Agency's bin Laden unit put through a call to Tenet's secretary and demanded to see him immediately. Tenet was in a meeting 'with the head of some foreign intelligence service', but they were booted out and Tenet let in the two top staff from the CIA's al-Qaeda unit:

> It wasn't just red lights and chatter. There were real plots ... There were pronouncements by Al Qaeda that there would be eight major celebrations coming. The world was going to be stunned by what would soon happen. Terrorists were disappearing. Camps were closing ... And this was building to a crescendo.

Immediately convinced, the Director of the CIA called the White House. Bush was away in Boston, so Tenet and the agents from the al-Qaeda unit met with National Security Advisor Condoleezza Rice and the Chief Counterterrorism Advisor on the NSC. Tenet had been unequivocal on the phone, insisting, 'I have to come and see you. We're coming right now.'

'Condi' Rice had grown up in the segregated South before attending university and completing a doctorate. She went from academia to advising the National Security Council on Eastern Europe during the George H.W. Bush years, and when George W. Bush began his campaign he brought her in as foreign policy advisor and then gave her the post of NSA when he won. Rice was the first woman and the first African American to be appointed NSA. She was calm in a crisis, confident in her own abilities and acutely aware that she had taken on a critically important role in the administration.

At their meeting on 10 July 2001, the head of the CIA's al-Qaeda unit, Richard Blee, told Rice:

> There will be significant terrorist attacks against the United States in the coming weeks or months. The attacks will be spectacular. They will be multiple ... This is an attack that is intended to cause thousands of American casualties somewhere. We cannot say it will be New York City or the United States, but it is geared towards US citizens.

Their recommendation to Rice was simple: the country needed to get on a war footing and take significant, coordinated action. Walking out to the West Wing car park, Tenet and the two al-Qaeda experts were convinced they had got across everything they needed to, but Rice remembered the meeting differently. In her memoirs, she wrote that her recollection of the 10 July meeting was 'not very crisp, because we were discussing the threat every day', although she did remember Tenet calling and asking if he could 'come over immediately'. Rice writes of 'a presentation that compiled the threat information that we had been reviewing daily along with some new intelligence'. Her belief at the time was that 'with the raised levels of alert for State and Defense, I thought we were doing what needed to be done'. Four weeks later, the President's Daily Brief warned that bin Laden was making 'preparations for hijackings or other types of attacks' and was 'determined' to strike at the USA.

Bush was certainly reading the warnings about al-Qaeda. Throughout the summer of 2001, whenever the Daily Brief contained information about possible attacks, the President would ask the CIA what information they had that 'might indicate an attack could come inside the United States'. The purpose of the now infamous 6 August Daily Brief item was to provide a summary of available information, ahead of Bush taking several weeks' holiday. Where the item lacked details, it was because there were none. As Tenet later conceded, 'We did not have and therefore did not convey information about any specific ongoing plot.' For the intelligence community, 9/11 was a sin of omission: they could not pass on to the President what they did not know, although there was an unflinching admission that they should have known more. But when it came to the next great failure of intelligence, it would seem that the President was being fed lies in the Daily Brief itself.

31

'Let Me Read'

The invasion of Afghanistan in 2001 was followed two years later by an attack on Iraq. The country's leader, Saddam Hussein, was connected to bin Laden on an axis of evil and possessed weapons of mass destruction (WMDs) that posed an imminent threat; or so the world was told. Two decades on, Iraq has become the totemic example of an 'illegal war'.

When the President-appointed WMD Commission – set up to investigate the WMD intelligence issue – reported back to George W. Bush in March 2005, it wrote the President a formal letter. It was a damning indictment of the Iraq WMD content Bush had received in his Daily Briefs. 'The daily intelligence briefings given to you before the Iraq war were flawed,' they noted. 'Through attention-grabbing headlines and repetition of questionable data, these briefings overstated the case that Iraq was rebuilding its WMD programs.' The intelligence community had not been guilty of distortion or fabrication of evidence, but simply of confirmation bias: everything that might support the narrative that Iraq possessed and was willing to use WMDs was seized upon, while contradictory intel or dissenters were ignored. There was also a habit of headlines that were more confident than the content beneath them, and an apparent desire to make sure the President was reading what they thought he wanted to read. Under the heading 'Rethink the President's Daily Brief', the commission stated that it wanted a new appointee to be 'ultimately responsible for the content'. In short, the CIA was losing the Daily Brief.

There were other arguments put forward as well: that it was a waste to have your best analysts briefing rather than analysing, and that the need to produce a single, feted analytical document for the Commander-in-Chief changed the nature of how intelligence was considered. As one anonymous former government official told a newspaper at the time, 'Everyone is doing current intelligence but not mining the vast amount collected … for important insights. They are getting the easily found, sexy pieces of collected information and pushing it up the chain to those who brief intelligence to the President.' The result was the creation of the Office of the Director of National Intelligence. The new Director of National Intelligence would be the head of the entire US intelligence community and, as well as bringing a more joined-up approach to the entire intelligence apparatus, they were given formal responsibility for the President's Daily Brief. As a headline change, it was the biggest shift in the Daily Brief since the CIA had been asked to start writing it.

However, the intention of the commission proved far more difficult to fulfil in practice. Other agencies and departments actively distanced themselves from having to get involved in producing the Daily Brief and, besides, the CIA knew how to write it, even if what they had written had been wrong. The result was that, from 2005, the President's Daily Brief no longer had the CIA seal, but it came out of the same office, produced by the same analysts, who were just officially seconded to the Office of the Director for National Intelligence, instead of working for the CIA. As the first new Director of National Intelligence himself admitted, 'I'll be damned if I can tell you that it's really that different. We left it all over at the CIA building. We were under no illusions that there was going to be some kind of revolution in the way things were done.'

There were in fact several changes, which were already being implemented before the WMD Commission's official, damning report, but they were primarily in tone, not in content; headlines were made less sensational and confidence assessments were included with items as a matter of course. There would be no ripping up of the President's Daily Brief. Instead, the Iraq intelligence debacle was a 'learning experience'. It was hardly what the WMD Commission had intended when they told Bush he needed to 'rethink' his Daily Brief, but there was another problem with that idea: the President liked his Brief just the way it was.

The irony was that, in Bush, the CIA had the most engaged and informed President it had ever had. He hardly ever missed an in-person briefing and religiously read the document itself. He even added in regular 'deep-dive' sessions, which resulted in CIA analysts used to the obscurity of their offices and intelligence dossiers finding themselves on the sofa in the Oval Office opposite the Commander-in-Chief, while he grilled them on their assessments of what was going on in their field areas. Perhaps on some level, Bush was so popular within the Agency – his father having been Director, then President, and Bush himself showing more personal interest than anyone could remember – that no one relished the prospect of contradicting the direction of travel toward war in Iraq.

There is also a parallel between Iraqi WMDs and the CIA's reports on the 'missile gap' during the Eisenhower administration. Faced with a gap in knowledge, it is always easier to assume the worst of your fears than to confront a complicated reality. The CIA and an entire administration had done exactly that previously, making the missile gap an 'imaginative creation of irresponsibility', as Eisenhower later phrased it in his memoirs. The human factor of confirmation bias contributed too, with lightweight evidence being attributed far more importance than it deserved. The President's Daily Brief was singled out for criticism after the Iraq War, but much of the intelligence community had been singing from the same hymn sheet.

What the fruitless search for WMDs proved was that even with twenty-first-century technology it was still possible to misread reality and present to the President intelligence that fitted a narrative, rather than allowing the information to write its own story. It seemed that the analysts who slaved away each night had long forgotten that mantra of Sidney Souers, the first man responsible for producing a written daily intelligence summary for the President: that information should never be interpreted 'to make it seem to support previously accepted policies or preconceived opinions'. As well as causing authors of the Daily Brief to lose focus, going to war in Iraq had also done something else: it had diverted attention, resources and effort away from Afghanistan, and that created problems for the President who would follow on from Bush.

★ ★ ★

On inauguration day 2009, the CIA briefer and the Director of National Intelligence entered the Oval Office and sat down. As the briefer lent forward to talk, the new President of the United States waved for him to stop and said, 'Let me read.' It was a moment that displayed much of Obama's character and set a precedent for how he wanted his intelligence. The Bush years had been full of deep discussions, in which the President would interrupt the briefers to ask for details or extra information, or to ask personal questions so he could get to know them. Obama was reserved and professional; at times his staff would find it difficult to decipher what he thought during a debate until he later made a decision.

Barack Obama had had one of the most storied journeys to the presidency in history. It wasn't just that he was the first African American President. He was an inspirational orator, a positive campaigner and a politician who breathed life back into the American Dream. The tall, classy Democrat had presence as well as poise and had managed to be nominated for a Nobel Peace Prize before he was even in office. His victory seemed to herald a new era for the USA, but Obama's grand aims would be restrained by the painful realities of politics. He was a man of letters, an inclination that would later hurt him, when problematic party politics would have been better served by a Johnson-style figure who walked the halls and talked to everyone.

Obama's personality meant that soon the daily intelligence meetings to discuss the content of the Daily Briefs began to slip. Where Eisenhower had wanted a staffer to talk at him about intelligence, it was the last thing Obama desired. The change in the dynamic was easily open to being misread. In 2012, *The Wall Street Journal* published an editorial which pondered 'Why is Obama skipping more than half of his daily intelligence briefings?' Citing the fact that, in his first 1,225 days in office, the President had conducted in-person intelligence meetings just 536 times, the paper implied that attending only 43.8 per cent of briefings was liable to leave a President uninformed. The author had in fact been somewhat overzealous in their sums: the Daily Brief was not published on Sundays, so Obama's attendance rate was actually above 50 per cent.

Critically, the President's diary was also more full of intelligence meetings than it had ever been: aside from the fixture of the weekly NSC meeting, Bush had also added a weekly terrorism discussion – which became known as 'Terrorism Tuesday' – which remained in Obama's diary. The fact that the

President was not having a daily intelligence meeting to discuss the Brief was hardly new; it was not the first time the 'First Customer' had not wanted to sit down in person and talk intelligence over breakfast. Even if he was not discussing it, it was clear Obama was reading it. CIA Deputy Director Mike Morell insisted that the evidence the President was still taking in his Brief was obvious for all to see in the weekly NSC meetings, remarking that he was 'impressed in NSC meetings that the PDB was informing him [the President]. He didn't refer to it explicitly, but you could see that he had internalized the analysis.'

Obama himself mentions the Daily Brief in his memoirs, or as his wife Michelle referred to it: 'The Death, Destruction and Horrible Things book'. Obama had a clear idea in his mind of the document's purpose, later writing, 'The goal was to have a continuously up-to-date sense of all that was roiling in the world, the large, the small, and sometimes barely perceptible shifts that threatened to upset whatever equilibrium we were trying to maintain.'

President Obama receiving the daily intelligence briefing on 3 February 2011. Nineteen days earlier, his Daily Brief had reported on a compound in Abbottabad in northern Pakistan, which was rumoured to be sheltering Osama bin Laden.

More than any other President, Obama's consumption of intelligence was like Truman's: he would privately pore over his Daily Brief, seemingly seeing it as a personal responsibility to ensure there were not any 'gaps' in his information.

For all the patterns of the past in Obama's intelligence methods, there was also one hugely significant change. On 14 February 2014, the CIA printed the last copy of the President's Daily Brief. The President's 'secret newspaper' had gone digital and was now delivered daily to the iPad that Obama carried around with him. The digital shift was openly publicised by the White House, which shared a photograph of Obama and his Deputy Director for National Intelligence sitting and staring at iPads in the Oval Office, which the White House press corps were assured were displaying that day's Daily Brief. The digital shift allows a deeper-level, immediate access to intelligence sources, as well as multimedia information, but the sense of mystery that for decades surrounded the TOP SECRET stamped cover has been diminished by the obvious technological advancement.

Like all the modern Briefs, Obama's remain classified and out of reach, so it is impossible to assess how often they contained information from Afghanistan. In the years since the 2001 invasion, the initial euphoria at the blinding success that swept the Taliban from power in weeks had been replaced by the realisation that creating a free and prosperous country was altogether more difficult. Speaking in April 2002, Bush insisted that the USA was 'helping to build an Afghanistan that is free from this evil and a better place to live'. He even drew a direct parallel with the Marshall Plan, which Truman had persuaded Congress to approve to help rebuild Europe after the Second World War. Between 2001 and 2009, the US Congress approved $38 billion in humanitarian and reconstruction assistance for Afghanistan, but following the mass deployment of US forces to Iraq, the fruitless hunt for WMDs and Iraq's descent into sectarian violence, events in Afghanistan often seemed a side note. The first surge in violence occurred in 2006, when there were 136 suicide attacks and more than 1,500 remotely detonated bombings. By the end of his first year in office, Obama had expanded the US force in Afghanistan to more than 100,000, and they faced a growing Taliban insurgency in the south of the country.

While the situation in Afghanistan was deteriorating, the CIA and the Obama administration were still obsessed with catching bin Laden, who seemed to have fallen off the edge of the world. For years, all their leads went

President Obama and Deputy Director of National Intelligence, Robert Cardillo,
read the President's Daily Brief on iPads.

nowhere. Then, on 13 January 2011, Obama's Daily Brief described a compound in the town of Abbottabad in northern Pakistan. The house had no internet connection and higher walls than normal, and its occupants burned their rubbish. It was hardly conclusive proof that the dwelling was sheltering the world's most wanted man, but the possibility was enough for it to make the Brief. Four months later, after a painstaking intelligence-gathering operation, US special forces raided the compound, shot bin Laden dead and carried off his body. The President had watched the operation unfold in real time from the situation room in the White House basement. However, while Obama received his Daily Brief on an iPad, could watch helmet-camera footage from special forces operations and deployed drones to loiter above the Afghanistan–Pakistan border region to stalk terrorists, technology and money alone were not enough to win in Afghanistan.

If there were maps in Obama's Daily Briefs, they would have shown the problematic reality that the Taliban still controlled territory in Afghanistan. Meanwhile, Afghan forces were struggling to keep major cities free from bombing attacks and faced concerted opposition in numerous outlying districts. And the complexities and corruption of Afghan politics hardly helped. The Americans needed another way out.

In 2013, the Obama administration announced it was beginning direct talks with the Taliban. The process had begun three years earlier, when a sleek business jet descended from the snow-filled November sky and landed on one of Munich Airport's cleared runways. Avoiding customs, where the main passenger might have been arrested, the Taliban representative was slipped through the airport to a safe house in the city's suburb, where he met with German and American intelligence officers; there was more than a passing resemblance to Henry Kissinger's secret negotiations over Vietnam. Discussions had been on and off ever since the clandestine meet but were formalised in 2013. They appeared to offer the solution to the problem that Afghanistan had become. With bin Laden dead, if the Taliban would guarantee no longer to harbour terrorists, Western troops could depart Afghanistan, leaving the security issue in the hands of the Afghan government while claiming victory and vindication for the post-9/11 invasion. It was an alluring prize.

Obama, however, did not have time to conclude a careful negotiation before the USA swung into election mode once more, and the outgoing occupant of the Oval Office faced the prospect of becoming an increasing irrelevance to world events. It is quite likely Obama read every single Daily Brief prepared for him during his two terms in office; like Truman, he had always wanted to be informed. The man who followed him would adopt a rather different approach.

32

'Something Will Be Missed'

His flaxen comb-over flapping in the breeze, unbuttoned coat sitting stiffly on his shoulders, Donald Trump spoke to the jubilant crowd in front of the Capitol of a new future, a new America. He slammed subsidising the armies of other countries and defending others' borders and announced, 'a new decree to be heard in every city, in every foreign capital, and in every hall of power ... America first'.

Eleven presidents had come and gone since Harry Truman peered through his glasses at the first Daily Brief in 1946, and with every new occupant of the Oval Office, the CIA had changed its processes or the pages of the Brief itself. Each version of 'The Book', as it was often called in the halls of Langley, had been modified to mollify the men – and they had all been men – who wanted their intelligence one way or another. But for many in the Agency, Trump's arrival triggered unique trepidation. There were no sweltering five-hour sessions of the type Jimmy Carter had received as President-elect. Instead, the briefers were turned away, managing to sit down with Trump and his team only once or twice a week. Once he was across the threshold, however, there was a change of tune. As even a critical journalist admitted, four months into the Trump presidency, 'in a White House with few steadying mechanisms – and one led by a Washington neophyte who bristles at structure and protocol – the daily intelligence briefing is the rare constant'. Trump quickly grasped the worldly realities, remarking one morning as he walked into the Oval Office around 10.30 a.m., 'All right, what's the bad news this morning?' Typically, he would sit behind the Resolute desk clutching a Diet Coke, although it was immediately clear that the new Commander-in-Chief preferred speaking to reading or listening.

Trump's appointee as CIA Director – a former West Point graduate, aviation industry entrepreneur and burly, plain-speaking Kansas congressman named Mike Pompeo – sat in on most briefings, primarily because Trump needed someone he knew in the room; he trusted few people and listened to even fewer. The meetings would often overrun, backing up the day's diary, but there were problems from the outset. Trump did not like to read the President's Daily Brief itself and did not ask to see it. He also frequently questioned what he was told. For all his willingness to sit down every day, it was hard to know how informed the President's Daily Brief was leaving the 'First Customer'.

Many of the criticisms levelled at Trump over his treatment of intelligence have, in fact, also been levelled at other occupants of the Oval Office. One

President Trump in the Oval with National Security Advisor John Bolton,
CIA Director Gina Haspel and Director of National Intelligence Dan Coats (right),
January 2019.

derogatory *Washington Post* headline read, 'Breaking with tradition, Trump skips president's written intelligence report and relies on oral briefings'. But Eisenhower also refused anything other than an in-person briefing, Nixon refused to believe that what the CIA told him was fact, and Kennedy wanted intelligence documents on single sheets with as little text as possible and would not sit still long enough to be briefed. The crucial difference was that Eisenhower brought decades of experience at the highest ranks of the military, Nixon was watched over by the hawk-like Kissinger and his intimidating intellect, while Kennedy's advisors managed to prevail upon him to increase his focus on intelligence by creating a special new version of the Daily Brief. The only thing that seemed to work for Trump was pictures. '[He] would not read things, did not like to be read to, did not like to be talked to, but he would look at pictures', recalled one close contact of CIA Director Pompeo.

The CIA prepared 'killer graphics', as Pompeo once described them, to supplement the Daily Brief that Trump did not read. In April 2017, when reports emerged that Syrian leader Bashar al-Assad had deployed chemical weapons against civilians in the country's long-running civil war, it was pictures which prompted Trump to take action. The result was a mass cruise missile attack launched against targets in Syria. Speaking afterwards, Trump said, 'It crossed a lot of lines for me. When you kill innocent children, innocent babies, babies, little babies, with a chemical gas.' But although they found images could sway the President, the document remained unread, and discussions at daily briefings were routinely consumed by whatever was uppermost in the President's mind. Several months into his presidency, Trump made it clear he no longer wanted to receive a personal copy of the President's Daily Brief. Somehow the story leaked out. Leon Panetta, CIA Director in the middle of the Obama years, told *The Washington Post*, 'Something will be missed … [if] he hasn't taken the time to read that intel.'

★ ★ ★

On the morning of 8 April 2019, Staff Sergeant Christopher Slutman was travelling in convoy on the looping dirt road that ran along the perimeter of the largest US base in Afghanistan. On one side, the terrain levelled out, the only promontories the occasional rocky outcrop and the walls and wire and guard towers of Bagram Airbase; on the other towered a rising mass of snow-capped mountains, jutting into blue sky. In a few days, Slutman, and the whole of his 4th Marine Reserve Division, would be leaving; finally, they were going home. The 43-year-old was used to uniforms: when he wasn't wearing the smudgy camouflage of his combat utility uniform, he was a New York City fireman and had been for fifteen years. That Monday, the convoy was targeted by a roadside bomb. Slutman was killed, along with Marines Corporal Robert Hendriks (aged 25) and Sergeant Benjamin Hines (31). Photos appeared on the wires the next day of grey-clad Afghan Army soldiers combing the area and standing guard by the mangled remnants of a vehicle. The Taliban had taken another three American lives in Afghanistan, and the context of the attack was awkward for the White House.

Two months previously, the Trump administration had begun direct talks with Taliban representatives in Qatar, with the intention, as Trump phrased it, to 'bring our people back home'; by 2019, US forces had been in Afghanistan for eighteen years and Trump seemed determined not to let the war become longer than Vietnam. The targeting of Slutman's convoy by the Taliban was problematic timing, but negotiations continued and, on 29 February 2020, the US government and the Taliban signed a deal. US troops, and those of their allies, would leave within fourteen months, while the Taliban committed to never harbouring terrorists again. The Afghan government, which had been excluded from the direct talks, was left to thrash out its own agreement with the Taliban, knowing that it was only a matter of time before it was left to battle alone. Trump was subdued in his announcement of the deal, noting the 'hard journey' Afghanistan had been, but clearly delighted to be the Commander-in-Chief who was pulling Americans out after such a long war. But the world would soon discover that Panetta's prophecy had come true: something had been missed, and it connected the convoy on the road outside Bagram Airbase and the document the CIA prepared for the President each day.

The New York Times' headline on 27 June 2020 was explosive. On the front page of the paper, beneath an image of a Florida health worker testing children for a newly discovered deadly virus, it read, 'Russia Secretly Offered Afghan Militants Bounties to Kill US Troops'. The article revealed that US intelligence officials had concluded that Russian operatives were offering cash to Taliban militants for killing coalition soldiers in Afghanistan. Two days later, *The New York Times* claimed that the focus of investigation into the bounties was 'on an April 2019 car bombing that killed three Marines'. The paper quoted unnamed sources that, on 27 February 2020, Trump's Daily Brief reported the CIA's conclusion that a Russian military intelligence unit was paying Taliban fighters to murder Americans.

When the story broke, the White House insisted Trump was not aware. Pointedly avoiding mention of the Daily Brief, the Press Secretary insisted that Trump was not 'personally briefed on the matter'. Even Republicans in Congress were livid. Nebraska senator Ben Sasse, who would later vote to impeach Trump, demanded, 'Congress should be asking and looking at: No. 1, who knew what, when, and did the Commander-in-Chief know? And if not, how the hell not?' The simple answer, it seemed, was that the Commander-in-Chief did not know because the President was not reading the President's Daily Brief. The following day, Trump tweeted late at night, 'Intel[ligence Services] just reported to me that they did not find this info [about Russian bounties] credible, and therefore did not report it to me.' He added that reports were 'by the Fake News *New York Times* … wanting to make Republicans look bad!!!' Never had there been so public a debate about the contents of the President's Daily Brief.

One of the issues seemed to be that when it came to Russia, Trump had a blind spot. Widely reported allegations that state-run Russian disinformation units had interfered in the 2016 US presidential election had always been trashed by Trump himself. But in the summer of 2020, the cross-party US Senate Intelligence Committee's three-and-a-half-year investigation concluded, 'Moscow's intent was to harm the [Hillary] Clinton Campaign, tarnish an expected Clinton presidential administration, help the Trump Campaign … and undermine the U.S. democratic process.' The Senate Committee only reported in 2020, but the CIA was certain of it in January 2017 and Trump was informed of the fact before he was even inaugurated. In office, he warmly embraced Russian leader Vladimir Putin whenever they met, and the Trump White House seemed 'soft' on the intelligence activities of the country which had tried to disrupt the USA's democracy.

Trump was almost certainly not 'personally briefed' that Russian intelligence was paying Taliban fighters, or of any connection to the deaths of Slutman and his colleagues. If there was a sit-down intelligence briefing on 27 February 2020, perhaps Trump was more interested in other matters and talked away the time on them, or perhaps the briefers in the room side-stepped what would have likely been a confrontational conversation. What is clear is that Trump did not read that day's Daily Brief, along with many, many others.

By the time the forty-fifth President of the United States came to leave the White House, it was reported he had not had an intelligence briefing for weeks. The Trump years had been tumultuous and uniquely problematic for the intelligence operatives tasked with keeping the President informed, and the President's Daily Brief had been almost entirely unread throughout. In his pre-recorded farewell speech, Trump did not mention the CIA or Afghanistan, although he insisted 'we are bringing our soldiers home', a remark that carried weight, with the deadline for withdrawal from Afghanistan set for 1 May 2021, less than three months later. In his speech, Trump also added that he was 'especially proud to be the first President in decades who has started no new wars'.

Having avoided new conflicts overseas, Trump had campaigned in two elections that had driven divisions within the USA itself ever wider: by 2020, US politics seemed more like open warfare to outside observers. In leaving, Trump was pettily protective of the document he had declined to read, refusing to let his successor have access to the Daily Brief until just over a month before he was due to sit down in the Oval Office. For once, it did not matter as much as it might have: the newcomer was in fact a reassuringly familiar face for the CIA and a man who had read many a Daily Brief before. But within eight months, Joseph R. Biden Jr would find himself accused of presiding over a foreign policy disaster in Afghanistan that stemmed from a failure of intelligence.

'The Best Decision for America'

Two days after Joe Biden entered the Oval Office, *NBC News* ran a cheery website article announcing, 'Biden puts the "daily" back into administration's intelligence briefings'. A White House official was quoted as saying 'The President is receiving the PDB daily and intends to keep doing so.' The same day, Biden's new Press Secretary, in answer to a reporter's question on assessing potential foreign interference in the 2020 election, told journalists that Biden was 'issuing a tasking to the intelligence community for its full assessment [of Russian interference]', which included 'the alleged bounties on US soldiers in Afghanistan'. From the very start of the new administration, it was clear that Biden would not only commit to reading his own Daily Briefs, he would also happily highlight the intelligence shortcomings of his predecessor.

Before he was inaugurated, Biden had already chosen a new Director for the CIA. William J. Burns was a former diplomat and looked like one: he had wavy white hair and a neat moustache and was comfortable in a suit and in a crowd. Importantly, he had an unimpeachable record. Mike Pompeo, Trump's first appointment as CIA Director, had been succeeded by the first woman to hold the post permanently: Gina Haspel. She was one of the most experienced field officers ever to become Director and one of the most contentious appointments. She had been a Station Chief in Eastern Europe in the late 1990s, but it was the calmly spoken, smartly dressed operative's next posting that caused the controversy. In 2002, Haspel ran a CIA 'black site' in Thailand, where suspected al-Qaeda members were secretly extracted to. There they were physically and psychologically abused, and some were waterboarded, in an attempt to get the detainees to reveal information about planned terror attacks against the USA. For many Democrats, her nearly three-year stint as Director (after Pompeo moved to become Trump's Secretary of State) was an acute embarrassment. The appointment of William J. Burns could not come soon enough; he was in post eight weeks after Biden's inauguration.

Joseph Biden became the oldest US President in history when he was inaugurated in January 2021. It had been a race of elders, with Trump in his seventy-fourth year and Biden four years his senior, although the Democrat liked to portray that only one of them was a statesman. Biden hailed from a family of Pennsylvanian Catholics and had been elected one of the youngest ever senators at the age of 29. He spent the next three-and-a-half decades as a Democrat in the upper house of Congress, failing in a bid for the presidency in 1988 after a series of clumsy episodes in which he plagiarised passages of other politicians' speeches, including British Labour Party Leader Neil Kinnock. In 1988, he had seemed a promising, youthful candidate, albeit one devoid of his own ideas. The opportunity had appeared wide open for a Democrat after two terms of Reagan rule, but the then 44-year-old Biden was one of seven candidates squabbling over the nomination, and the Democrats handed the Republicans another term and George H.W. Bush the White House. After supporting Obama as Vice President, Biden decided against running in 2016, leaving the way open for Hillary Clinton as the Democrat heir apparent. It was four years of Trump that forced his hand. When he arrived in the Oval Office, he faced the ongoing crisis of the global Covid-19 pandemic. Afghanistan was therefore not his primary concern, but the upcoming departure date loomed large.

In April 2021, three months after entering office, Biden shunted Trump's May deadline. There were concerns that hitting the 1 May date was not logistically feasible, while the Afghan government had been unable to negotiate with the Taliban, who were continuing a campaign of violent attacks. The new date to have all US troops home was 11 September 2021, clearly chosen for its symbolism above all else. Even the delay of four months came with no guarantee of long-term stability once the foreign troops left. Speaking to a House of Representatives' committee in March, the Department of Defense's special inspector for Afghanistan said that without continued US military and financial support, the Kabul government might fall: 'The Afghan government would probably lose the capability of flying any of its aircraft within a few months and, to be quite blunt, would probably face collapse.'

★ ★ ★

On arriving in the White House, Biden had handed the post of National Security Advisor to a Yale graduate who had worked for Hillary Clinton's 2008 campaign, before becoming the youngest Director of Policy Planning in State Department history. Jake Sullivan had much in common with McGeorge Bundy. Although he had never crossed the political aisle to work for the other side, he had a rapier-like mind and an air of youthful confidence that was backed up with the hard knowledge of an operator twice his political age. Sharp featured, with a side-parting and suit, he can often be spotted in the background in images of Hillary Clinton prior to 2021. He went from Yale to Oxford to finishing second in the World Universities Debating Championship and applied a love of ideas to the role of NSA. He also had an unashamed love of his country that would have done a Republican proud: 'I was raised in Minnesota, the American Midwest,' he once told a journalist, 'in the era of ... the fall of the Berlin Wall. That gave me a deep, abiding belief in this country, in American leadership and capacity for good in the world.' Like several former NSAs, Sullivan took it upon himself to manage the President's daily intelligence, although he did not exclude the CIA, like Tony Lake had under Bill Clinton, or sit enthroned holding all the threads of information, as Kissinger had done during Nixon's years. Under Sullivan's watch, the President's Daily Brief was circulated more widely and more top officials were invited to take part in the daily intelligence briefings, where their expertise might be relevant. But despite all the experts in the room, no one seemed to have unequivocally informed the President that the writing was on the wall when it came to Afghanistan.

★ ★ ★

In May and June 2021, the Taliban stepped up their attacks. Fifty-five people, mostly female students, were killed in a car bomb and mortar attack on a school in Kabul in early May, and by late June the Taliban had control of 50 of Afghanistan's 370 districts, focusing their efforts on isolating regional capitals. In July, the last US forces departed Bagram Airbase in the dead of night, without notifying the Afghans, with the result that the base was ransacked by opportunistic looters. As the evacuation centred around Kabul, the Taliban besieged the cities of Herat, in the west, and Lashkargah and Kandahar, in the south. By 11 August, Reuters was quoting anonymous US officials who revealed intelligence assessments that Kabul might fall within ninety days. Five days later, the capital of Afghanistan was in the hands of the Taliban and US and UK forces were holding a narrow perimeter around Kabul Airport, as thousands of desperate locals tried to secure places on planes to flee. Suddenly the media were comparing the departure from Afghanistan to the humiliation in Saigon.

Biden holed up in Camp David as rumours swirled about what the President had known (or not known) when it came to intelligence assessments about the speed of the Taliban advance. His earlier words were coming back to haunt

US Marines embark Afghan evacuees onto a US Air Force plane.
Kabul Airport, 21 August 2021.

him. At a press conference on 8 July, a reporter had asked Biden, 'Do you see any parallels between this withdrawal and what happened in Vietnam?'

The President replied, 'None whatsoever ... There's gonna be no circumstance where you're gonna see people being lifted off the roof of an embassy.'

By mid-August, the media was showing on loop footage of US helicopters doing just that. There was even one image – of a chinook coming in to land on the flat-roofed Kabul Embassy building – that was so strikingly visually similar to one from Saigon in 1975 that the social networking platform Twitter was awash with posts of the two pictures side by side. With the evacuation still ongoing and the Taliban going door to door in Kabul searching for Afghans who had worked for the US-backed former government, *The New York Times* broke the news that 'classified assessment by the American spy agencies' had 'warned of the rapid collapse of the Afghan military'. At the very moment Biden was assuring the world Kabul was unlikely to fall, it was revealed the intelligence services were providing contrary assessments: that there was risk of a 'cascading collapse' that could reach Kabul.

★ ★ ★

We do not know what was written on the digital pages of Biden's Daily Briefs over that calamitous summer, but they would have included much about Afghanistan. The pictures have probably been toned down since the time of Trump, but any diagrams of the Taliban's sweeping advance should have been shocking. It was clear Kabul might fall and, if the leaks to the press can be believed, the CIA was stating as much, at least by July. US diplomats in Afghanistan even took matters into their own hands; twenty-three of them sent a collaborative, confidential memo to Biden's Secretary of State, Antony Blinken, warning the Taliban could swiftly take the capital.

In the past, telegrams from desperate diplomats had been heeded in the White House. When George Kennan dictated his missive from his Moscow sickbed in 1946, the mention of it in the Daily Brief had so intrigued Truman that he asked to read the full Long Telegram. The following year, when Mark F. Ethridge dispatched his message back to Washington that the fall of Greece was imminent, the warning made its way into the Daily Brief and Truman appeared to react within days. The message from the Kabul Embassy seventy-four years later was a formal 'dissent cable' – designed to allow diplomats to send bad news without fear of repercussions – but it is claimed it never reached Biden. The Brief writers may not have been aware of it, or it may have been assumed that such a significant intervention would obviously have made its way from the State Department in-tray to the desk in the Oval Office. But even without the warnings from diplomats, the CIA had enough easy evidence to hand as the Taliban swept towards Kabul.

However, Biden defiantly painted the intelligence as wrong. In a stumbling television interview in late August 2021, the President insisted, 'Number one, as you know, the intelligence community did not say back in June or July that, in fact, this was gonna collapse like it did.' When pressed by his interviewer, he admitted intelligence had warned the Taliban could take over, 'But not this quickly. Not even close.'

The CIA's Counterterrorism Chief for South and Southwest Asia until 2019 hit back in a published article soon afterwards, stating, 'The decision Trump made, and Biden ratified, to rapidly withdraw U.S. forces [from Afghanistan] came despite warnings projecting the outcome we're now witnessing.' Dismissing that it was a debate about dates – how long Kabul might hold out – he said, 'Ultimately, it was assessed, Afghan forces might capitulate in days under the circumstances we witnessed, in projections highlighted to Trump officials and future Biden officials alike.' The strong suggestion from the CIA was that the intelligence Biden received – and surely some in his Daily Briefs – had been different to what the President now claimed.

On the afternoon of 30 August, the last US military plane left Afghan airspace. It had taken off from Kabul Airport at midnight local time, with the acting US Ambassador to Afghanistan and the commander of the 82nd Airborne, which had been sent to oversee the withdrawal, being the two last men to step on the C-17's ramp. An aide brought a note to the Oval Office, where Biden was in a late afternoon meeting. The President cleared the room, except for Sullivan and Secretary of State Blinken. He then asked the two men to join him in his private dining room, where he telephoned the Defense Secretary to confirm the news.

In an address to the American people the following day, Biden asserted that the withdrawal was the 'best decision for America'. He called the operation 'one of the biggest air lifts in history', an apparent comparison to the huge operation in Berlin about which Truman had received detailed, daily updates in his Brief. We are unlikely ever to know if Biden received similar, detailed statistics; perhaps instead of noting the number and type of food stocks as the CIA had done for Truman over Berlin, Biden was updated daily on the number of Afghan interpreters or US-connected officials extracted, and those who were likely to be left behind.

Biden appeared tone deaf to the reality of what had taken place, referring to the evacuation as an 'extraordinary success' and painting it as a choice between leaving or 'extend[ing] this forever war'. It was an incongruous address, delivered at the very moment there were calls in the press for Sullivan to resign as NSA for the failure of foresight. In an echo of the sentiments of previous presidents regarding Vietnam, Biden noted he was the fourth Commander-in-Chief who had faced Afghanistan, insisting, 'I refuse to send another generation of America's sons and daughters to fight a war that should have ended long ago.'

Events in Afghanistan had followed a similar trajectory to Vietnam: initially secret negotiations with an ideological enemy, a phased military withdrawal and eventual abandonment of a former ally to their fate. As it had been in 1975, it was hard to escape the impression that what the world was witnessing in Afghanistan was a superpower in full retreat. Biden's treatment of his intelligence also raises the question of whether, privately, there was a Kissinger-style policy of a 'healthy interval' – one not openly acknowledged, but which is perhaps supported by the apparent disregarding of intelligence warnings of the impending fall of Kabul.

There was a final act in the shadows, too, away from the roar of aircraft engines and shouting soldiers. Four days before Biden announced the end of US involvement in Afghanistan, CIA Director William Burns travelled the opposite way to the throng of would-be refugees, heading from Kabul Airport into the city to meet with one of the Taliban's senior representatives. There has been no official comment on the meeting, but in the changed world it seemed a long time since George W. Bush had condemned the Taliban for 'brutalising' the Afghan people. Now their leaders were receiving personal visits from the head of the CIA.

Biden had seemed unheeding to the information he was receiving about Afghanistan. Perhaps it suited the President not to publicly know what his intelligence services felt he should know, although there remains the lingering question whether those in the room during meetings that summer tried to make sure the President comprehended how badly things might go wrong, or how clearly it was spelled out in writing in the Brief itself. The fact that the unravelling happened so soon was a chastening blow for Biden's popularity and the perception of the USA on the world's stage. So much so that the Biden administration was more comfortable blaming an intelligence failure (and the Afghans) than taking responsibility. If indeed Biden's Daily Brief warned that the Taliban might imminently capture Kabul, it was a warning the President chose to ignore, because it was politically inconvenient.

Epilogue

Just before 1 p.m. on Wednesday, 16 September 2015, a crowd gathered at the Lyndon Baines Johnson Presidential Library in Austin, Texas. Escaping the 30°C outside heat for the air conditioning of the library's auditorium, they sat and waited expectantly. They were there to see secrets revealed. The event marked the release of the Daily Briefs from the Kennedy and Johnson years, including the ones from the Cuban Missile Crisis and the intelligence Johnson received as he plunged the USA ever deeper into the quagmire of Vietnam.

CIA Director John Brennan was the keynote speaker. After being introduced, he strode to a lectern, straightened his broad shoulders and launched into his prepared speech. 'For students of history,' he said, 'the declassified Briefs will lend insight into why a President chooses one path over another.' The suggestion was that, now we know what presidents knew, it will be clear why they did what they did. In a few cases, that has proved correct: Truman aided Greece seemingly at least partly because his Daily Brief warned the country would collapse and fall to Communism.

However, tracing cause and effect is complicated, and presidents have always received more intelligence than just what is in their Daily Briefs. Even when there has been specific intelligence, it has proved possible for presidents to take insufficient action, as was the case with Bush and warnings ahead of 9/11, or to ignore the intelligence completely because it was not the answer they wished to hear, as Biden seemingly did with Afghanistan. Often what the Briefs have not contained has been as historically influential, from the deliberate avoidance of comments on clandestine CIA operations, to the great gaping gap of knowledge on the Soviet missile programme that spurred Eisenhower into the U-2 flights over the Soviet Union.

Brennan concluded in his 2015 address, 'Today, the PDB is so vital to the White House, one wonders how they could operate without it.' It has proved a largely true statement, although the following year, a President was elected who often attempted to do just that. The document itself has gone from a binder to an iPad, but it still relies on each President making time, or being persuaded to make time, to read it. For CIA Directors, getting the Brief in front of every President in a context in which they are willing to listen has proved an ongoing challenge. As Truman described it, it is 'information of vital importance' – despite the numerous times the CIA analysts have been wrong – and every one of the USA's leaders still has the Agency to thank for ensuring that they are 'briefed every day on all the world'. The intelligence included in the President's Daily Brief, and what is missing, still shapes history.

A selection of declassified Kennedy and Johnson Daily Briefs. The open page covers Central America, noting, 'Colombia is coming in for its share of trouble from two brands of Communist guerrillas.' A paragraph from the top item on Venezuela is redacted.

Chapter Notes

The President's Daily Brief or 'PDB' has been through many iterations and several name changes. President Truman first received a 'Daily Summary' in 1946, but as the document evolved it was retitled, first as the 'Current Intelligence Bulletin' and then as the 'Central Intelligence Bulletin'. President Kennedy's revised version was known as the 'President's Intelligence Checklist', which eventually morphed into the 'President's Daily Brief'. For the sake of simplicity, every version of the document has been described in the text as the 'Daily Brief', although the specific intelligence reports are referenced by their official names below. The entire declassified collection is available to view on the Central Intelligence Agency Reading Room website.

Introduction

News of the world's first electronic computer was carried in *The New York Times* on 15 February 1946 in an article headed, 'Electronic Computer Flashes Answers, May Speed Engineering. NEW ALL ELECTRONIC COMPUTER AND ITS INVENTORS.' Truman's first Daily Summary was the same day and can be found in the Daily Summary Collection in the CIA's online library.

1 Long Telegrams

Kennan's dispatch of the 'Long Telegram' is recounted in his account of the first half of his career: *Memoirs, 1925–1950* (Random House, 1988).

The CIA's own biography of Souers describes Truman's light-heartedness at the appointment of the first Director of Intelligence.

The first meeting of the National Intelligence Authority took place on 5 February 1946, where Souers insisted the President did not want the information in the Briefs interpreted. The minutes of the meeting can be found in *Foreign Relations of the United States, 1945–1950: Emergence of the Intelligence Establishment* (Government Printing Office, 1996). Souers' comments on the interpretation of intelligence were made in a letter to Clark Clifford, one of Truman's aides, in December 1945.

Anthony Eden recounted the Washington representative's views of Truman at Roosevelt's funeral in *The Reckoning* (Cassell, 1965).

It was Winston Churchill who credited Truman with 'obvious power of decision' in his memoirs, *Triumph and Tragedy: The Second World War*, Volume 6 (Rosetta Books, 2014).

Truman mentioned his efforts to get abreast of his briefs in *Memoirs by Harry S. Truman: Year of Decisions* (The New American Library, 1955).

Kennan's second message on 'the lifeblood' of the Soviet political system was quoted in the 21 March Daily Summary. The 'Long Telegram' is widely available both in printed sourcebooks on the Cold War and also on the digital archive of the Wilson Center.

Churchill's letter to Truman was dated 29 January 1946, and the text is printed in Martin Gilbert's *Never Despair, Winston S. Churchill 1945–1965* (Random House, 1988).

The *Chicago Sun*'s criticism ran under the headline 'Churchill's call for World Domination' on 6 March 1946, with *The Wall Street Journal*'s editorial published the same day. The Soviet response to Churchill's speech was reported to Truman in his 12 March 1946 Daily Summary.

Journalist Arthur Krock revealed the existence of the Daily Briefs in his *New York Times* article, 'The President's Daily Newspaper' on 16 July 1946.

2 Helping Friends

Alistair Cooke's first *Letter from America* was broadcast on 24 March 1946. It would go on to become the longest-running radio speech programme in history, continuing for fifty-eight years.

Comments on the state of readiness for war of Soviet troops in Korea appeared in the 6 March 1946 Daily Summary, with notes on Soviet rumours of a US departure within three years in the 10 August 1946 Summary.

Lieutenant General John Reed Hodge's warning that remaining in Korea would lead to war was printed in the 29 April Daily Summary, with his warning of an invasion by a Soviet-trained Korean army appearing on 29 October 1946. He sent repeated similar warnings. The First World War veteran had led US soldiers in the brutal island-hopping battles across the Pacific, finally landing his troops at Incheon in September 1945.

Churchill's animal analogy of the two great powers was made at the Tehran Conference in late 1943 and included the observation that Britain was 'a very small country' in comparison.

Reports of a twelve-year plan for the 'complete communization' of Western Europe appeared in Truman's Daily Summary on 7 August 1946, information shared by the British.

Soviet 'sensitivities' to being underestimated were noted on 7 June 1946; a week later, on 15 July, reports arrived from Berlin of the sudden change in attitude on the part of Soviet officials. The slogans scrawled on the side of Soviet tanks were spotted in the autumn, being noted in Truman's Summary on 16 November.

Notes on Ural tank factory production reached Truman on 28 August, including the comment that the armour factory at Nizhnii-Tagil was producing thirty-five tanks a day. On 7 September, Soviet total ground force strength was assessed at 3.1 million men.

Truman's 26 September 1946 diary entry was published in *Off the Record: The Private Papers of Harry S. Truman*, ed. Robert H. Ferrell (Harper & Row, 1980).

Ambassador MacVeagh's note on Greece was printed in the 30 July 1946 Daily Summary. His follow-up on the 'serious fighting' involving UK forces appeared on 5 August.

Secretary of State James F. Byrnes' proposal of 'helping our friends in every way' reached the President on 26 September 1946.

The message warning of Greece's 'imminent fall' was in Truman's 18 February 1947 Daily Summary. Mark F. Ethridge's recollections of his 1947 visit to Greece, composing the telegram at the American Embassy in Athens and the response to the announcement of the Truman doctrine were recalled in a 1974 interview with Richard D. McKinzie. The interview is now held in the oral history collections of the Truman Library.

A copy of Truman's speech before the joint session of Congress on 12 March 1947 is available online via the Yale Avalon Project. While it became later known as 'the Truman doctrine' it was not titled when it was proposed.

Truman's diary entry on the intelligence reports on 'what goes on all around the world' was written on 20 February 1952.

3 Winged Angels

The first warning of the Berlin Blockade, which the CIA wrongly interpreted as a Soviet plan to create an 'emergency' to force discussions, can be found in Truman's 14 June 1948 Daily Summary.

George C. Marshall's own insistence that the recovery was directed against poverty was made in a speech at Harvard University on 5 June 1947. Seven years later, the Marshall Plan earned him the Nobel Peace Prize.

Nikolai Novikov's message to Moscow on the nature of the Marshall Plan was sent on 9 June 1947. It can be found in the Woodrow Wilson International Centre publication, 'New evidence on the rejection of the Marshall Plan, 1947' by Scott D. Parish (Woodrow Wilson International Centre for Scholars, 1994).

The CIA's use of Marshall Plan funds is detailed in Sallie Pisani's *The CIA and the Marshall Plan* (University of Kansas Press, 1991).

The definition of current intelligence as information of 'immediate interest and value' was made in the National Security Council's (NSC) 13 January 1948 Intelligence Directive No. 3, entitled 'Coordination of Intelligence Production'. The document is quoted in the CIA publication, *The First 'First Customer'* (2018).

The CIA's 'Review of the World Situation as it Relates to the Security of the United States' was published on 26 September 1947. A copy is available online via the Truman Library.

Berlin Governor Frank Howley's delight at the sight of the first planes is retold in his memoir, *Berlin Command* (G. Putnam & Sons, 1950).

The New York Times' wary analysis of the showdown in Berlin appeared in the 27 June 1948 edition.

The CIA's note that Berliners would support the Western powers 'unless it becomes obvious that the US can no longer feed the Germans' was appended to the 26 June 1948 Daily Summary item on Germany and the Berlin situation.

Truman's 19 July 1948 diary entry can be found in *Off The Record: The Private Papers of Harry S. Truman*, ed. Robert H. Ferrell (Harper & Row, 1980).

The 'critical period' in the airlift was identified as August and September in Truman's 24 July Daily Summary.

The US Embassy in Moscow reported Moscow's apparent complete unwillingness to negotiate in the 12 January 1949 Daily Summary. It also reported on the cementing of Soviet influence over eastern Germany, something the Berlin Ambassador had highlighted on 26 November 1948, describing the actions as 'Soviet efforts to split Berlin'.

Truman's comment on the Berlin Airlift as a 'symbol' of the USA's dedication to the cause of freedom came in his memoir, *Years of Trial and Hope*, Volume II (Doubleday, 1956).

4 Genbaku

Dr Terufumi Sasaki's story appeared in John Hersey's article, 'Hiroshima', in the 31 August 1946 issue of *The New Yorker* magazine.

Truman's note on his decision to use the bomb was made in his diary on 25 July 1945. Truman's diaries are held in the archives of the Harry S. Truman Library and Museum.

Truman's criticism of 'depriving' the USA of nuclear assets was voiced in his memoirs. His comment about the USA not 'throwing away the gun' was made in a letter to Bernard Baruch – US representative to the United Nations Atomic Energy Agency Commission – on 10 July 1946.

The reports of the pilot appeared in the 17 September 1946 Daily Summary. Earlier rumours of bomb tests in Kazakhstan were in the 29 July Daily Summary.

The warning about Frédéric Joliot-Curie came in the 7 May 1949 Daily Summary. As it transpired, he was fired by the French and (as expected) stayed in France.

A detailed account of the efforts to catch up with the US atomic weapon programme can be found in David Holloway's *Stalin and The Bomb: The Soviet Union and Atomic Energy, 1939–1956* (Yale University Press, 1996).

Hillenkoetter delivered his memo to Truman on 9 September 1949. It was released in September 2019 and can be viewed on the National Security Archive website. For a narrative of the impact of the Soviet bomb, see Michael D. Gordin's *Red Cloud at Dawn: Truman, Stalin and the end of the Atomic Monopoly* (Picador, 2010).

Hillenkoetter sent his first memo to Truman on 6 July 1948, a copy of which can be viewed on the National Security Archive's website titled 'Director of Central Intelligence R.H. Hillenkoetter, memorandum to the President, "Estimate of the Status of the Russian Atomic Energy Project", 6 July 1948, Top Secret'. The CIA's Nuclear Energy Branch confirmed there had been no change in that assessment in a 1 July 1949 report, 'Status of the USSR Atomic Energy Project'.

The Soviet Union did not develop the capacity to assess atomic debris through air sampling until six years later. In a Brief prepared for President Eisenhower (Current Intelligence Bulletin, 5 March 1955), the movements of a specialist unit of Soviet Tu-4 aircraft – the Poltava division – were analysed in detail. It had been sent to China when the USA was conducting tests in 1954 and that autumn had been posted to Turkestan, in Kazakhstan, where Soviet atom bomb tests took place.

The update from the US Embassy in Moscow in the 30 September Daily Summary was sound intelligence, but covered the giant gaping hole in information: the US spies who pretended to be diplomats in the Soviet capital had, to a man, also failed to pick up on news of the test.

5 A Re-Examination

Truman's 31 January 1950 directive is reprinted at the top of the declassified NSC-68 report, officially titled 'United States Objectives and Programs for National Security', dated 14 April 1950. The text is available on the History and Public Policy Program Digital Archive, US National Archives (Wilson Center).

The Daily Summary report on Soviet atomic capabilities by 1952 was an assessment from the Belgian General Staff printed on 7 October 1949, who were now working on the assumption that the Soviets would be happy to start a war by that date.

The NSC met to consider the report on 20 April 1950. Minutes of the fifty-fifth meeting are held at the Harry S. Truman Library.

Truman recounted how he found out about the start of the Korean War – and his musings on the flight back to Washington – in the second volume of his memoirs. His recollection differs slightly from the narrative in David McCullough's prize-winning biography, *Truman* (Simon & Schuster, 2003).

The Moscow Embassy's unequivocal message on the Korean situation was printed in Truman's 25 June 1950 Daily Summary.

Truman's concern over 'a general Asiatic war' was confided in his diary on 30 June 1950. The internationalist nature of the response was already becoming evident, as the UK, Australia, Canada and the Netherlands were already providing ships.

Acheson was speaking at a meeting of US policy makers at a 'Princeton Seminar' held on 15–16 May 1954. Records of the meetings are contained in the Harry S. Truman Library's Acheson Papers.

Truman finally approved NSC-68 as the policy approach at the sixty-eighth meeting of the NSC on 30 September 1950.

6 Information of Vital Importance

Truman's comments on Korea being a 'police action' were made at a press conference on 29 June 1950. The text of the question and answer session with reporters is available online via the American Presidency Project.

The performance of South Korean troops was the subject of Truman's 1 July 1950 Daily Summary. It was suggested in the same report that if the North Koreans got across the Han River, 'a rout of the defenders would be a prospect'.

B-29s had been deployed to the UK during the Berlin Airlift as a warning shot to the Soviet Union, but the aircraft were in fact not nuclear capable, although the Soviets mistakenly assumed they were.

The smoke from the Soviet Embassy in Havana was reported in the 8 July 1950 Daily Summary.

The warning of the capacity of the Chinese to influence the Korean conflict came in the 3 October 1950 Daily Summary. Two days later (5 October Daily Summary) it was reported that 20,000–30,000 Chinese-trained troops of Korean origin were already fighting for the North Korean Army.

The CIA's insistence that China would not intervene in Korea came in the 30 and 31 October Daily Summaries. Six weeks after insisting the Chinese Communists would not intervene, the analysts found themselves eating their words. The rationale for the assertion in the 16 October Daily Summary was repeated four days later, with the claim that neither the Soviet Union nor China was 'considered at this time to be willing to assume the increased risk of precipitating a third World War which would result from direct Chinese Communist intervention in Korea'.

The reports of 'unknown jet fighters' – MiG-15 interceptors that outclassed all Western aircraft in the theatre at the time – were in the 2 November 1950 Daily Summary.

The accusation that General MacArthur had walked 'into a baited trap' appeared in Truman's 9 December 1950 Daily Summary.

Criticism of the Daily Summary and its development into the Current Intelligence Bulletin (CIB) is narrated in *The First 'First Customer': Harry Truman*, an internal CIA summary of intelligence development released in 2018.

Smith's letter to Truman outlining the contents of the new Daily Brief, which was now called the CIB, was enclosed with the revised document on 28 February 1951. Truman's positive feedback was sent on 8 March. The text of both letters is available to view on the State Department historical website. The inclusion of 'live' intelligence in the CIB has encouraged more aggressive redacting of their contents than with the Daily Summaries. Often, whole sections of CIBs are whited out, although the usual practice in declassifying has been to remove the hard intelligence itself but leave the CIA assessment intact. At times, analysis therefore relies on guesswork on the part of the historian to, quite literally, fill in the blanks.

The assessment on Mao and rumours of a coup in Panama appeared in the 8 March 1951 CIB.

Truman's speech to CIA officers took place on 21 November 1952 and is quoted in the CIA's internal history, *The CIA under Truman*.

Truman's letter to 'Ike' was dated 16 April 1952 and was published in *Off The Record: The Private Papers of Harry S. Truman*.

Eisenhower's response to his pre-election briefings from the CIA is narrated in the CIA's own record, *Keeping the President Informed: Current Intelligence Support for the White House* (CIA, 1973).

The text of Truman's farewell address to the American people on 15 January 1953 is available online through the American Presidency Project.

7 Briefing the Commander-in-Chief

Sputnik was the front-page article in *The New York Times* on 5 October 1953.

The launch was reported in Eisenhower's CIB on 5 October 1957, with 'additional data' included in the report on 6 October and the Chinese reaction recorded two days later.

The assessment of Soviet Premier Malenkov's speech was published in the 9 August 1953 CIB.

The lament from the CIA Office of Current Intelligence (OCI) on the lack of interest in the CIB on the part of the President is revealed in G. Fred Albrecht's internal 1967 CIA publication, *A History of the Current Intelligence Bulletin*. Further details of the experience of Brief-writing for the Eisenhower administration can be found in the CIA's report, *In the Military Style: Dwight Eisenhower* (undated), declassified 14 March 2019.

The first image in the Briefs was in Eisenhower's 22 February 1954 CIB. It showed French and Viet Minh positions near Dien Bien Phu.

The OCI Director's quote on the new Brief, which landed on 14 January 1958, is published in G. Fred Albrecht's internal 1967 CIA publication, *A History of the Current Intelligence Bulletin*.

The admission that the change to the CIB made no difference to the lack of interest from the President, and notes on NSC Briefing practices, are contained in *In the Military Style: Dwight Eisenhower*. It notes, 'No comments about the CIB from Eisenhower or White House principals have been recorded.'

Details of the practice of pre-NSC meeting briefings are contained in the CIA's 1973 publication, *Keeping the President Informed: Current Intelligence for the White House*. Most of the recollections come from the then Director of the OCI, Huntington Denton Sheldon.

8 Reconnaissance

Hitler watched the film of the A-4 rocket launch on 7 June 1943, an event recounted by Albert Speer in his memoirs, *Inside the Third Reich* (Macmillan, 1970).

The update on the Soviet rocket development at Peenemünde was included in Truman's 12 and 14 August 1946 Daily Summaries.

Dulles' 'Reconnaissance' memorandum of 24 November 1954 was declassified in 2002. The requested figure for the aircraft project is redacted, but it is visible on the authorisation memo by Andrew Goodpaster produced later in the same day, titled 'MEMORANDUM OF CONFERENCE WITH THE PRESIDENT 0810 24 November 1954'. Both memorandums are available on the CIA's online Reading Room.

Details of the camera to be carried by the U-2 were printed in the CIA's 7 January 1955 project 'AQUATONE' outline memo, which was declassified in 2011.

Dulles' memoirs were published in the early 1960s and were mostly a deliberately vague, wider discussion of the nature and gathering of intelligence, which was combined with a hugely restrained account of his own career. See *The Craft of Intelligence* by Allen Dulles (Harper & Row, 1963).

The report on the Soviet Ministry of General Machine Building – assumed to be a front for a new missile programme – appeared in the 6 April 1955 CIB.

Details of the potential interception of the missing RB-47 over Kamchatka were printed in the 19 April 1955 CIB. The revelation that it was shot down did not come until 1993, during an exchange between US and Soviet members of the Joint Commission of POW/MIAs, when Soviet representatives confirmed they had downed the aircraft thirty-eight years previously. The list of the thirteen downed reconnaissance aircraft can be found in the National Security Agency's *Cryptologic Quarterly*, Spring 1993 edition, 'Maybe You Had To Be There: The SIGINT on Thirteen Soviet Shootdowns of U.S. Reconnaissance Aircraft' by Michael L. Peterson.

The story of the U-2 flights over Kazakhstan is revealed in the CIA's internal history, *The Central Intelligence Agency and Overhead Reconnaissance: The U-2 and OXCART Programmes, 1954–1974* by Gregory W. Pedlow and Donald E. Welzenbach (1992). It was released to the public in 2011, although sections remain redacted.

The successful Soviet ICBM test took place on 26 August 1957 and was covered in detail in the 28 August 1957 CIB. The 2011 declassified version of the 28 August CIB, released as part of a CIA document collection on the 'Missile Gap', had the first item redacted. The 2019 release includes the first item, which is titled 'Evaluation of the Soviet announcement of successful ICBM test'.

Special Intelligence Estimate 11-10-57, entitled 'The Soviet ICBM Program', was published on 10 December 1957.

9 'There was Created a Myth'

McElroy's comments during his interrogation by the Senate subcommittee were in fact quite nuanced and highlighted US missile developments and military improvements, but that was not what made the headlines. The story ran in *Time* magazine on Monday, 9 February 1959, under the heading, 'DEFENSE: What about the missile gap?'

The 10 May 1960 Central Intelligence Bulletin shared details of the creation of a new 'missile command'. The intelligence was mostly quoting Soviet speeches mentioning it, with some speculation that the new man in charge might have attended the known ICBM launches the previous year. In the final line, it was noted that active communications were still coming from the 'suspected' ballistic missile division under the control of the Soviet 5th Long Range Air Force group. The first comment on the U-2 incident appeared the following day.

The Central Intelligence Bulletin's reports on the U-2 were non-existent until 11 May. On 16 May, the Brief noted that the 'U-2 incident' was potential ammunition for those trying to critique Khrushchev as 'soft' on capitalists if he continued with discussions with Western leaders at the planned Paris conference. On 17 May, there was a chronology of 'Communist exploitation of the U-2 incident', which listed events to date. On subsequent days the Brief was primarily concerned with the international reaction in the context of the Paris Summit. Another ICBM launch from Tyuratam was reported in the 6 June Brief.

The laboured investigations of the Guided Missiles and Astronautics Intelligence Committee were published in the paper, 'Report of the GMAIC Deployment Working Group, "Soviet Surface to Surface Missile Deployment"', 1 September 1960, quoted in the CIA publication, *Closing the Missile Gap* by Leonard F. Parkinson and Logan H. Potter (undated), declassified 2011.

Penkovsky's letter was actually written in July 1960, but not passed on until a month later. The translated version is available as part of the CIA's declassified collection entitled 'Lt. Col. Oleg Penkovsky: Western Spy in Soviet GRU', available in the CIA online Reading Room. His story is detailed in Jerrold Schecter's *The Spy Who Saved the World* (C. Scribner & Sons, 1992).

Eisenhower's memoirs, *Waging Peace, 1956–1961: The White House Years*, were published by Doubleday in 1965. In his memoirs, the President also recounted his decision to 'weather the storm' over the U-2 incident.

The 'missile gap' was a topic of the fourth televised debate of the 1960 campaign which took place on 21 October. The full transcript of all the presidential debates is available online on the website of the Commission on Presidential Debates.

The conversation between Secretary McNamara and JFK was recounted by Director of the John F. Kennedy Presidential Library and Museum, Tom Putnam, at an event to mark the fiftieth anniversary of the missile gap controversy in April 2018. The Oval Office audio recording can be heard on the YouTube video of the event, available on the JFK Library channel, dated 11 April 2018.

10 'The CIA is the Place I Have to Go'

The New York Times article on 7 April 1961 was in fact a restrained version of what the paper was aware of. Correspondent Tad Szulc had uncovered far more detail than was printed, including that the invasion was imminent and that it was backed by the CIA.

Kennedy's reaction to the Bay of Pigs and his determination to be more involved in future events were shared with White House Counsel, Clark M. Clifford, and recorded in his memoir, *Counsel to the President: A Memoir* (Random House, 1991).

Kennedy met with senior aides to discuss the Cuba invasion plans on 8 February 1961. The memorandum of the meeting was declassified in 1998 and is available through the John F. Kennedy Presidential Library website.

Bundy penned his blunt memo to Kennedy on 16 May 1961. The note is recorded in Volume XXV of *The Foreign Relations of the United States, 1961–1963*, labelled 'Memorandum from the President's Special Assistant for National Security Affairs (Bundy) to President Kennedy', which is available on the State Department's website of the Office for the Historian.

Clifton's meeting with the two CIA analysts is recounted in David Priess' *The President's Book of Secrets: The Untold Story of Intelligence Briefings to America's Presidents from Kennedy to Obama* (Public Affairs, 2016), which also reports the enthusiasm Kennedy's interest in the document created in the team who wrote it.

Jackie Kennedy's note to her husband was found between the pages of a May 1963 President's Intelligence Checklist (PIC).

The 17 June Central Intelligence Bulletin and 17 June PIC are both available to view on the CIA Reading Room website. The huge popularity of the Central Intelligence Checklist, derived in part from the massive circulation the document had developed during the Eisenhower years, meant that it was carried on as a daily intelligence update. However, the new 'Daily Brief', with its close-knit circulation and additional information, began to diverge significantly.

The 17 June report of Soviet-made MiGs being shipped to Cuba was confirmed in the next PIC (19 June 1961), when aerial photographs of a San Antonio airfield revealed a partially assembled MiG-17.

11 Soviet Merchant Ships

The comment on Soviet merchant ships was note 'D' on the final page of the 4 August 1962 PIC. Further details of Soviet shipments appeared on 9 August.

The Phase One report on Operation Mongoose was dated 25 July 1962 and is available as part of the collection of documents relating to Operation Mongoose held by the National Security Archive of the George Washington University.

State Department Legal Advisor Abram Charles' memo on 'Cuban Sugar' was sent in August 1962. It is also part of the George Washington University Mongoose papers collection.

The 24 August 1962 exiles' attack on the Havana hotel was covered in Kennedy's 31 August PIC.

The intelligence supplied by staff from the UK Embassy in Havana was in Kennedy's 23 August PIC.

The 29 August PIC stated there was 'no sign of a let-up' in shipments, which in the previous six weeks had totalled eighty voyages to Cuba by Cuban vessels, with a further twenty to thirty-five other ships under 'Communist Charter'.

The map of SAM sites on Cuba was printed in the PIC on 6 September 1962, with the commentary of missiles that had shot down Powers' U-2 appearing the next day.

The mention of submarine escorts for a Soviet convoy 700 miles out of Cuba came in the 21 September PIC. However, it was noted, 'A check by one of our navy aircraft verified the presence of five Soviet merchantmen in the area, but say no submarines.'

The downgrading of one SA-2 site appeared in the 24 September PIC, with the addition of two more on 28 September.

Kennedy's 9 October PIC noted the closing of the gaps in anti-aircraft missile coverage over Cuba. The figure of twenty sites potentially operational was included the following day.

Details of the Special Group Augmented meeting on 9 October can be found in Max Holland's CIA publication, 'The "Photo Gap" that Delayed Discovery of Missiles', *Studies in Intelligence*, Vol. 49, No. 4 (2005).

Bundy's decision not to tell Kennedy immediately about the discovery of nuclear missiles on Cuba has since been criticised. He justified it in a memo to Kennedy, dated 4 March 1963, which he included in full in his later book, *Danger and Survival: Choices about the Bomb in the First Fifty Years* (Vintage, 1990).

12 Offensive Weapons

Bundy recounted giving Kennedy the news on the morning of Tuesday, 16 October, in his book *Danger and Survival*.

The first official memo on the Cuban Missile Crisis was published in 1992 as part of the declassified CIA collection, 'CIA Documents on the Cuban Missile Crisis'. The memo is dated 16 October and titled 'Probable Soviet MRBM Sites in Cuba'.

The transcripts of the audio recordings of the 11.30 a.m. and 6.30 p.m. meetings at the White House on 16 October are available on the State Department's online archive under *Foreign Relations of the United States, 1961–1963*, Volume XI: *Cuban Missile Crisis and Aftermath*, Documents 18 and 21.

The Vienna 1961 summit and Khrushchev's evisceration of Kennedy are detailed in Frederick Kempe's book, *Berlin 1961: Kennedy, Khrushchev, and the Most Dangerous Place on Earth* (Penguin, 2012).

Kennedy's famous 22 October address is available from multiple channels on YouTube and the transcript is published online by the JFK Library.

The full headline of *The New York Times* Late City edition on 22 October read: 'U.S. IMPOSES ARMS BLOCKADE ON CUBA ON FINDING OFFENSIVE-MISSILE SITES; KENNEDY READY FOR SOVIET SHOWDOWN'.

Kennedy's 22 October letter to Khrushchev can be viewed online on the JFK Library resource collection for '13 Days In October'.

13 Men of Letters

The declassified version of the 23 October PIC does not include the document covering the CIA's review of the worldwide reaction to Kennedy's speech, which was separate to the Checklist itself.

Kennedy's 24 October PIC reported the number of MRBM sites unchanged and noted the efforts to camouflage the sites.

Khrushchev's 24 October letter is open to view as part of the JFK Library's online collection on the Cuban Missile Crisis.

The Soviet premier's admission of his aim to 'frighten' the Americans is narrated in Michael Dobbs' popular history of the crisis: *One Minute to Midnight* (Knopf, Doubleday, 2008).

CIA Deputy Director Marshall Carter's biography is outlined in his own words in the US Senate Committee on Armed Services nomination hearing prior to his appointment, which took place on 29 March 1962. The transcript of the hearing was declassified by the CIA in 2006. The senator who described him as 'a man that people trust' was Republican Leverett Saltonstall.

Director McCone's warning that Soviet SAMs might be used to hide the deployment of nuclear missiles was sent to Deputy Director Carter on 16 September 1962. His message was released in 1992 as part of the CIA collection, 'CIA Documents on the Cuban Missile Crisis, 1962, volume 10, Cuba, January 1961–September 1962'.

The CIA analyst's jibe that the Director was not occupying himself in the traditional manner while on honeymoon is recounted in the Centre for the Study of Intelligence's two-part biographical on McCone: *John McCone as Director of Intelligence 1961–1965* by David Robarge, CIA History Staff. The short book was released publicly, with some redactions, in 2015.

The Director's message to Kennedy warning that the USA should not create its own 'Pearl Harbor moment' was sent to the President on 17 October and was entitled 'Memorandum for Discussion'. The memorandum is printed in *Foreign Relations of the United States, 1961–1963*, Volume 11: *Cuban Missile Crisis and Aftermath*.

LeMay's comparison of the Cuban blockade with the Munich agreement took place at the meeting of the Joint Chiefs of Staff on 19 October and is recounted in Serhii Plokhy's *Nuclear Folly: A History of the Cuban Missile Crisis* (Penguin, 2021).

McCone's frustration at the slowness of Navy intelligence is revealed in the CIA's *John McCone as Director of Intelligence 1961–1965*.

The minutes of the 25 October ExComm meeting are part of the JFK Library's Cuban Missile Crisis online archive. The official title is 'Record of Action of the Fourth Meeting of the Executive Committee of the National Security Council.'

The 26 October PIC included the comment that the atmosphere in Havana was 'one of slowly rising tension'.

Portions of the Checklist are redacted. It is the first time that a map of the missile sites is visibly included with the daily updates.

Khrushchev's 26 October letter is open to view as part of the JFK Library's online collection on the Cuban Missile Crisis.

Roger Herman's obituary is published on the website of the Patriot Guard Riders of Texas. He died three days before his seventy-ninth birthday. He was one of the eleven pilots who flew U-2 missions over Cuba and would go on to be the first pilot to fly U-2s over Vietnam, eventually retiring from the Air Force with the rank of Lieutenant Colonel. His exchange with Major Anderson is quoted in Dobbs' *One Minute to Midnight*.

The transcript of the 27 October morning ExComm meeting was published in the *MIT Press International Security Journal*, Vol. 12, No. 3 (Winter, 1987–88).

14 A Missile Misadventure

The transcript of the 27 October afternoon/evening ExComm meeting was published in the MIT Press journal, *International Security*, Vol. 12, No. 3 (Winter, 1987–88).

Kennedy's letter of condolence to Mrs Anderson was dated 28 October. An early, pre-prepared version is available to view as part of the JFK Library's online resources relating to the Cuban Missile Crisis.

General Maxwell Taylor delivered the update to the Joint Chiefs of Staff around 6.30 p.m. on 27 October. His comment is recorded in *History of the Joint Chiefs of Staff: The Joint Chiefs of Staff and National Policy,* Volume 8 (Historical Division, Joint Chiefs of Staff, 2011).

Kennedy's 27 October letter to Khrushchev is published online by the JFK Library.

The English translation of Dobrynin's coded, secret telegram to Moscow on the evening of 27 October is published by the Wilson Centre archive: 'Cable, Ambassador Dobrynin to the Soviet Foreign Ministry, Meeting with Robert Kennedy, October 27, 1962, History and Public Policy Program Digital Archive'. His description of Bobby Kennedy's physical state was recalled by Khrushchev himself in his memoirs *Khrushchev Remembers*, translated by Strobe Talbott (Little Brown, 1970).

Kennedy's comment about 'hard praying' was made to his Appointments Secretary Dave Powers.

The news that all Soviet MRBMs on Cuba were operational came in Kennedy's 28 October 1962 PIC.

Dobrynin recalled the message from Moscow at 4 p.m. on Sunday, 28 October, in his memoirs, *In Confidence: Moscow's Ambassador to America's Six Cold War Presidents* (Crown Publishing Group, 1995).

Khrushchev's Radio Moscow address confirming the back-channel communication of a few hours before is available as part of the JFK Library's online archives.

The notes on the progress of the dismantling of the missile sites in Cuba appeared in Kennedy's 30 and 31 October PICs.

The PICs in the first week of November 1962 include multiple comments on the progress of the missile deconstruction. Initially photographs were 'not conclusive enough' (3 November), and on 4 November, there was 'no readout yet of yesterday's U-2 mission' as the analysts were still going over the films.

Missile transporters began to arrive at the docks at Mariel port on 5 November, until the final proof of departure came in Kennedy's 6 November PIC, which was officially confirmed by the Soviets at the UN (9 November PIC).

Operation Mongoose was put on a pause, which became permanent, on 30 October 1962. The directive, entitled 'CIA, Director John McCone, Memorandum for General Marshall S. Carter, "Urgent"', stated, 'The activities of Operation *Mongoose* are to be stopped during the next several days and therefore all prior approvals for sabotage, infiltrations, guerrilla activities, cashing of arms are to be temporarily suspended.' It can be viewed on the National Security Archive's website.

15 A More Reliable Government

The report of Mosaddeq's comments to Ambassador Loy Henderson was printed in the CIB on 22 January 1953.

Truman's 13 and 14 March 1946 Daily Summaries covered Iran and the Shah's fear of a 'blitzkrieg'. George Kennan and the team in Moscow believed the Soviet Union 'must make some effort in the near future … to establish a regime which will accede to such major Soviet demands as the retention of troops and the granting of oil concessions' (18 March).

The warning of the 'depressing effect' of the fall of Iran to the Soviets came from the US Embassy in Moscow on 14 March 1950, almost exactly a year before Iran's nationalisation of the country's oil industry.

Acheson's criticism of Mosaddeq was included in his memoirs, *Present at the Creation: My Years in the State Department* (W.W. Norton, 1987).

Mosaddeq's exchange of letters with Eisenhower took place in June 1953. The text has been preserved by the American Presidency Project and can be viewed online under the title, 'Exchange of Messages Between the President and Prime Minister Mossadegh on the Oil Situation and the Problem of Aid to Iran'.

The State Department memo was written by Henry Byroade (Assistant Secretary of State for Near Eastern, South Asian and African Affairs) on 26 November 1952 and entitled 'Proposal to Organise a Coup d'état in Iran, Department of State'. The document was made public by the National Security Archive.

Kim Roosevelt's heavily censored and in places inflated account of events in 1953, *Countercoup: The Struggle for Control of Iran*, was published in 1980 (McGraw-Hill).

SIS agent Christopher Montague Woodhouse's admission of the change of tactic to persuade the USA to support the Iran coup to stop the country going Communist is quoted in Stephen Kinzer's popular account *All the Shah's Men: An American Coup and the Roots of Middle East Terror* (John Wiley & Sons, 2003).

The 4 March 1953 CIB is published in the CIA Reading Room online, while the minutes of the 4 March NSC meeting and the prepared but unused memos (4 and 11 March) on Iran covert operations can be found in the State Department's official historical document collection on Iran, *Foreign Relations of the United States, 1952–1954*, Volume X: *Iran, 1951–1954*.

The US Embassy report on the Shah's personality is quoted in the State Department's
Foreign Relations of the United States, 1969–1976, Volume E04: Documents on
Iran and Iraq, 1969–1972.

US Ambassador Loy Henderson's garden chat with the Shah was recorded in a
memo that he sent back to Washington on 30 May 1953. It is included in the State
Department's Iran Foreign Relations Collection.

The CIA Director's warning about Communist control of world oil is recorded in
the minutes of the 4 March NSC meeting.

The collection of dispatches from the Embassy in Tehran collated and forwarded
to Eisenhower reached the President on 23 May 1953. The memorandum, titled
'Memorandum from Acting Secretary of State Smith to President Eisenhower',
can be viewed as part of the State Department's Iran Foreign Relations collection.

16 Counter-Coup

Allen Dulles' April money authorisation of $1 million for the Tehran Station is noted
in the CIA's official internal history of Operation Ajax, which was leaked by *The
New York Times* in 2000.

The influence of the Shah's support was noted in the CIB on 9 June 1953. The Shah's
comments on the possibility of General Zahedi being Prime Minister were shared
with Loy Henderson in his 30 May memo.

The 2 and 4 August CIBs contained Mosaddeq's accusation of the alignment of UK
and US policy.

The New York Times reported on the Shah's arrival in the Iraqi capital on 17 August
under the headline 'Shah Flees Iran After Move to Dismiss Mossadegh Fails'.

Under Secretary of State Smith's 18 August message to Eisenhower is published in
the State Department's *Foreign Relations of the United States, 1952–1954*, Volume X:
Iran, 1951–1954, under the title, 'No. 346 Memorandum by the Under Secretary
of State (Smith) to the President.' The attached message, including the US
Ambassador in Iraq's description of his 17 August meeting with the Shah in
Baghdad, is in the same volume under 'No. 345 The Ambassador in Iraq (Berry)
to the Department of State'.

The positive news of the counter-coup was carried in the 20 August CIB.

The note on CIA asset efforts to spark the 19 August demonstrations is included the
CIA official internal history of the coup.

Reports that the Soviets were offering aid to Iran's new government appeared in
the 29 August CIB.

The note on UK wishes to get an Iranian oil deal was in the 2 September CIB, with
the comment on Zahedi's knowledge of the situation appearing on 18 September.

Zahedi's policy checking with Henderson was noted in the CIBs on 3 and
4 September 1953.

Eisenhower's rather selective recollections of events concerning Iran were included in
his memoir, *Mandate for Change, 1953–1956: The White House Years* (Doubleday, 1963).

The CIA's handover of $5 million was revealed in the secret official internal history of the coup leaked by *The New York Times* in 2000.

Kim Roosevelt's concern over the conduct of future covert ops, expressed to Eisenhower on 4 September 1953, was mentioned in his memoir of the operation.

17 Banana Republic

The first approach over a coup of Guatemala appeared in Truman's 6 May 1946 Daily Summary.

The authorisation for operation PBSUCCESS was granted by Eisenhower and the NSC on 12 August 1953.

The United Fruit Company 'executive' was Thomas McCann, who worked for the company for twenty-three years and subsequently wrote *An American Company: The Tragedy of United Fruit* (Crown, 1976).

Arévalo's allegorical story, *The Shark and the Sardines*, was first published in 1961. The English translation is published by Papamoa Press, 2017.

The history of the United Fruit Company is narrated in *Bananas: How the United Fruit Company Shaped the World* by Peter Chapman (Canongate, 2007).

The plan for the first Guatemala CIA coup, named Operation PBFORTUNE, is covered in the CIA's originally classified internal history of the 1954 coup, *Operation PBSUCCESS: The United States and Guatemala, 1952–1954* by Nicholas Cullather, published internally in 1994 and declassified in 2016.

The United Fruit Company's 'Report on Central America, 1954' was only ninety-four pages long, but had a huge impact on policy makers in Washington. It articulated precisely what many of them assumed or wished be true of Árbenz's administration in Guatemala.

The admission of apparent close US involvement in equipping the Árbenz operation can be found in the 12 September 1953 CIB.

The 'Liberation Air Force' is covered in detail in the first popular history of the coup, *Bitter Fruit: The Story of the American Coup in Guatemala*, written by Stephen Schlezinger and Stephen Kinzer (Harvard University Press, 1982).

Guatemala featured in the CIB in many of the days running up to the launch of the coup. The reports of 'planted caches' of US weapons appeared on 10 June. On 15 June, the Bulletin reported that the Army was still anti-Communist and was even threatening the President: it was 'believed still to have the capacity for decisive action against the regime'. The day before the Castillo Armas invasion, Colonel Monzón, who would briefly head the junta before Castillo Armas, was apparently 'pressing ... for the immediate ouster of President Árbenz'.

The CIB item on Guatemala for 19 June is redacted, although the analysts' comment that 'the unknown degree of support for Castillo Armas among active army officers would appear to be the crucial factor' is still visible. The revelation of the inserted Daily Brief item on the Guatemala invasion was included in G. Fred Albrecht's originally secret 1967 internal CIA history of the Brief, *A History of the*

Current Intelligence Bulletin. Albrecht also reveals that Deputy Director of Plans, Frank Wisner, was not happy with the OCI insistence on including the dictated item as incoming cable. Wisner's penning of an item for the Brief is one of only two known cases when items have not been written by analysts. The other came in 1957, when then CIA Director Allen Dulles wrote a piece on the situation in Cuba.

The initially negative news of the coup effort in Guatemala appeared in the CIB on 20 June 1954.

Reports of an attack on the US Embassy in Guatemala City appeared in the 24 June CIB. The report of 'only limited' territory being in the hands of rebels appeared the following day. The instruction to destroy written evidence of PBSUCCESS held at Guatemala City Station came on 1 July and is noted in *Operation PBSUCCESS: The United States and Guatemala*.

The concerns of Army officers that the USA was preparing for a full invasion are related in Piero Gleijeses' *Shattered Hope: The Guatemalan Revolution and the United States, 1944–1954* (Princeton University Press, 1992).

The success of the coup was reported as a 'late item' on 27 June 1954. News of the outlawing of the Communist Party in Guatemala was carried in the 29 June CIB. Monzón was positively viewed as 'a strong anticommunist', and he had already ordered the arrest of all Communist leaders in the country. The strong position of Castillo Armas was commented upon on 3 July 1954.

William Prescott Allen, publisher of the *Laredo Times* in Texas, cabled Eisenhower about the number of West Coast Communists on 24 June 1954. His message is quoted in Jean Edward Smith's *Eisenhower in War and Peace* (Random House, 2012).

An account of the presentation to Eisenhower in the East Wing of the White House can be found in former CIA officer David Atlee Phillips' *The Night Watch* (Ballantine Books, 1982).

A number of US diplomatic staff in the region expressed concern about US interventionism years before the Guatemala operation. In the 4 December 1948 Daily Summary, Ambassador Warren in Paraguay insisted, 'The use of US arms and munitions by the groups accomplishing such military coups [as in Peru and Venezuela], may lead democratic elements in Latin America to blame the US for such coups ... The US recognition policy plays into the hands of military groups and could contribute to eventual dominance by the military caste throughout Latin America.'

18 One Man

Head of Congo CIA Station Larry Devlin's telegram was received just before the 18 August NSC meeting. It was revealed in Madeleine Kalb's *The Congo Cables: The Cold War in Africa from Eisenhower to Kennedy* (Macmillan, 1982).

Minutes of the 18 August 1960 NSC meeting are available on the State Department's Office of the Historian website, Document 180 of *Foreign Relations of the United States, 1958–1960*, Volume XIV: *Africa*.

Eisenhower's wish to 'eliminate' Lumumba was reported by the minute taker at the 18 August NSC meeting, Robert Johnson, in private interviews with the Senate Intelligence Committee in 1975 during the post-Watergate inquiry into US covert action. It became public knowledge in 2000. The veracity of Johnson's allegations has been disputed, but it is something he claims he 'vividly recalled' and whether Eisenhower said it in as black white terms or not, assassinating Lumumba (if the opportunity presented itself) became official CIA policy within less than a fortnight.

The telegram stating that the removal of Lumumba was a 'high priority' of covert action was sent to the CIA Station in Leopoldville (Kinshasa) on 27 August 1960. The text can be viewed in the State Department's *Foreign Relations of the United States, 1964–1968*, Volume XXIII: *Congo, 1960–1968*.

Frank Wisner's mental health battles are recorded in Thomas Evans' *The Very Best Men: Four Who Dared, the Early Years of the CIA* (Simon & Schuster, 1995). Wisner's 'breaking point' was said to be the Soviet crushing of the 1956 Hungarian Revolution. The 'high-level muttering' in Washington was that the CIA (and Wisner's DDP office) had encouraged the revolution and then abandoned the Hungarians to the incoming Soviet soldiers. It was largely untrue and ignores the fact that the Eisenhower administration was navigating the Suez Crisis at the same time, but it was reportedly the moment when Wisner's mental health deteriorated to the point at which he could longer carry on his role.

The US Embassy's description of Mobutu was quoted in the 20 September 1960 CIB.

News of Mobutu's success made the CIB on 15 September 1960. The extended commentary on 'Situation in the Congo' was 'as of 0430' Eastern (Daylight) Time, with Leopoldville five hours behind Washington. The description of Mobutu was printed in the same item.

Quotes from minutes of the 21 September NSC meeting are contained in the State Department's *Foreign Relations of the United States, 1958–1960*, Volume XIV: *Africa*, Document 223.

Leopoldville CIA Station Chief Larry Devlin received the 'eyes only' telegram on 19 September. He later narrated his experiences in his book, *Chief of Station, Congo: Fighting the Cold War in a Hot Zone* (Hachette, 2008).

19 Allies Overseas

Devlin's cable requesting a 'third country national' was sent on 7 October 1960, with his suggestion of the rifle coming ten days later. In October, the CIA also sent an additional field officer to Leopoldville, Michael Mulroney, who was a senior officer in the Directorate of Plans. His actions and the insertion of QJWIN, the foreign assassin, are evidenced in the 1975 report by the Senate Select Committee 'to study governmental operations with respect to intelligence activities', titled 'Alleged Assassination Plots Involving Foreign Leaders', dated 20 November 1975. Devlin testified in person at the Senate hearings under the pseudonym Victor Hedgeman.

Records relating to QJWIN were released as part of the President John F. Kennedy Assassination Records Collection Act of 1992. They can be viewed on the

National Archives and Records Administration website. The summary of QJWIN is labelled 104-10059-10223. QJWIN is widely believed to be a German national by the name of Jose Marie Andre Mankel. The Mary Ferrell Foundation's collection of related records includes CIA contracts in that name. Interest in Mankel has often centred on his alleged involvement in a later CIA assassination programme that has been allegedly linked to President Kennedy's assassination.

Details of the plan to use UN vehicles and uniforms as cover were revealed in a telegram from the CIA Station in Leopoldville on 29 November. The message can be viewed as part of the State Department's historical collection in *Foreign Relations of the United States, 1964–1968*, Volume XXIII: *Congo, 1960–1968*.

The planned withdrawal of Moroccan UN forces was reported in Kennedy's first CIB on 21 January 1961.

Kennedy's perspective on Africa is mentioned in Richard D. Mahoney's *The Kennedy Brothers: The Rise and Fall of Jack and Bobby* (Arcade, 1999), along with his discussions about the potential to 'save' Lumumba.

The cables from the CIA Station warning of the threat of Lumumba re-entering politics (dated 13 January 1961), and admitting knowledge of the plan to transfer him to Katanga on the day it took place, came to light in the Senate Select Committee's 1975 assassination plots report, along with the message from Elisabethville Station on 19 January 1961.

The 'Analytical Chronology of the Congo Crisis' was dated 25 January 1961. Only twelve copies were distributed, one of which went to the Oval Office. The document has been digitised and can be viewed as part of the online archives held by the JFK Presidential Library.

The impact of Lumumba's disappearance on debates at the UN was reported in the 13 February CIB. The note on Lumumba's death appeared the following day and analysts noted it would 'further discredit Tshombe's government' and warned 'there may be reprisals by Lumumba's supporters against whites and Africans in the Congo'.

Items on the Congo appeared in the 17, 18, 19, 20 and 21 June 1961 PICs.

Dean Rusk's stormy meeting with Kennedy took place on 25 July 1961. An account of the efforts to sway the vote can be found in *Kennedy's Quest for Victory in American Foreign Policy, 1961–1962* by Thomas G. Paterson (Oxford University Press, 1992).

The Embassy warning of a 'bandwagon' psychosis in favour of Gizenga was made in a cable from Leopoldville dated 28 July. It can be found in *Foreign Relations of the United States, 1961–1962*, Volume XX: *Congo Crisis*.

20 A Situation

Lady Bird's *A White House Diary* was published in 1970 (Holt, Rinehart & Winston).

CIA analyst Dick Lehrman revealed the Agency's information approach to Johnson in an interview for David Priess' *The President's Book of Secrets*.

The PIC dated 22 November 1963 in the CIA archives is a special, backdated memorial edition created for Jackie and Bobby Kennedy by OCI staff. The PIC prepared for Johnson's first full day was dated 23 November.

Sentiment for a US withdrawal from Vietnam was noted in the 24 November 1963 PIC.

Truman's 9 August 1946 Daily Summary warned of 'anarchy' in Indochina.

Ho Chi Minh's reported 'direct contact' with Moscow was an item in the 30 November 1946 Daily Summary.

Truman's Daily Summary on 1 February 1950 warned the USA could 'soon be faced in Indochina with a situation'. The note from the Ambassador in Paris was quoted on 17 February.

Ambassador Kirk's message from Moscow urging 'everything short' of troops for Indochina appeared in Truman's Daily Summary on 17 February 1950.

21 The Jungles of Indochina

Eisenhower's first CIB, dated 21 November 1953, noted the Viet Minh's use of river mines in Tonkin.

Eisenhower's address to the Governor's Conference in Seattle took place on 4 August 1953. The full text has been made available online by the American Presidency Project.

The CIA analysts' warnings that repeatedly reinforcing Indochina was not a long-term solution appeared in Eisenhower's 2 August 1953 CIB.

US financial aid to the French in Indochina is detailed in the Pentagon Papers.

British Pathe's film of the Eisenhowers' 1953 Christmas can be viewed on the British Pathe YouTube channel, titled 'Ike's Xmas Aka Christmas At Home With Eisenhower (1953)'.

Eisenhower's 1 January 1954 CIB noted the forthcoming attack on Dien Bien Phu and warned of the threat from Viet Minh artillery.

Officer Tran Do's recollections of the Viet Minh efforts to get artillery pieces into the heights above Dien Bien Phu are quoted in Max Hastings' *Vietnam: An Epic Tragedy* (William Collins, 2018).

Tennessee senator Albert Gore narrated how Johnson described to him and three other senators after the 3 April meeting 'in the Johnson manner' how he had 'pounded the President's desk', although the meeting was not held in the Oval Office, so the senator's recollections may have been somewhat hazy, or Johnson's description misleading. Either way, Johnson was against going to war over Dien Bien Phu. See Anthony J. Badger's *Albert Gore: A Political Life* (University of Pennsylvania Press, 2018).

Churchill's reply to Eisenhower is quoted in Martin Gilbert's *Never Despair: Winston S. Churchill, 1945–1965* (Minerva, 1990).

The fall of Dien Bien Phu appeared in Eisenhower's 8 May 1954 CIB.

Kennedy's remarks on Indochina were made in the Senate on 6 April 1954. The text of his speech can be viewed on the JFK Library's online archive.

22 Boots on the Ground

Kennedy visited Fort Bragg in October 1961. His comment on the 'form of warfare' was made in his post-visit message of thanks to General William P. Yarborough.

David Halberstam's *New York Times* piece on the 'uncertain struggle' was published on 21 October 1962. He subsequently wrote his own account of the descent into war: *The Making of a Quagmire: America and Vietnam during the Kennedy Era* (Knopf, 1988). Before going to Vietnam, he had reported from the Congo during the Congo Crisis.

Kennedy's 31 December 1962 PIC covered missile launchers still waiting to be removed from Cuba. Vietnam appeared on 2 January, with the report on the Viet Cong attack on the special forces training base.

The NSAM-263 memo, dated 11 October, can be viewed on the online archive of the JFK Library. It is titled, 'National Security Action Memoranda [NSAM]: NSAM 263, South Vietnam'.

Cronkite interviewed Kennedy on CBS on 2 September, during which the President insisted the USA 'should not withdraw' from Vietnam.

Clifton's concerns were mentioned in a 9 January 1964 report. It is quoted in Foreign Relations of the United States, 1964–1968, Volume XXXIII: Organisation and Management of Foreign Policy; United Nations.

The NSC Executive Secretary's concerns about the PIC becoming 'just another intelligence paper' were voiced in a memo to Bundy in February 1964. The text can be found in *Foreign Relations of the United States, 1964–1968*, Volume XXXIII: *Organisation and Management of Foreign Policy; United Nations*, entitled, 'Draft memorandum from the Executive Director of the National Security Council (Smith) to the President's Special Assistant for National Security Affairs (Bundy)'.

Johnson's insistence that his Brief was adequate was reported by McCone in a memo of his conversation titled 'Wednesday 29 April 4.45 p.m. in Oval Office'. The CIA Director's note is available as part of the collections of the Lyndon Baines Johnson Presidential Library.

UN Secretary General U Thant's comments on Vietnam appeared in Johnson's 30 April 1964 PIC.

23 Wider War

The attack on USS *Maddox* was reported in Johnson's 3 August PIC.

The transcripts of McNamara's telephone calls with Johnson are in John Prados' *The White House Tapes* (The New Press, 2003). Recordings can be listened to on the National Security Archive website.

The transcript of Johnson's address to the American people on the night of 4 August is available from the University of Virginia's Miller Center archive.

News from Vietnam appeared in PIC almost every day in July 1964. Quoted extracts are from 6, 7, 8, 10, 11, 13, 16, 22, 24 and 25 July.

The note about Khanh's desire for 'carrying the action north' appeared in Johnson's 24 July Checklist. The claim it was not encouraging US action against North Vietnam was printed a day later.

The positive feedback is scrawled in the return memo to Bundy and recalls Truman's response to receiving the first of his updated Daily Briefs in 1951 that the analysts had 'hit the jackpot with this one'.

The admission that the contents of the President's Daily Brief were the same as the document that had preceded it is contained in the CIA's own publication, *OCI and President Johnson's New Administration, 1964–1965: Supporting the President*, author unknown, declassified November 2000.

Johnson's 11 August PDB reported on the loss of a Douglas A-4E Skyhawk bomber around 52 miles south-west of Hanoi. By the evening the President read the note, McGuire's 'Eve of Destruction' was already all over the radio.

24 America's Soul

The 5 January 1967 PDB led with a labelled image of Launch Complex B at the Shuang-Cheng-Tzu missile centre. The image was from a Gambit-3 satellite launch – one of three in 1966 – recorded as Mission 4303, which ran from 15–22 December.

Martin Luther King's 'Beyond Vietnam' speech was delivered at Riverside Church in New York City on 4 April 1967. The video of him reading the 15 April petition outside the UN building in New York is available on the United Nations YouTube channel.

Johnson's 13 May 1967 PDB contained the warning from the CIA that the North Vietnamese were now seeking 'a war of attrition' in Vietnam.

President Johnson's memoirs, *The Vantage Point*, were published by Holt, Rinehart & Winston in 1971.

The quoted PDBs referencing the Tet Offensive are from 30 and 31 January and 24 and 29 February 1968.

Johnson announced his decision not to run again on 31 March 1968. He records his personal motivation for doing so in his memoirs.

25 A Healthy Interval

Nixon's long fostered anger at the CIA is revealed in Kissinger's *The White House Years* (Little Brown, 1979).

Allen Dulles' comments on briefing Kennedy were made in an oral interview in December 1964 with Thomas Braden. The transcript can be found in the JFK Library.

Kissinger's criticism of the Brief's coverage can be found in *Getting to Know the President: Intelligence Briefings of Presidential Candidates, 1952–2004* by John L. Helgerson (Military Bookshop, 2013).

The CIA officer's suggestion that Nixon and Kissinger 'didn't give a crap' about the Daily Brief – and Kissinger's own comment on knowing 'a lot about foreign policy' – are quoted in *The President's Book of Secrets*.

The admission of Nixon viewing the PDB as of little more worth than the daily papers came in an OCI internal memorandum dated 27 February 1970, titled 'Current Intelligence and Its Audience'.

Helms' memoirs are entitled *A Look Over My Shoulder: A Life in the Central Intelligence Agency* (Presidio Press, 2004).

The sympathetic insider memo from the NSC was sent to Helms on 18 June 1969. A copy can be viewed in the State Department's historical collection, *Foreign Relations of the United States, 1969–1976*, Volume II: *Organisation and Management of U.S. Foreign Policy 1969–1972*, Document 191.

Nixon's suggestion that *The New York Times* was a better source of information than the CIA was recorded by his Chief of Staff H.R. Haldeman in *The Haldeman Diaries: Inside the Nixon White House* (The Book Service Ltd, 1994).

Nixon's sentiment on the war is revealed in Walter Isaacson's *Kissinger: A Biography* (Simon & Schuster, 2005). Kissinger's lauded January 1969 article in *Foreign Affairs* was titled 'The Viet Nam Negotiations'.

Kissinger's memo to Nixon recommending a 'healthy interval' was sent in September 1971. It is quoted in Isaacson's biography, although truncated versions have appeared elsewhere.

Kissinger's negotiation memos can be read on the US State Department's website of the Office of the Historian, *Foreign Relations, 1969–1976*, Volume XLII: *Vietnam: The Kissinger–Le Duc Tho Negotiations*.

The 25 October 1972 PDB noted a possible imminent ceasefire in Vietnam.

26 What Happens If?

Helms quotes the note from Haldeman's September meeting with Nixon in his memoirs; it was first revealed in an Associated Press account of Nixon's time in office.

Helms' uncertainty over how often Nixon saw the PDB is noted in the CIA publication, *The President's Daily Brief: Delivering Intelligence to Nixon and Ford*, which was published alongside the 2015 PDB release.

The 9 August 1974 PDB included a map of South Vietnam, with labelled areas of interest.

The PDBs referencing the fall of South Vietnam quoted in the text include 2 January, 28 March and 16, 17, 29 and 30 April 1975.

President Gerald R. Ford's public appreciation of the PDB came at the swearing-in ceremony of George H.W. Bush as DCI, on 30 January 1976.

27 Under Attack

The video of the moment President George W. Bush's Chief of Staff, Andy Card, informed him of the second plane attack during the visit to Sarasota's Emma E. Booker Elementary School is widely available online. Bush's assertion that he restrained his reaction so as not to 'rattle' the kids was made in a National Geographic Channel interview which aired in 2011.

The redacted 6 August 2001 President's Daily Brief was declassified on 10 April 2004 and can be viewed on the George Washington University National Security Archive website.

The insistence on avoiding 'another Pearl Harbor' was made by 1950–52 Assistant CIA Director Kingman Douglass and is quoted in G. Fred Albrecht's internal 1967 CIA publication, *A History of the Current Intelligence Bulletin*.

Accounts of the critical 15 September meeting at Camp David were published by Rumsfeld and by CIA Director George Tenet in *At the Center of the Storm* (Harper Collins, 2006).

Osama bin Laden's early years in Afghanistan are detailed in Lawrence Wright's *The Looming Tower* (Knopf, 2006). CIA officer Gary Berntsen has given a number of interviews about the operation to catch bin Laden in 2001 and has written a memoir of the experience (*Jawbreaker*, Crown Publications, 2005), which was published with extensive CIA redactions. Other details were also revealed in the November 2009 report to the US Senate Foreign Relations Committee, and in Delta Force operative Dalton Fury's book, *Kill bin Laden: A Delta Force Commander's Account of the Hunt for the World's Most Wanted Man* (St Martin's Press, 2008).

The text of George W. Bush's 20 September 2001 address to Congress is available on the White House archives.

28 Failures

Francis Fukuyama's now famous article was published in the journal *The National Interest*, Summer 1989, No. 16, under the heading 'The End of History?'

Details of Carter's 28 July 1976 intelligence briefing in Georgia can be found in John Helgerson's *Getting to Know the President*. Lehman later recalled the meeting in an interview with Richard Kovar, published in the Summer 2000 edition of the journal *Studies in Intelligence*, entitled, 'Mr. Current Intelligence: An Interview with Richard Lehman'.

The transcript of Carter's 15 July 1976 speech accepting the Democratic nomination is held by The Jimmy Carter Library.

Carter's speech in Tehran was on New Year's Eve, 1977. His diary entry for 25 October 1978 was included in his autobiography, *Keeping Faith: Memoirs of a President* (Bantum Books, 1982). He also states in his memoirs that reports he was 'receiving from the CIA, the State Department' led him to believe the Shah would have to leave the country for reform to be enacted, but there is no claim he was warned that the government would collapse.

The Shah's televised speech was made on 6 November 1978.

Former Defense Secretary Brown's comment on the Daily Brief's inadequacies when it came to Iran can be found in *The President's Book of Secrets*.

29 Freedom Fighters

Ronald Reagan's approach to the Daily Brief is summarised by Richard J. Kerr and Peter Dixon Davis' article in the Winter 1998–99 issue of *Studies in Intelligence*, 'Mornings in Pacific Palisades: Ronald Reagan and the President's Daily Brief', available online on the National Security Archive. Kerr was former Deputy Director and Davis held a number of positions in the Directorate of Intelligence; they also lamented how administrations saw intelligence as a silver bullet, or a waste of time.

Reagan's in-flight comment during the briefing on the Palestine Liberation Organization is recorded in Helgerson's *Getting to Know the President*.

The Reagan Diaries were published by Harper Collins in 2007. Reagan recorded watching the classified CIA film on India's Prime Minister on 7 June 1985.

Journalist Phil Gailey's *New York Times* article, 'Reagan Views Films to Get the Diplomatic Edge', was published on Christmas Eve 1981.

The transcript of the 1985 State of the Union address, which Reagan gave on 6 February, is available on the Miller Center website from the University of Virginia.

George H.W. Bush released portions of his diaries after leaving office in 1993, including some entries relating to the Iran–Contra affair and 5 November 1986.

President George H.W. Bush's fondness for the Daily Brief was mentioned in correspondence with the authors of *Mornings in Pacific Palisades*.

Deputy Director of Intelligence John Gannon's delight at working for George H.W. Bush is recounted in *The President's Book of Secrets*.

President George H.W. Bush gave his 1991 State of the Union address on 29 January.

30 'A Jungle Full of Poisonous Snakes'

George Tenet's lament at the state of the CIA when he became Director is included in Chris Whipple's *The Spymasters* (Simon & Schuster, 2020); and also in the 28 November 2015 Showtime documentary, *The Spymasters: The CIA In the Crosshairs*.

Bill Clinton's PDB recollections are included in *The President's Book of Secrets*.

Woolsey's admission that he did not have a relationship with the President was made in a *National Review* interview. His comment that the CIA was now in a jungle full of snakes came during a talk given at the Hudson Union Society on 9 June 2016, which can be viewed on the hudsonunionsociety YouTube channel.

The 4 December 1998 PDB, with redactions, was published in the *9/11 Commission Report* in the section 'Responses to Al Qaeda's Initial Assaults'.

There are multiple accounts of the 10 July 2001 meeting at the White House. Rice's own recollections can be found in her memoir, *No Higher Honour* (Simon & Schuster, 2011).

The President's interest in potential al-Qaeda attacks on US soil is mentioned by Tenet in his memoirs.

31 'Let Me Read'

The 31 March 2005 letter from the Commission on the Intelligence Capabilities of the United States Regarding Weapons of Mass Destruction to President George W. Bush can be viewed on the State Department Archive website.

The indictment of the Brief processes in the press came in *The Washington Post*'s article, 'CIA to Cede President's Brief to Negroponte' by Walter Pincus, 19 February 2005.

First Director of the Office for National Intelligence John D. Negroponte's admission that the PDB has not undergone any radical reimagining is noted in *The President's Book of Secrets*.

The Wall Street Journal article, 'Why is Obama skipping more than half of his daily intelligence briefings?' by Marc Thiessen, appeared on 10 September 2012.

CIA Deputy Director Mike Morell's assertion that Obama was a student of the Brief is made in *The President's Book of Secrets*

Obama's memoir *A Promised Land* was published in November 2020 (Viking).

The contents of Obama's 13 January 2011 PDB are mentioned, but not directly quoted, in *The Spymasters*.

32 'Something Will Be Missed'

Trump gave his inauguration speech on 20 January 2017.

The first account of intelligence briefings in the Trump White House appeared in *The Washington Post* on 29 May 2017: 'How President Trump consumes – or does not consume – top-secret intelligence' by Philip Rucker and Ashley Parker.

The Washington Post article accusing Trump of 'breaking with tradition' by not reading his PDB appeared on 9 February 2018.

The comments on Trump's love of pictures during briefings was made by Bruce Riedel, Senior Fellow at the Brookings Institution, to Chris Whipple in his research for *The Spymasters*.

Trump post-strike comments were quoted in *The Guardian* on 6 April 2017: 'Syria chemical attack has changed my view of Assad, says Trump', by Julian Borger, David Smith and Jennifer Rankin.

Panetta was quoted in *The Washington Post*'s 9 February 2018 article.

The article exposing the Russian bounties in Afghanistan was published online on 26 June 2020 and ran on the front page of *The New York Times* the following morning.

All the volumes of the Senate Intelligence Committee's lengthy report titled 'Russian Active Measures Campaigns and Interference in the 2016 US Election' can be viewed on the Senate Intelligence Committee's website.

Trump's farewell address was released on Tuesday, 19 January 2021.

Biden, along with his Vice President-elect Kamala Harris, only received access to the Daily Brief from 1 December 2020, although both had been receiving more general briefings from intelligence officers prior.

33 'The Best Decision for America'

The *NBC News* article, by Carol E. Lee, Mike Memoli and Elyse Perlmutter-Gumbiner, was entitled 'Biden puts the "daily" back into the administration's intelligence briefings' and published on the *NBC News* website on 22 January 2021.

Press Secretary Jen Psaki's mention of the alleged bounties was made during the 21 January 2021 press briefing. The transcript is available on the White House website.

The extent of Haspel's involvement in the CIA 'black site' in Thailand was revealed after a National Security Archive Freedom of Information lawsuit forced the publication of heavily redacted cables sent by Haspel while she was in charge of the site.

Biden's embarrassments in 1987 that torpedoed his bid for the nomination are noted in *Time* magazine's 30 July 2019 article, 'Why Joe Biden's First Campaign for President Collapsed after just 3 Months'.

John Sopko, the DoD's special inspector for Afghanistan, was speaking on 16 March 2021. His remarks were quoted in *Al Jazeera*'s article of the same day, 'US official warns Congress on troop withdrawal from Afghanistan'.

Sullivan was speaking with Elise Labott in an April 2021 interview for *Foreign Policy*.

The Guardian reported on 26 September 2021 that Sullivan had 'changed the nature of the President's Daily Brief': 'Jake Sullivan: the Biden insider at the center of the Afghanistan crisis', by Julian Borger.

The report quoting unnamed officials revealing the new assessment that Kabul could fall in ninety days was published by *Reuters* on 11 August 2021: 'Taliban could isolate Kabul in 30 days, takeover in 90 – US intelligence', by Idrees Ali.

Biden was answering questions on 8 July 2021. His remarks were widely quoted in the press – and dredged up after the withdrawal a month later – and the video of the press conference can be viewed on YouTube.

The New York Times, 17 August 2021: Mark Mazzetti, Julian E. Barnes and Adam Goldman, 'Intelligence Warned of Afghan Military Collapse, Despite Biden Assurances'.

The memo from the Kabul Embassy was reported in *The Wall Street Journal* on 19 August: 'Internal State Department Cable Warned of Kabul Collapse' by Vivian Salama.

The transcript of Biden's 19 August *ABC News* interview with George Stephanopoulos has been released on the *ABC News* website.

Douglas London, former CIA Counterterrorism Chief, dismissed the claim Biden had not been informed, writing for *Just Security* on 18 August 2021.

The transcript of Biden's address was released by *Al Jazeera* on 31 August 2021.

Epilogue

The recording of the LBJ Library Event, 'The President's Daily Brief, delivering intelligence to the First Customer', is available to view on the TheLBJLibrary YouTube channel, dated 24 September 2015.

Index

Numbers in *italics* denote illustrations